362.1963720092

TEN
923

D0571409

SALTY BABY

WATERFORD CITY AND COUNTY
WITHDRAWN
LIBRARIES

SALTY BABY

A Memoir

ORLA TINSLEY

WATERFORD
No. 0051611156
CITY LIBRARY

HACHETTE
BOOKS
IRELAND

Copyright © 2011 Orla Tinsley
First published in 2011 by Hachette Books Ireland
A Hachette UK Company

1

The right of Orla Tinsley to be identified as the Author of the Work has been asserted by her in accordance with the Copyright, Designs and Patents Act, 1988.

All rights reserved. No part of this publication may be reproduced, stored in a retrieval system, or transmitted, in any form or by any means without the prior written permission of the publisher, nor be otherwise circulated in any form of binding or cover other than that in which it is published and without a similar condition being imposed on the subsequent purchaser.

A CIP catalogue record for this title is available from the British Library.

ISBN 978 1 444 7 0412 9

Typeset in Sabon by Hachette Books Ireland
Cover design by Anu Design, Tara, Co Meath
Printed and bound by CPI Group (UK) Ltd, Croydon, CR0 4YY

For reasons of privacy and to protect identities, names and identifying details have been changed in some instances.

The publisher would like to thank *The Irish Times* for kind permission to reproduce articles by Orla Tinsley in the book's appendices.

Hachette Books Ireland policy is to use papers that are natural, renewable and recyclable products and made from wood grown in sustainable forests. The logging and manufacturing processes are expected to conform to the environmental regulations of the country of origin.

Hachette Books Ireland
8 Castlecourt Centre
Castleknock
Dublin 15
Ireland

www.hachette.ie

A division of Hachette UK
338 Euston Road, London NW1 3BH
England

To my ever-supportive family.

And to all people dealing with CF,
past, present and future.

Contents

Foreword by Róisín Ingle   1

Salty Baby   5

Appendices   354

Acknowledgements   369

WHAT IS CYSTIC FIBROSIS?

Cystic Fibrosis (CF) is the most common potentially fatal inherited disease in the world. There are over 1,200 people with the illness in Ireland, where 1 in 19 people are carriers of the gene that causes it. Cystic Fibrosis affects the glands, including the lungs, digestive system and reproductive system. It causes thick, sticky mucus to be produced that blocks the lungs and intestines, making it easier for bacteria to grow. The mucus also blocks essential enzymes, which help break down food. This means that a person with CF must take medication throughout his/her life to counteract infection and mucus build-up in the lungs and to aid the digestion of food. A person with CF must also follow a demanding daily regime of treatment to stay well. Other organs can be affected, too, which can lead to diabetes, osteoporosis and arthritis, among other issues. The biggest difficulties are the threat of constant chest infections and malnutrition. Over the last decade treatment has improved significantly for people with CF, and there are now more adults than children with CF. There will soon be pensioners with CF.

Foreword

Six years ago my mother fell down a steep flight of stairs and fractured her arm. She was recuperating well from surgery when I visited her in St Vincent's hospital. While I was there she told me about the person lying in the next bed, a young woman who was surgically attached to earphones while mainlining an impressive variety of jellied sweets. This person wanted to be a writer. She had Cystic Fibrosis. Her name was Orla Tinsley.

My mother told me that this Orla Tinsley was kind, that she looked out for others in the room, seeking out medical staff to help older patients in distress. She also said that Orla was something of an irritant to staff. Every day my mother could hear her behind the curtain educating doctors and nurses on the intricacies of her condition, instructing them about the kind of treatment she did and did not need.

My mother said I should talk to her. So I did.

I had never met anyone like the beautiful young woman behind the hospital curtain. She told me she was 18 but when she spoke she seemed much older, partly the result, I later understood, of a childhood spent mostly around adults in hospital.

Within minutes I went from having little understanding of Cystic Fibrosis to being overcome by the kind of anger that causes your throat to constrict and your eyes to burn. She was articulate and quietly passionate as she told me the story of CF in Ireland and of her frightening new life in the adult hospital services. I suggested she write about her experiences in the newspaper where I work, *The Irish Times*. She worried that she would bore people. I told her she might be surprised. Eventually she agreed.

I remember the relief I felt when she filed her first article. Phew, I thought. She can write. I remember worrying as she did her first live radio interviews, feeling responsible for having put her in that stressful situation. In fact, she was a natural born campaigner and spoke with authority and humanity about the unacceptable medical realities for her and the rest of CF community. It was as though she had been doing it all her life.

Our friendship grew. I discovered that Orla had a gorgeous singing voice – don't let her tell you otherwise – which made her stiff competition in the Karaoke stakes. I discovered she was effortlessly stylish, that she loved Audrey Hepburn and idolised Judy Garland.

I discovered, quite by accident, that CF made her an extra-salty person. One day she came round to my house while I was on maternity leave. One of my twin girls, then just a baby, started sucking on her arm as though it was a particularly tasty lollipop. Orla asked me whether I minded. "You know, the salt levels in my system," she explained. This incident came after months spent ensuring those precious babies weren't exposed to so much as a whiff of salt. I instigated an immediate sucking ban.

Over the past six years I have also discovered that Orla Tinsley is an intense, determined and driven person. She has had to be. The expression "lives life to the full" isn't really adequate for Orla. It's more accurate, but not nearly as catchy, to say that she grabs life by the hair and noisily demands that it offer up every last drop of experience, whether professional, cultural, romantic or otherwise. She is forensically self-aware, as intimate with her weaknesses as she is with her great strengths. She is tenacious and tough, a total terrier of a campaigner. She makes me want to raise my game on a regular basis and even though she grew up hating people for saying it, I am going to say it anyway: My friend Orla Tinsley is one of the most inspirational people I've ever met.

This book you are holding in your hand is important on so many levels. It's a fascinating insight into what being a hospital "lifer" looks like from the inside. It's a powerful testament to how things can change when a vulnerable person decides to speak out and keeps on speaking when people in authority would like nothing better than for them to lie back on their A&E trolley and think of Ireland.

It's about how that expression can give other people, a whole community, permission to shout about something they didn't feel they could articulate before. It's an inspirational book about growing up and finding your voice.

Many other people and groups have been crucial in the campaign for improved Cystic Fibrosis services in this country. As Orla points out in this powerful memoir, this was not a solo run.

I can only say what her fight for the Cystic Fibrosis unit looked like to me, a friend watching from the sidelines, cheering her on.

For so long that unit seemed an impossibility, an unattainable goal, like trying to shift a shattered limb which logic dictates cannot, will not move. And yet with every sinew of her being, Orla willed that unit into existence. She risked her own health in the process. She risked aggravating people who administered her drugs or decided whether or not she got a hospital bed. She risked censure from those within the CF community who didn't always take kindly to having an unelected spokesperson or frowned on her campaign strategy of trusting her own gut instincts above almost everything else.

Despite all those risks she worked diligently, many times from her hospital bed, to achieve justice for people with CF. And finally there was movement. Documents signed. Diggers turned on. Bricks laid on bricks. For this and for so many other things unrelated to her campaign or her medical condition I am proud to call her my friend.

Róisín Ingle, Dublin, July 2011

Prologue

The idea of writing a book all about yourself is a strange one. I consider myself pretty boring in general, so I couldn't see why anyone would be interested. My friend Róisín Ingle told me back in 2005, when I was writing my first piece for *The Irish Times*, that what you find boring about yourself other people may find fascinating. It reminded me of that question about Patrick Kavanagh that appeared on the Leaving Cert English exam one year: *'Kavanagh turns the ordinary into the extraordinary.' Discuss.* Kavanagh and his poetry made me roll my eyes. I didn't understand him. I didn't see his charm. I was more of a Plath girl. Six years older, I love his work.

Now, I appreciate the ordinary so much. Waking up in the morning, running in the sunshine, sitting on the grass in the park with my friends, cooking a good meal – that simple stuff is what makes me tick. I know now that the ordinary qualities of reality can be mesmerising, but I still wasn't sure about writing this book. I think partly it was because I have always tried to protect myself from the tag of 'inspirational sick girl'. I've heard that phrase in numerous ways, many times in my life and it has always irritated me. On the other hand, I recognised that making best friends with doctors and nurses and sleeping much of the year away from your parents is not a normal childhood. But then, what is normal? As my dad likes to say, 'It's all relative'.

I suppose my biggest fear is that people will read this and think this is how someone with CF lives their life or turns out, or that it is typical of the challenges faced by all people with CF. This is just one story of a great many. There are people who have CF who have fascinating lives, and people who don't do much at all. I'm just one voice, but because of all of the campaigning, I've become *the* voice, which hasn't always sat so well with me.

I started writing this book in 2007, but in a way I had been writing it my entire life. The first time I thought about writing my life story was when I was fourteen and unaware that this was an unusual ambition. I was sitting in the playroom of St Philomena's Ward in Temple Street Children's Hospital. I was 'in crisis', though I didn't really know what that meant then. I was stuck, emotionally, and I couldn't make sense of my situation. My dad was always telling me to write down my feelings, to sort out my emotions on the page, so I asked a nurse to look up the meaning of *Meconium Ileus* in a medical journal. It was, after all, how this had started, how I had been diagnosed with Cystic Fibrosis (CF) and I figured that if I knew how it had started, I would then know how to get out of it. I would write my way into understanding and everything would all be happily sorted.

That wasn't the case, of course. Crippled by adjectives and poetic illusions, I remained stuck. The words I wrote at that time were short, wispy and don't make sense when I read them now. They were born out of confusion, anger, resentment, aggression and a desperate need to be good enough. I was sinking into teenage angst. Back then I would have said my writing was 'creativity'. I felt no-one understood 'real writing'. (I totally blame my father and his love of adjectives for this.) At that time, I thought creativity was something that could be defined, that you had to pillage your own soul and dredge the depths of the human condition to find it. I had no idea that living, instead of constantly examining, was the most rewarding, liberating experience of all, that it was in itself the real story and that it wasn't wise to pay too much attention to it.

In 2007 I found myself writing an article about CF care in Ireland. I had written about it before, but this time was different. In the previous few months I had experienced two friends with CF dying and I was becoming increasingly politically aware. But at the same time, I didn't want to be 'the girl who writes about cystic fibrosis'. I didn't want to be chained to the cliché of 'brave girl' for life. Then I watched the pre-election political party leaders' debate on television in my apartment in UCD and what I saw and heard infuriated me. I stood there, in front of the television, shaking with anger at the blatant ignorance displayed on the screen. These men knew nothing about CF when it was mentioned and what was worse, they didn't care. The article I wrote then, in anger, confusion and as a desperate attempt to motivate someone into doing the right thing, was published in *The Irish Times* just before the general election. It changed my life. Within a few hours of its publication a documentary film company had called asking if they could chronicle my ordinary days, which they insisted would be fascinating. My mother called from home to say a publisher had telephoned and wanted to publish my life story. I had to run in and out of our apartment in Roebuck Hall because there was no phone reception inside. Each time I ran back in, it got more ridiculous. How could one article do so much?

My biggest fear was revealing myself in all of these things. To put myself out there was to stare Truth in the eye and just say it. My life isn't perfect, it's boring and rough and complicated and exciting and amazing. It's normal. I hadn't yet accepted that though, and so I hibernated and thought: who am I to write a book on CF? Writing a piece in a newspaper was different. It was shorter for one, and I was talking about my personal experience. Róisín argued my experience was valid and that kind of gave me permission to write, but I had never wanted to be defined by CF.

I stayed on campus that summer in an attempt to write this thing; 'Thing' because it was a sort of creature that took over my life. Stopping only to see the Rolling Stones at Slane and get manhandled by a bouncer while trying to get backstage to Mick Jagger, I was consumed by it. I started off and ended up slumped in depression, caught in a loop of my own madness. Who was I anyway, what was I doing here and could I really tell the truth about myself? So basically I had the same self-indulgent thoughts that I imagine most people have at twenty, particularly if you're trying to slot your life into a book. I looked at my life and didn't see how it was interesting, all I saw was shame and fear, a not so dazzling academic record and an inability to ever really complete anything I'd started. My dream was to write fiction, to write something as far away from me as possible. I was of no real interest to me.

It took me another entire year to get my act together and get the writing flowing. Examining one's own life is no laughing matter. It's tough and dirty. But the writing of this has helped me grow in ways I didn't think possible. It has taught me a lot about my good sides and my downright ugly sides. Take it or leave it, it is what it is.

PART 1

Carpe Diem – Sieze the day

1.

In 1987 my father was standing on a ladder, painting the new nursery. I was hanging out in my mother's womb. She was relaxing on the couch in the sitting room. I wasn't kicking and screaming for once, I was pretty quiet. In fact, I hadn't moved in quite some time. A sudden screech from downstairs nearly knocked my dad from the ladder. 'Brian, come quick.' My mother could feel the warm wet between her legs. She was bleeding. I was ready to get out of there nine weeks early, or die in the process.

My father raced downstairs and found Mom lying across the couch. There was blood dripping from the couch onto the floor. Mom was scared, but she was also very calm. She was a nurse and she slipped into professional mode immediately. They rang the GP and the hospital, then got into the car. My mother brought a handful of towels to try and stem the flow of blood. Every few minutes she gave Dad an update: 'There is slight movement, it's still alive.' They broke a lot of red lights, then double-parked outside the hospital doors. Once inside, my mom was taken straight to theatre to be examined.

The bleeding stopped and she was put in a cubicle, with

a review planned for the morning. With morning came a further haemorrhage and the decision was taken to deliver immediately by Caesarean section. It was that or the baby would die, but my mother told me it was still a difficult decision to make. In 1987, delivery at thirty-one weeks was a high-risk proposition for a baby because its lungs wouldn't be fully developed. There was no other option.

At 11.00am on 22 March, a team of doctors introduced me to the world. Years later, I would revel in telling medical students that I was born the weight of a bag of sugar and could have fit into the palms of their hands – their eyes never failed to widen in disbelief. I couldn't breathe on my own and was put into an open incubator to give me oxygen and keep me alive. My mother remembers waking up after the C-section and looking over to where the cradle should have stood beside her bed. Instead, there was a Polaroid picture of me. She had to wait for my father to arrive to wheel her up to the Special Care Unit (SCU) and my incubator. My parents couldn't hold me because I was too small. I was literally a baby in a bubble. My premature body weighed only three pounds, but I had long, freakishly spindly legs and arms and liked to stretch around in my oxygen bubble amid the intravenous lines and the heart rate monitor leads. A doctor came to the ward and gently told them that I might not survive because of the complications resulting from being so premature. My lungs hadn't developed fully and had to be treated with surfactant, which helps them to develop faster. I also had a small hole in my heart and had to be given medication to help that close over. For the first few weeks after my birth I was on and off life support, tentatively holding on to life.

It was about two weeks after I was born that the doctors began to realise something else was happening. My mother had started to suspect something, too. I had a distended stomach, which at first was treated as another complication, but Mom had a feeling that something was wrong. She was right. They did some tests and when the results came back, my doctor diagnosed an obstruction of the bowel – *Meconium Ileus* – which would require surgery in Temple Street Children's Hospital. His main concern was whether I would survive the transport: by now I was just three weeks old, which meant I was still only thirty-four weeks and therefore not even full-term and I was still on life support. The night before the transport, a priest came and gave me the Sacrament of the Sick.

I made the journey safely and the surgery was a success. Indeed the operation was the first one of its kind performed by this surgeon and was reported in a medical journal. Professor Fitzgerald, who would be my primary consultant for the next eighteen years, removed my appendix too. Years later he told me it was 'because it was in the way' and he was saving me 'the trouble' of having it removed later in life. He squeezed out the meconium blockage with his hands. It was the first time he had carried out such a procedure, and I still have the small, crooked scar above my belly button as testament to his skill. After the surgery, he urged my parents to go home and get some sleep. There was nothing they could do, and in those days there was no accommodation for parents. My mom says while they didn't want to leave they knew they could do nothing and they lived only half an hour away. Getting some rest was the best option. The professor called them later to say he didn't think I would survive the night; there was very little hope and they reacted in different ways. Dad recalled sheepishly that he drank spirits to deaden the anxiety – something he would never normally do. My mother coped by taking control of the situation, in her mind working through the practicalities that would be involved in the event that I didn't make it. It was a long night. They 'comforted' themselves with the thought that death would be peaceful release; that if I did survive, perhaps I'd be in too much pain.

In the morning, the doctor phoned to say I was still alive and my condition was stabilising. My father says that moment was simply indescribable. They drove straight up to Temple Street to see me. For the next while, that was all they could do. They weren't allowed to hold or lift me from the incubator, so they sat beside me, putting their fingers through the glass barrier to touch my skin. They talked to me non-stop, telling me about their lives, my home, my family. Mom says they wanted to make sure I knew who I was.

When I was four weeks old, a nurse handed me into my mother's arms for the first time. She remembers that moment as being very emotional and surreal. I was still tiny, with long, skinny limbs, fingers and feet. My parents were now allowed to stay with me all day. They could hold me regularly by reaching inside the incubator and even change my nappy there too. Taking me out of the incubator was dangerous because it meant a loss of body heat. It must have been a strange relationship – intense and remote at the same time.

By the time I was five weeks old the doctors were fairly sure I had cystic fibrosis, but would have to wait until I was twelve weeks old to carry out the test on my sweat glands that would confirm it. But as they were 99 per cent sure I did have it, they started treating me with enzymes that break down food and intravenous antibiotics. Their theory was confirmed when the tests were performed seven weeks later: I had CF. After almost four months in hospital, on Derby Day, 15 July, my parents finally took me home to Kildare and the nursery my father had painted.

That was my dramatic entry into the world and my parents' unexpected crash into CF world. I would need extensive treatment every day of my life and for a long time they would have to give it to me. I would need to breathe in a steamed antibiotic from a nebuliser to loosen the sticky mucus in my lungs. They would have to give me postural drainage physiotherapy every single day by holding me over their shoulder slightly to help drain the loosened mucus down from my chest. My bowel blockage meant that I would need digestive enzymes to combat the gathering mucus in my intestines which would continuously block the natural enzymes that my body secreted to break down fats. I would already be at a disadvantage with my inability to naturally absorb fats because of the mucus. In technical terms, I had no lipase, amylase or protease in my system and without them, any fats I consumed would get caught by the mucus and lodge in my gut.

It would be a vicious circle, however, because my parents' other job would be to get me to eat as much as possible, whether it was 'good' or 'bad' food. I had to work harder to breathe, which meant I burnt more calories than the average child. They were warned that this would get worse when I got an infective exacerbation. I would lose most of the weight I had gained, which wouldn't be very much in the first place, because my body would burn so many calories just staying alive. My mother said it felt like we would have to start fighting right now, and continue every single day, if we were going to beat this. There is no cure for Cystic Fibrosis, they were told. The only thing they could do was keep me as well as possible until one came along. It was what my dad reminded me any time I tried to get out of doing medication: 'You need to be as well as possible so that when a cure comes along, we're ready for it.'

This was my parents' approach from the start – to be positive, always. They made a rule when I was young that if we were going to manage CF and the unpredictability of it properly, wrapping me in cotton wool wasn't going to work. They starting researching the best options for me and decided to relocate to Australia because it offered the most beneficial and healthy environment for a child with CF. My life would be better there because the health care was more advanced. Although my dad didn't have a professional qualification then, my mother was a qualified nurse which should guarantee entry to Australia. My mother was determined. In the visa application interview at the Australian Embassy she outlined my medical needs and we were permitted entry to the country. All the plans were in place for the big move, but a month before we were due to leave, Mom received a phone call. She says an official told her that I would be too much of a burden on the state and therefore Australia wouldn't accept us. Undeterred, they started planning how they would give me the best life possible at home in Ireland, with as few restrictions as possible. They believed, right from the beginning, that I could lead a full and happy life with CF.

I didn't hear the story about Australia until I was twenty-one years old. I wished I had heard it earlier. It quelled something that had been niggling at me. I had often wondered why we hadn't moved to somewhere better, wondered if they had ever even thought about it. On occasion, I had even been bitter about it. In the early days of campaigning for the CF unit at St Vincent's Hospital people would ask me, 'Why didn't your parents just move countries?' In private, I wondered if the reason was that CF appeared more innocent back then, less threatening. To those who asked, I said my life was here. I got older, and started to mean it. Why should I leave my country because the people in charge of it won't do their jobs? Nothing would ever change if people just left when they encountered a problem. I had never allowed CF to be the critical factor in any of my decisions, and now I'm glad it didn't decide where my parents chose to live. The cards fell where they did. Whether it was Ireland, Australia or someplace else, my parents' attitude and fighting spirit, which they passed on to me, would have been the same and in the end, that's what has really made the difference.

2.

In my bedroom at home there was a white-and-pink wardrobe. At nighttime I imagined if I opened it Narnia would be there, waiting for me. Occasionally, after I finished my bottle of Ribena, I'd turn off the light and stick my head into the wardrobe just in case I caught a glimpse of snow further on. I never did, but it never stopped me secretly hoping. I loved the idea of imaginary worlds and loved reading and making up stories with my dad. Imagination was greatly valued in our household.

My bed had been built by my uncle Frank. Above it were pinned my two favourite things: Mom's race number from the Flora Ladies Mini-Marathon 1992 and an adult-sized red bath towel featuring Mickey Mouse's grinning face. My mom says he was my favourite Disney character when I was very small, but I'm pretty sure it's always been the Little Mermaid. Although it's also true that I had a toy Mickey Mouse that was my bedtime partner, even though his worn-out nose hung on by a stitch. My dad said it was because he'd been on so many adventures to Dublin, to the hospital.

Mom had taken part in the tenth year of the mini-marathon and I remember that she trained all year, walking everyday. My mom loved walking and the house was buzzing with excitement on the day of the race. Afterwards, Dad and I huddled together in a pub waiting for her to arrive. He remembers it because it was the day he turned his back on me for a second and when he turned back, I was gone. The few seconds of blind panic until he found me chatting to some random women were enough to convince him to keep a sharper eye on me. I was terrible like that – I'd talk to a chair. I remember staring up at the sweaty bodies filtering in and out, anxiously looking out for Mom. When she arrived and showed off her medal, we were so proud.

The Mickey Mouse towel was purchased some months after the race, when my dad was in Cape May, New Jersey, in the USA. He went there for four months one summer to finance himself through the rest of his degree. He and his best friend, Ken, had completed one year of their degree courses and needed funds to see them through the rest. Before my dad left I told him I wanted him to bring me home a red or a pink-and-white tape recorder. It was very specific: it had to be able to record voice and play tapes so I could interview people. When Dad reminded me about this request, I felt a little sceptical, but I know I was good at communicating from an early age. Dad says that's just the way I was – I knew exactly what I wanted. We still have no idea how I knew which one I wanted. I think it was probably in an American TV programme, which was where most of my wild ideas came from.

Dad worked two jobs in Cape May, one at a hotel from 5.00am to 6.00pm and the other from 7.00pm to 11.00pm at a shop selling Irish goods and souvenirs. Between jobs he spent his time trying to figure out the next installment in 'The Adventures of Nutty and Notty', two squirrels that lived in a tree outside his house. He claims I harassed him for the next episode on the phone or by letter. I reject these accusations, of course. His other preoccupation was hunting down that tape recorder. After scouring Cape May, he eventually managed to discover there was a similar one in Pennsylvania, and nothing would stop him until he got it. To me, my dad was like Flash Gordon or Batman, he could do anything. He sent a picture of himself home in a letter: he was standing with his foot on top of a giant shark which was beached near where he worked. I imagined my dad wrestling the shark in the water, brute strength, cunning and a sharpened seashell his only weapons.

On the day Dad was due to return from America, in late September, Mom and I walked along the lane beside our housing estate to visit Snowy, a white pony, naturally, who lived in a field on Blackberry Lane, which was on the south periphery of our estate. We went there often to feed Snowy slices of apple, and this time I climbed a red fence nearby and we searched the sky for airplanes with my dad inside. Our world wasn't the same without him.

When we were all together our house was a place of magic. My Mom made mouthwatering Rice Crispie buns with marshmallows and Smarties. When my dad came home from work he would open his hands and orange-flavoured sparkle ice pops would fall from the sky. I never caught him throwing them up in the air first. In my eyes, he was a magician. Anytime I had a problem he would tell me the same thing: 'There's always a way. Just think outside the box. If you can't do it one way, try another.' My earliest memory of him telling me this is when I was sitting in my red high-chair in our kitchen. He told me over and over again that the people who did well in life were the ones who remembered to think positive and positivity was addictive; there was never a reason to be sad. That lesson was my first. He called it Positive Mental Attitude and it became the mantra I lived by. Whenever I was faced with a difficult situation, which of course was often, I would take a deep breath and repeat to myself in a whisper, 'Positive Mental Attitude, Positive Mental Attitude ...' My dad was fanatical about this idea and he made me the same. I'm glad now, looking back over my life, because many times it was the only life-ring I had to cling to, especially when facing doctors and needles and unpleasant treatments on my own.

My parents never tried to hide the fact that I had CF, they were open and easy about it. Our neighbours, Mr and Mrs Cullen, started burning smokeless fuel in my honour, so the smoke wouldn't waft into our garden and make me cough. My mother was mortified as we secretly stuck to the regular. The truth was that, unlike cigarette smoke, coal smoke didn't cause me irritation and anyway, smokeless fuel was more expensive. The Cullens were on one side of our two-storey house and on the other side were Tom, Mary and Brian. Every morning, when I was leaving for school and Tom was leaving to go to work, he would call out to me, 'Thumbs up for Tom, thumbs down for Mr Cullen'. When I was five it was a constant competition between those two as to who was my favourite neighbour.

My dad loved theatre. He'd spent his spare time before I came along in any local play that was being put on. He loved the stage and really appreciated people who enunciated properly. My parents enrolled me in Speech and Drama classes in the Christian Brothers' primary school, which I went to until I was nine. I wasn't really interested in studying for the grades, like the rest of the girls. I just went for the role-play and the fun of it. I don't think my parents knew about the grades system in the beginning, which was similar to piano grades, and I wasn't interested by the time they did. In truth, I was kind of intimidated by the other girls in the class, like when I went to Irish dancing. It was a funny dynamic: I wanted to beat them all to prove I was the best. I liked to tell them riveting dramatic tales or stomp the hardest. This did not gain me friends. My dad loved to recite the words 'This That These Those and Them', enunciating the 'th' sound carefully. He made me say them anytime I slipped up and fell into the *Dis* and *Dat* that was part of the flat midlands accent. My dad maintained that the way you spoke could make a difference to how people regarded you.

Posture was also a big thing in our family, and this was mostly because of CF. Ken, Dad's best friend, was training to be a physiotherapist and he did his final year thesis on exercise and CF. Ken warned me that coughing would create a natural hunch that stemmed from my body protecting my chest when I coughed. He said that a lot of adults with CF ended up with a hunched back as a result. My father scared the hell out of me, reminding me constantly of this and warning me not to do it or I would end up looking like Quasimodo. Every now and again he'd randomly bark, 'shoulders back, chest out', and it worked. Even while sitting on my space hopper watching *Mork and Mindy*, I had good posture. It also resulted in some people in school thinking I was a snob. To them I walked around with my head in the air and talked 'funny', which of course I did. It wasn't easy.

I did physiotherapy twice a day with my parents. The massive V-shaped foam platform was kept in the spare bedroom and all I had to do was lie over it as they clapped my back. They started doing it for me when I was just a baby, and apparently I found it really relaxing. So much so, in fact, that clapping my ribs with a lightly cupped hand and loosening the mucus sometimes made me doze off. Not the desired result of a session! They would have to decide who would be the evil one to wake me up to so I could cough it out. My parents tell me I loved doing physio and never had any trouble with it, until I hit the teenage years. They came up with ingenious ways to get the mucus moving around in my chest so I could cough it out – minus the sleep. My dad got me a grey trampoline that I loved bouncing on and for my birthday my Granny Tinsley got me that red space-hopper. It was great craic. Dad told me a different story each time he did the physio. My favourite was the long saga of Sally and and her horse, Silver, who became stranded on a desert island.

The Ketts house was at the top of our road. Their mom, Marie, minded me after school until I was nine because my

WATERFORD
No. 0051611556
CITY LIBRARY

mother worked as an ICU nurse. Marie's daughter, Niamh, was like the sister I never had and Barry and Rory were like my brothers. They all played musical instruments, so I started learning piano too. Mom said if I got that right, then I could play anything, that's what she'd heard. I became a pupil of our neighbour, Joe, who had written successful music for the Eurovision Song Contest. The problem with piano was that I kept missing so many lessons. In the beginning I just practiced on a piece of paper that had the keys drawn on it, but as time went on hospital interrupted my plans and thus began my love/hate relationship with finishing things. If I didn't care enough and couldn't do it well enough, I wasn't going to bother finishing it. This seemed like the right way to go about things. It didn't mean I was a 'perfectionist' or that it might make my life a little complicated down the line.

It is a difficult trait for someone who also doesn't like losing. When my Uncle Paddy visited from England he would photograph everything – he had records of our family from before I was born. When Uncle Paddy arrived on one particular visit, the neighbourhood girls were playing in our backyard and I decided we should have a race on camera. I was daydreaming so much that when they yelled 'Go', I still stood there, hand on skirt, twirling around. When I finally did set off, they were on the way back. Naturally, I demanded we do it again. My cousin Edel said to run it in slow motion, like they do after a big race on television to determine the winner. So they ran slow motion and I ran ahead of them, while they roared at me to come back and stop cheating. It was completely my fault that I hadn't gone the first time, but I didn't know how to lose.

I was six years old when Dad brought me hurriedly up to the Ketts one day as Mom was going into the hospital to have a baby. 'Your Ma's not really going to have him today,' my friend Niamh said. 'It's too early.' Mom was at the hospital, about to give birth to my brother. Some hours later I ran to my dad's car as it turned into our driveway. Niamh was right after all. Mom was still in hospital; it was a false alarm. Why? Why wouldn't he just come out? I was impatient to see him. Ten weeks later he did come out – four weeks late. His name was Jack and they immediately did a test to check his health status. He didn't have Cystic Fibrosis. Our family was complete.

3.

I was in hospital a lot when I was young but as a good friend said once, if you asked a fish about its life it would probably never mention water. CF was simply an integral part of life; I didn't know any different. Spells in hospital were so much part of the fabric of my life that separating it from 'normal life' was difficult. I knew other kids in my class and in my town didn't have to go there, but I didn't feel bad because of being in hospital or having CF. Everyone told me I was special and I felt that I was. I didn't feel lucky or unlucky to have this childhood. I just knew I was different and that was okay. I felt like I knew more than most kids my age.

Hospital was my second home from the start, at times my first home. I spend my first four Christmasses there with acute infections. My earliest memories all involve CF, but in different ways. My first is of moving between different rooms on the children's ward, trying to find the handheld computer game of *The Lion King* my dad had got me. It had gone missing on the ward while I was in the schoolroom. I searched the different rooms to find it and eventually saw a boy playing it with his mom. She said she had bought it for him, so I thought it couldn't be mine. Later that day my dad went to talk to the boy's parents. When he came back, he told me they had taken it and that he had gotten it back. I felt kind of bad about taking it back.

The public ward on the top floor of Temple Street Children's Hospital was known as Top Flat. I attended there from the age of two until eleven. My earliest memory of Top Flat is when I was five or six. Colette was another patient in hospital, she was thirteen and I slept in the room opposite hers. I shared with five other kids, but she was in a large room on her own. Her room had one other bed in it, but it wasn't being used. She had Cystic Fibrosis, too, but that didn't mean anything to me then – I had no conception of cross-infection and the dangers we posed to each other. I loved to go into her room and colour beside her, chatting about my day. My mother says I used to put on shows and sing to her, too. We were friends and I didn't understand why the nurses and my mother tried to keep us apart.

One of my roomies liked to drive the Fisher Price car around after midnight. I didn't mind. He never had many visitors and it gave me an excuse to stay up. Not that you'd need it on that ward. The adults nicknamed it Beiruit because of the rapid rhythm of the days and the harebrained antics that went on day and night. One night a nurse was thrown into a bath full of leftover dinners, mostly baked beans, to mark her last shift before changing jobs. There was a great sense of character to the ward, and there was always time for fun.

The morning always brought a fresh set of challenges. If the nurse didn't get to me first, my alarm call was the strong waft from the cleaning lady's mop and bucket and the rackety noise of the floor polisher banging against my bed. *Thud. Wake up!* It still happens to this day. Shower, breakfast and IVs followed and hopefully my line would work and the morning wouldn't be disrupted by people trying to re-site it. There was no getting out of going to the schoolroom, but that didn't stop me trying. I wanted to be good and go, but some mornings the atmosphere on the ward was much more fun. I would put it off as long as possible by saying I was too tired. If I was lucky, Dr Murphy or a nurse might wander in at just the right moment with some drugs and delay me legitimately for a while. They were on to me though, and I rarely got away with it. Listening in on the nurses' love lives and what dresses they wore out at the weekend – these were fascinating things when you're six.

The primary school was run by the principal, Mrs Dawson and aided by one teacher, Mary. Mrs Dawson had curly grey hair and Mom remembers how kind she was to me: 'She treated you as if you were her own. I knew you were safe.' In my eyes, Mrs Dawson would let me away with murder. Mary was the complete opposite. She was kind, but stern. There was no messing about with her. If Mary started talking in Irish to another adult in the room, you knew something was up or worse still, that you were the reason for this *as Gaeilge* conversation.

Around 9.30am Mrs Dawson would arrive at the foot of my bed. I could always get away with staying in bed longer if I told her I didn't feel like getting up – despite the fact that I was dressed beneath my bedsheets. There was no hope of it with Mary though. She'd march right up to the top of the bed and say things like, '*Amach as an leaba!* ' or '*SUAS!*' The words hurt my head and there was no way to escape her.

In retrospect it must have been so difficult for them to try to keep their pupils interested. Most of us were doped up on drugs with the average attention span of a goldfish. The school had limited resources, but Mom always made contact with my school to find out the books my class was doing and to keep me up-to-date. Sometimes, if I was tired or unwilling to continuously focus, I got to play on the computer for a break. And sometimes when I wanted to do more I was made to take a break, because I would wear myself out. When I look back now, I wonder if it made me a bit of a slacker in some ways, but how else could the adults have handled that situation?

The school day lasted from 9.30am to 3.00pm. The schoolroom was a small room on the first floor near the front of the hospital. We walked there in single file most days – 'we' usually meaning me and some post-surgery kids, most likely recovering from tonsillitis or appendicitis. Sometimes there were other regulars like me, kids with chronic illness who knew how things worked. If some other kid had CF, we couldn't ever be in the same room together because of the risk of cross-infection. There was generally always one or two children I knew I couldn't ever mix with, so I always checked with the teacher first to find out whether they were in that day. If anyone presented an unknown risk, the school or playroom staff would have to contact infection control to find out if we could share the same space. If you found yourself in a situation with someone you shouldn't be mixing with, it was usually by accident: they would be walking out of the school room when you were on your way in, for example. When that happened, we'd shove our backs up against the wall as we passed each other or fold our bodies into the grooves in the narrow corridor so we didn't pass any bugs to each other. It's just the way it was. I never really thought about what sort of infections were in the 'outside world', as I called it. The idea that sitting beside someone on a train might infect me, for example, was not even on my radar. I was aware of people with colds, coughs or running noses – all visible dangers. I was angry if someone didn't follow the rules in the hospital and I usually made it known. I wasn't afraid of anybody, though, inside or out, which wasn't always a good thing.

Most of the time there were around four or five children in the schoolroom. It was a rectangular room that had a computer on the right as you went in the door and a bookcase on the left. On its shelves were the books for each curriculum and opposite it was a smaller bookcase, full of novels. There were two sets of grey tables placed together, like the ones in a normal classroom, where the students and teachers would sit side by side. Everyone learned at their own pace, so each child was usually learning something different from the person beside him/her. It was the teacher's job to keep track of everything.

The unpredictable happenings of the schoolroom kept me occupied throughout the day. Every morning the blackboard would show the day, the date, what the weather was like and what was happening. *It is Monday the 22nd of March. It is Spring. It is Orla's birthday.* At 12.15 we gathered back on the ward to sit on the blue and orange plastic chairs and eat lunch, which was usually shepherd's pie, heavy on the peas and slim on the meat. I would open my Creon capsules and sprinkle them onto my shepherd's pie and gobble it up. Up next was the softest, creamiest ice cream and green-on-orange jelly. Afterwards the classroom assistants would round us up for school again for an afternoon of Art or Computer.

When I was very young, I would stay downstairs in the afternoon with Colette, painting on the large printing paper with green on the back while leaning against the hospital table. My mom remembers that she would arrive and drag me out of there, horrified because she knew the risk of cross-infection was high. Colette had a very different bacteria from me, one that could make me very sick. It was hard to understand at that age. One day Colette's room was empty. A nurse told me that Colette had 'moved to another ward'. I always knew when adults were lying – too much smiling involved. I had to wait for my mom to come in that evening to find out what had happened. The 'other ward' turned out to be ICU. She died a few days later. My parents explained to me that she had been very sick, but it didn't register until much later in life that she had the same illness as me and that the boundaries they had tried to impose on us, the boundaries I broke again and again, were to protect each of us against the bacteria the other had.

An average day in hospital felt like it lasted much longer than at home. The best part was that there were no real rules. Despite their being rules regarding medication and therapy, the compensation was the lack of social restriction. There were things my parents found difficult – more so than me. My mother says, 'It was so hard when we watched some of those ridiculous young doctors trying to put lines in on you in A and E.' I remember those moments, where an hour and seven or eight needle jabs would go by before my dad would tell the doctor to stop and call for someone else. I had 'floppy veins' that were overused and the heavy IV antibiotics I was on twice a day had ruined them.

Those moments were always balanced with some sort of reward at the end – like a toy, or even a story from my father. I was good at being strong. The Power Ranger session probably had a lot to do with this, with its line about leading a double life and that you must be strong and fearless, because that in turn makes you stronger. I stared right at the needle when they told me to look away. I became immune. The only option was to smile and tolerate and get on with it. These moments were always balanced out by my parents being there. Dad would firmly tell me that 'the power of the mind controls', and I felt like I was the one who was in control, that I was strong enough and powerful enough to overcome anything.

The truth was, as much as I missed my friends, I really enjoyed hospital. Apart from the needles and the inexperienced doctors, I loved connecting with older people. I wanted knowledge and I wanted it fast. I wanted to know everything. Back then, infections weren't as big a deal as they are for me now. There was no real pain involved, no coughing up blood, no really debilitating factors. CF was a breeze When I saw someone with CF who had a 'bad' bacteria, I always felt sorry for them and then was secretly thrilled that I was healthier than them. I was winning. That was always the goal: stay healthy, eat whatever I wanted and be creative. CF was like a pair of shoes I put on every once in a while, and usually had fun prancing around the hospital in them until I went home. The needles and the doctors and the screaming as the interns tried for sometimes the eleventh time to get a needle in my vein were all manageable. It just wasn't a big deal.

The hospital always had a warm feeling to it. And then there were the frequent visits from celebrities who wanted their picture taken with the inspirational sick kids. It was a joke to me, of course – 'inspirational sick children' meant nothing. I was just getting on with it. The porters at the front door knew my name and there was a human-sized brown teddy bear sitting in a wicker chair that I always passed on the way in. He was chained by the foot because he was there for charity. People saw him and put money in the box beside him. The corridors were long but familiar. It was like walking into my own home, except the ceilings were higher and instead of three friendly faces, there were hundreds. The ladies in the pink and green uniforms who worked in the canteen always said hello and snuck me a chocolate bar whenever I passed by.

Across the road from the hospital stood a group of flats with brown walls that had faded to a mucky colour with age. There were spiked red iron fences around them and sometimes I imagined there was a secret vortex of people swirling about inside. I had a clear view of the flats from the treatment room. I usually stared at them out of boredom while waiting for some doctor to come down to put in a new IV line. There was something warm and thrilling about all those people and all of that life just heaving around. I saw glimpses of those people every day – someone decorating a Christmas Tree or lighting up a cigarette – but I would never really know them and that fascinated me. I wanted to know what they were doing and why and how and what it all led to. I could hear arguments, see women walking around, getting ready for a night on the town. Once, at around one o'clock in the morning, I saw a man corner a woman up against a wall and she screamed so much I had to go and tell the nurse. There were children hanging around at night too, swigging from bottles and making noises like they were banging timber. One time, when I was ten, a boy waved up at my window, pulled down his pants and stuck his bum up in the air.

I always watched the kids who hung around at walls after school. They were so exotic to me. Back home I waited on the green beside the church for my parents to pick me up after school, which they did without fail. I ate a packed lunch, not stuff bought at the shop during break. The kids in the flats often walked home with a bread roll in their hands. At first I thought it was cool and kept begging my parents to let me buy my lunch when I went back to school, but my mom said it wasn't cool at all, that it was sad because their parents didn't take the time to make them lunch. I still thought it was cool though, like those kids had a responsibility I didn't have.

Fundraising events were a regular part of hospital life. I had my first introduction to them at age two when I had my picture taken with Friar Tuck and Little John from the local pantomime, *Robin Hood*. In the photo is a little girl with a big bouncy mop of golden curls looking slightly startled at the camera which the guy dressed as Friar Tuck is pointing at. It was published in a national paper and my parents framed it.

Whenever I was an inpatient I passed the time between drugs, physio and school getting involved in whatever event was on. I didn't feel any desire to lie in a bed all day. My lungs may have been stuffed up, but my brain was bored by lack of movement. I wanted to talk and sing and entertain. I loved having my photograph taken and as I got older I hung out in the fundraising office between school and needles and played with the free toys or chatted about what celebrities were coming next, what the newest fundraising incentive might be. They called me Ms Tinsley because I loved sauntering around like a little lady of importance, sorting it all out. It was a welcome distraction and I would get so caught up in it I'd forget why I was really there.

Back then, it was interesting because I saw the wide gap between the people who needed the equipment and those who had the power to give or withhold it. Money was the mediator. It was the difference between care and abject cruelty, between life and death. All that was missing was money, and I found it so strange that the government wouldn't provide it. The fundraising efforts were amazing, but even then I was aware that everything took so long. A machine or piece of equipment would be needed urgently, but it would take years of chipping away at the cost for the fundraising team to finally be able to purchase it for the hospital. Everyone knew it needed to be bought and everyone spoke about it and helped out, but the biggest bit of the jigsaw – the government input – was missing. Here was this unified sense of goodness aiming towards the one goal, yet despite all the hard work of the team, it never came easy.

During one hospital admission in 1994, when I was seven, my favourite nurse asked me take part in a fashion show she was holding in aid of the genocide victims in Rwanda. She explained to me that thousands of little girls and boys just like me had nothing left after the genocide, and that we could help them. I remember sitting on my hospital bed and telling Mom that I was going to be in a fashion show and it would be amazing and I would wear designer clothes from Clery's in Dublin. I figured she would like that because both she and Nana liked Clery's. She raised an eyebrow. Just who was it that wanted to parade her daughter around in a fashion show? I told her it was just Liz and it was for the orphans and it was fine. My mother was less than impressed. She was very protective of me and I can only imagine what extreme thoughts were going through her head when she heard the words, 'Your seven-year-old daughter' and 'fashion show', given that I was so precocious and loved to perform. My dad was all for throwing me up on stage because he loved performing, but my mother was more level-headed. She had a practical side that I didn't always give her credit for. Sometimes she worried too much, whereas if it made sense in my head I just wanted to do it.

When the nurse came in and explained that it would be for charity, that there were other children from the hospital involved and youth groups too and that there would be plenty of adults there, my mother finally said yes. Phew! Although if she had said no, I would probably have just asked Dad. We had to drive to Dublin for rehearsals and I was paired with another girl who had long wavy blonde hair that fell right down her back. She was eleven to my seven, but I was tall for my age. Before the show we lined up to get our make-up applied in ten seconds flat by a woman with a handheld mirror. We had to walk down the catwalk, high-five each other and then walk in a circle before standing back-to-back, arms folded, and smirk with satisfaction My green check trousers and red blouse with white collar made me feel extremely cool.

Each day in hospital the physio would come. Deirdre. There were four with the same name, which was also the name of my best friend in school. But much of the medical detail from my hospital spells eludes me – it's like I saw it as a place where life just unfolded, rather than a place that was outside the norm, that was to be feared in any way. I trusted most of the people looking after me, but from a young age I was assertive when I needed to be.

I always remembered what Dr Murphy had told me: the patient knows best. He had been a consultant of mine since I was three weeks old. He had a moustache and sometimes mumbled his words. He often thought out loud, which made his moustache ruffling even funnier. My mother says he was a father figure to me. Strange as it may sound, I had to trust him with my life. Just like I had to trust the numerous nurses and physiotherapists and then the dieticians and others when they came along. I didn't feel different in a bad way from my friends, but I did feel like parts of me were separated out and existing in different places. I imagined that my friends were coherent, all the pieces of them held tightly together within their families. But emotionally and spiritually I was connected to all these different professional people from a very young age. I knew about their lives, their boyfriends, their families, their decisions and I was learning from all angles. Sometimes this was confusing. I got close to someone in hospital, they told me all about their life and then I went home and didn't see them for months. At home, I'd talk about the details of something they'd said or done and it must have been strange for my mother, listening to my banter about people whose personal lives she was not privy to, from a part of my life where she was in some ways more the outsider than they were.

When I asserted myself to doctors it was usually around the issue of needles. It was self-protection. It wasn't that I was scared of needles, they didn't actually hurt that much. I learned early on that, apart from luck, when it came to site-ing cannulas, a bit of style and a lot of patience were required. Unfortunately, this was lost on many doctors, particularly junior ones. I would sit in the treatment room waiting to be seen, hoping the person who walked through the door was a registrar or a doctor with proper experience. If it was an intern, I would usually tell them to leave. Interns, the cool dudes of the doctor chain, breezed into the room as though surfing their own private wave. They were here, they were ready and they had put in a cannula before and wanted to do it again, man. I learned from a young age who could and who shouldn't be allowed to perform this procedure. They weren't all bad.

As a kid I felt sorry for interns because they had no idea what they were in for with me. My veins are particularly difficult to insert a needle into. My mother says it's because I was so premature – my veins weren't yet grown fully when I was born and they never recovered. Interns would typically come in, try and distract you with some natter about how clever you were for telling them which needle was better for your tiny veins and just feel along your arm and jab you. Sometimes they forgot to strap on a tourniquet and would simply spring their finger on a spot that looked blue and felt spongy and just shoot. Needless to say, once I learned to identify them, I gave them the boot quickly or we would have been there all night. Sometimes we were. When I was nine and telling them what to do or that there were no good veins in the area they were looking in, they would smile and ask to wait for the IV nurse in the morning. I badgered them really, but it was necessary.

I usually knew within minutes of them walking into the room what kind of needle-handler they were going to be. If they came in munching a bag of Tayto crisps, took one glance at my hands from over the edge of the sink as they washed off the salt and said, 'No problemo!', I still couldn't be entirely sure. There were other indicators that had to be taken into account. Was his hair gelled or natural? Was he actually looking at you, or through you and the next six patients he had to see to the couch in the doctor's lounge? Gelled hair usually meant they spent time on their appearance, which would sometimes mean they didn't spend much time looking for a vein. Their conversation fillers were usually tiring and unoriginal. They were the type of guys who couldn't deliver. They would ask me to talk about school, or ask me how many brothers and sisters I had. Sometimes they'd tell me I was brave and say how much they'd love to have my hair, if only they were a girl. I had been through it so many times it made me cynical and bored. I respected them more when they didn't play the distraction game. When the female doctors started showing up as I got older, it got more complicated. I never understood how they could work all day and night in high-heels. I always had more respect for the girl running around in scrubs and runners. I felt like she had seen some gritty stuff, like she had more experience. In retrospect, this is all bonkers, but as a kid this was the sort of coding that helped me assess the situation. Or rather, that kept me thinking I was in control.

I learned to say things like 'So now you are asking me about this to try to distract me? Stop. It won't work. Thanks,' or 'No I don't want to look away'. My most familiar lines were, 'You're looking in the wrong place. They disappear when you go in, so don't try there. Try here and here. If you can't do it, it's okay. Not many people can.' They responded better to that approach because their egos were less bruised. 'I always get it, I never miss,' they might say. When they didn't manage it, mostly I would just tell them it wasn't a reflection on their ability and I would head back to bed so that my team could sort it out in the morning. I was a precocious child, but I always dreaded those nights when an IV was necessary, they were the most frustrating part of hospital.

There were only two people I really trusted when it came to affairs of the veins: Eileen and Carmel, the official intravenous nurse and the phlebotomist. Carmel was always perfectly made up, with electric red lipstick and matching nails. Her short blonde hair and glamour were like an ad for Chanel. When Carmel stuck her head out the door of the blood-testing clinic, she would wink at me conspiratorially and usher me in with one perfectly manicured finger. Eileen, on the other hand, was always in a hurry. I didn't go down to see Eileen – she came up to the ward to see me, and woe betide any patient who wasn't ready when Eileen came calling. It was poor Eileen who had the experience of trying to get in the trickiest long line ever. A long line was much worse than a peripheral cannula. There isn't much I hate in life, aside from cigarette smoke and spiders, but long lines were right up there. For a long line, the cannula was threaded up through the vein in the arm. On this occasion, Eileen could only get so far and no further, so she tugged the line to try to pull it through. You know if you get smacked in the stomach with a football and winded? You feel sick deep inside your stomach? That's how my arms felt as she was tugging with the tube deep inside my veins, like weaving thread through a doll. She was just as traumatised as me and ended up crying, too. After that experience they decided to look at alternative ways to give me antibiotics. I'm sure Eileen was as relieved as me to hear that.

4.

Getting back to home life after hospital was always difficult. My mother says I was giddy and it would take me while to calm down into family life. Hospital life was faster; I was always alert and aware of what was going on and there wasn't a lot of relaxing involved. From a young age I was bad at relaxing. I felt like it was giving in to the idea of being ill. I hated the idea of staying in bed all day and would only do it if it meant not having to get up for school.

Just like not hating having CF, I didn't hate the absences from school that came with it, but I really missed the friendships. I had two great loyal friends and though it was always hard to get back into the groove of school, it never took too long to settle in again. I played soccer and auditioned for shows and sang in anything I could get myself into. School was a breeze. I was good at most subjects and I was one of the top two best singers in the class. The other was my best friend, Deirdre. She had straight black hair that was always neatly tied up in a bun or ponytail and she spent painstaking time colouring inside the lines. Her crayoning was so heavy that you could scratch through it and make funny shapes. It usually took her all of colouring time to do it, whereas I just threw a few colourful lines on the page and it was done. I really admired her work, but for me, the faster I was done, the more quiet time I had in our junior infants library, which was much more fun. Deirdre and I were partners in crime at school.

In senior infants our teacher entered us into the *Feis Ceoil* competition. We were all learning to play the tin-whistle and our play, *Froggy Went A Courtin'*, was selected to compete. Deirdre played an elf, hard at work with other elves who sat in a circle in front of a tree. I was the tree. My mom was so proud and made my costume out of brown and green crêpe paper and velvet. Standing still for a whole half hour was extremely difficult, but it was exciting to be on stage and I knew if I worked hard enough I could be better than a tree.

That summer my dad brought me to the auditions for the *Babes in the Wood* pantomime in Newbridge, and I ended up being cast as a fairy, along with twenty other children, singing 'I Can Sing A Rainbow'. It went something like, 'Listen with your heart, listen with your eyes and sing everything you see.' I remember the dance rehearsals and how I wanted to practice over and over, but we only had an hour because we weren't the most important fairies. I had inherited the acting bug from Dad and I loved being on stage. Some weekends, instead of renting a movie or watching *Murder She Wrote*, we would watch my father perform his role in 'Charlie's Aunt', just for us. On nights like that we sucked sparkle ice-pops and he would entertain us with stories of when he was treading the boards. He wanted to go back to it, but he had too much work to do.

For my sixth birthday I got a grey and blue typewriter, just like Jessica Fletcher in *Murder, She Wrote*. My father loved that I was so into writing and being creative like him, and always encouraged me. I was going to solve mysteries and then come home and eat two tea cakes or Fry's chocolate creams and drink my Ribena. As a result of my need for extra calories, I was encouraged to eat anything and everything, including two tea cakes every night, 'roundies' as my dad called them. These were teacakes of marshmallow with jam in the middle and a thin layer of chocolate on top. They worked until I was about eight and started craving something richer. Fry's Chocolate Cream became my poison: seven slices of delicious perfection – eaten all at once for mind-blowing greediness or slowly devoured by nibbling along the sides and peeling off the chocolate bit by bit to reveal the gooey fondant in the middle.

I loved most food. I adored potatoes – mash was good, crispy roast potatoes were better, but my absolute favourite was potato dauphinoise, which my dad started cooking when I was around ten. The creamy goodness that floats in your mouth after biting into the crunchy top layer is the most satisfying feeling in the world. And I could eat as much as I liked for as long as I liked. Most people with CF avoid food when they are sick, and my parents and medical team always marvelled that I didn't. Sure, the IV antibiotics sometimes put a stopper in my hunger or made me nauseous, but when that happened I just reminded myself that *The power of the mind controls* and I made myself mentally hungry. It was mind over matter and I was scarily good at it.

I made my First Holy Communion in Cill Mhuire, the church beside our school. I remember standing in line in our classroom waiting to taste my first practice Communion wafer. It shrivelled on my tongue like skin in the bath. I didn't think much of it. The most important thing about the day was, of course, the dress. My best friend Deirdre was wearing a pearl-covered number, complete with headdress. I told Mom I wanted to have something similar, and she said that next time we went to Dublin to the hospital, we could have a look around.

We usually drove up to hospital appointments listening to Frances and Mary Black on the *Only A Woman's Heart* album, singing along. I knew all the words and rolled my eyes at Mom when she got them wrong. After the appointment we would walk past the Garden Of Remembrance and into town for our soup. If it had been a particularly tough session I got chips and a delicious Café Kylemore bun. Nana came with us on occasion and I trailed behind them as they shopped in Arnotts or Clery's, tolerating the boredom of the clothes racks for a spell in the early learning centre or maybe some McDonalds on the way home. Other times we went to Bewley's Café on Westmoreland Street for a bowl of soup. For the communion dress hunt, Mom brought me to Laura Ashley on Grafton Street. The name alone made me snore. Who named their shop after themselves? Where was the creativity in that? Serious, sober, sensible dresses hung on mundane hangers. In my mind's eye I could see the pink Café Kylemore bun: it would get me through this. The chosen dress was white and plain but for a sailor-type collar. It wasn't anything like Deirdre's pearl-covered dress. I was not to appreciate my mother's sense of style until much later in life.

On the big day, my classmates and I stood alongside each other, hands placed together, angelic and true. After the ceremony my family gathered at our house. My cousin Elaine was having hers an hour before mine, so my Nana had to hightail it from one end of the town to the other to fit us both in. Three hours after I had stood at the altar in my pristine white dress I was playing football in the cul-de-sac with the neighbourhood boys. My neighbour and one of my best friends, Daniel, arranged for cookies and Coke in his tent afterwards; his dad was in the army, hence the tent. You couldn't sit upright in it, though, so we lay down and ate our goodies.

When I finally arrived home I realised I had lost a fifty-pound note while diving for a goal at the gate of the abandoned house no one wanted to buy because it was in front of the train tracks. There was also the small problem of the grass stain smeared along the back of my Laura

Ashley dress, gained during a hard-fought contest to see who could throw the most sticky-backs at the other person. I had won, but not exactly with my mother, who was less than impressed.

This communion lark didn't really mean much to me anyway. Dad didn't believe in the God stuff much; Mom did. I had cousins who didn't have to go to Mass at all, and some who went all the time. The idea of God was never pushed on me. My father's view on life was more philosophical in all areas. He loved exploring words and language, looking for the hidden meaning in something someone said. He loved figuring out people and stories and the endless possibilities of life. My mother was more into rules, like the importance of college and family and tradition. I'm not sure why I didn't entirely believe in God at that point. I guess I had just seen so much that I didn't really see how one guy could be okay with all that happened in the world. And Mass was so boring. I just wanted to be out in the world.

Visits to Temple Street often meant a trip to Walton's Music Shop, if there was time. If I needed to be admitted into the hospital, there was usually a bed available. Sometimes there was a one or two-hour wait for our appointment, and Mom and I would split up and go to our own favourite places: she to the Hugh Lane Gallery on Parnell Square and me to Walton's. At that time I hated art galleries. There was nothing bright and exciting about them. Even just walking into the place froze me up inside. There was no vibrant colour and I didn't understand the appeal.

My mother and I would walk along the grey pavements, past the flats, avoiding things like groups of youths huddled in the corner or the smash that made us jump out of our skin once. It was a woman who had thrown a glass down from the flats. Mom said she did it because she was bitter. I liked walking past Belvedere College, the boys' school on Great Denmark Street, and watching the boys in their black and navy uniform congregate on the street outside the gates.

Dublin was a place of endless possibilities. Here, boys had their lunch break in the streets and the city was their playground it seemed. There was no such thing as not being allowed to cross a certain line in the schoolyard, like in my school. There were no lines. After the gates of Belvedere, Mom and I would part. I would rifle through the sheet music in Walton's and find sheet music to dement my piano teacher with and distract him from scales and grades. Mom would cross at the traffic lights and head into the Gallery.

When I was eight my mother sent me to swimming lessons and I hated them. I loved swimming, but this was boring. I hated holding onto a bar in a line with other children and kicking the water as it splashed and smacked. I didn't see swimming as a sport or competition. Instead it was something natural and free, like breathing. I loved jumping into the river and just swishing around, whatever way I felt like. Sometimes I flopped like a mermaid, hands by my sides, just using my body.

Some of our summers were spent in Wexford, near the seaside. At first we stayed in my aunt and uncle's holiday caravan in Kilmuckridge, then in a little wooden cabin my parents rented near Morriscastle beach. When I was nine and my brother three, my parents rented their own green-and-white mobile home, which was parked a five-minute walk away from a stony beach. At seven o'clock each night, when the beach was bare, Dad would bring my cousin Elaine and me down for a swim. The Irish Sea was chilly in the evening and the sky hanging over us was coloured like Turkish Delight. Elaine squealed before she even got into the water, but I ran right in. I had to or my dad would have tickled me into it. I couldn't handle tickles. 'The power of the mind controls,' he'd say whilst swirling his hands around his head in faux-hypnotist style. *If you think it, you can do it.* The chill of the water was never an issue, I just dived right in and swam underwater until I warmed up.

The site held around twenty mobile homes and a tennis court. Near our caravan balcony an orange woman lay tanning her toned yet bizarrely wrinkled body. 'Sun worshipper,' Mom muttered.

'What does that mean?'

'You know, someone who only cares about their body and lies around getting skin cancer. It's so dangerous.' I looked at the skinny woman in her electric pink bikini against the deep brown tan and shuddered.

Mom's friend from work brought her boys down too, David and Neil, and we played tennis on the court, sometimes for the entire day. One day a girl and boy came along to play, so David and I played doubles with them. The girl's name was Clare and we played tennis together most days after that. One morning she didn't turn up, so I went over to her caravan, in case she had forgotten. She had slept in so I sat at the kitchen table to wait for her to get ready. Her brother was there and he took out his nebuliser. I was flabbergasted and told him I had one too because I had CF. Did he? His mom, who was lovely, asked me to leave and said Clare would meet me at the court.

That night when Dad and I came back from swimming, Clare's mother was just leaving our place. Mom sat me down and tried to explain to me what was going on. Clare's brother didn't know he had CF, he thought he had asthma. *But why?* I kept asking my mother. *Why would they lie to him?* I couldn't get my head around it. His mother had come over to make sure that I was okay, but she didn't want me to talk about CF around her son. If someone said to me, 'You have an awful cough,' I simply said, 'I have cystic fibrosis so sometimes I cough, it's no big deal'. It was no big deal, so why was this woman making it such a big deal?

I suppose everyone deals with it differently and as I got older and entered into adult services, I met people who had told no one growing up that they had CF. These people didn't tell employers as they got older either. I also met the other side of the coin, people who think CF is a blessing and that because of it they have greater knowledge than people who don't have CF. This can in fact give them a sense of superiority, which they carry into adulthood. I definitely equated more with the second type as a child, but not so much now. For me now, that thinking ends up being false. No one is better than anyone else, we're all where we're meant to be. I still hate when I hear that parents deny their child personal information about their illness, but I understand it too.

Many years later I met Clare's mother again and she said that meeting me when her son was that young had changed her perception of CF and slowly they had started explaining things to him. It must have been really hard for him, and for his parents. My parents were never into keeping secrets – there was nothing to hide. Their approach to CF helped me because it meant it was never an enemy for me. I never said what a friend of mine with CF says regularly and with great feeling: 'I HATE CF'. Hearing her say it, and say it like that, really forced me to examine why I didn't share her feeling. In later life, as I got sicker with CF, I was frustrated to extremes that I didn't know were possible. I felt out of control, I lashed out and cried and fought. But I didn't hate it. Hate didn't seem to belong with it. It wasn't my identity but it was so close to me that hating it would have been like hating myself.

5.

When I turned nine my family moved to a house in downtown Newbridge, just beside the River Liffey. The house belonged to my uncle, and he, my father and their brothers had been raised there. It was a temporary solution while our new house in Hawkfield, or 'the countryside', was being built. My father was very proud that he and his siblings had been raised in such a small house and with so little. The house was full of things that reminded him of childhood. One night my mom showed me a photo of a woman in a long Victorian style dress with elegant top hat. She looked like Audrey Hepburn in *My Fair Lady*. I was dumbfounded. This was my father's mother. She died in 1950, they weren't sure from what. Maybe a clot or a hemmorage. My dad had two Moms, one whom I had never met and who died before he was five. This was serious stuff to digest and I prodded about it, but didn't get anywhere. I always saw my dad as the most positive, motivated person in the universe. It was unthinkable that a tragedy like this had been thrust upon him at a young age. To my mind, it made him even more brilliant.

This news and our change of environment coincided with

my arrival into third class – the class of doom. Our teacher's first love was Maths. Every morning, after our prayer of thanks – which I was wearing thin of saying not least because of the slew of religion flitting around my neighbourhood in the form of Novenas and holy water bottles from neighbours for the sick child – the numbers went up on the board. Every single morning was like torture as I surveyed the symbols scattered across the blackboard and my heart sank. That year the school took part in a creative writing competition. I remember sitting with Dad at the small wooden table in our claustrophobic kitchen, binding together the sheets containing my story in a black folder with golden rims. I came first in the competition, but when I asked for my prize-winning entry back, my teacher couldn't find the folder. I was devastated and Dad said the lesson was to always keep a draft copy of my work – he said it could be worth millions some day when I was Jessica Fletcher!

When we moved house I joined the same choir as my cousin Elaine, in Milltown church, because Mom thought it was a good way to get to know people in our new community. That summer we both started in the Milltown summer camp on a production of *Les Miserables*. After two weeks of rehearsing every day our director, who stamped and roared comically when he got angry, realised he couldn't secure the rights to perform it. He called us all into the carpeted hall of Milltown school to inform us that we were changing the show to *Joesph and the Amazing Technicolour Dreamcoat*. We had just three weeks to put it together and even now, twelve years later, I can recite every single song from *Joseph*, word and note perfect. This musical changed my life. I made friends at a rapid pace in musical theatre. It was full of drama and hijinks. I particularly bonded with a girl who was slightly older than me. There was something so incredible about her. When she stood up and sang, 'Joseph's mother she was quite my favourite wife', I lit up. Of course, I was just an Ishmaelite;

I hadn't been there in time for the auditions. My cousin Elaine was a narrator. She says I was pretty mean to her around this time because I didn't have a main part. It was tough because I saw how nervous she was, but I didn't understand nerves or fear. I would have gladly taken her place.

When the summer ended, we were still living in Dad's old house. We ended up living there for almost a year. It was tough. I missed playing Power Rangers with Daniel. Our 'home' was now an old terraced house, built in the 1950s, small and draughty. There was no front garden and the back garden was just a tiny, secluded area, raised off the ground and riddled with weeds. There were no trees to jump out of, pretending to be GI Joe.

'Go on, Orla,' Mom said one day, ushering me down through the corridor when she spotted children outside. I didn't want to make new friends. I liked the ones I had. As I made for the door she whipped my hands together and placed the dreaded mittens on them. They were cream and puffy, as though made for the Arctic and embroidered with a cheesy Christmas jumper pattern. I wanted to wear my elephant-leather horse-riding gloves, but my mom said I would ruin them. She placed the homemade gold thread that held the mittens together between my lax wrists and smiled. She had made the mittens herself, but they were so uncool and heavy on my hands. I walked outside and took a deep breath of the town air. There was a boy and a girl sitting on concrete stumps near the green area and the boy looked up.

'Well, well, well. Orla Tinsley.'

That was his opening line. He wasn't new, it was Jimmy, the boy to whom I had given my first Valentine's card. He lived here? I hadn't known. Jimmy was small and skinny with blonde hair in a pudding-bowl hair cut. There was a girl with long blonde hair with him and she beckoned me over. She introduced herself as Karen.

I got a Power Rangers Megazord from Santa that year.

The Megazord was the amalgamation of all the Power Rangers' powers to create the ultimate superhero robot. My mom ended up enlisting my Aunt Eilis to get it in London during a business trip because they were sold out everywhere in Ireland. I was over the moon. My mother told me to slow down with as I pieced it together. 'Looked at the instructions,' she called. I didn't need instructions! We fought, but after the first thrill of assembly, it didn't matter so much anymore. Power Rangers and Captain Planet weren't appreciated in this neighbourhood.

I was very fickle about things anyway. I was passionate and when I loved something, I became completely obsessed with it, but my mom says that as soon as something else came along, I dropped it like a hot potato. Even so, I never wanted to throw anything away. My wardrobe was filled with things I didn't use but couldn't throw away. It was when we moved to the 'temporary' house that I got very messy. Now my space was small and limited, so I should have been more picky about my possessions, but I wasn't. I didn't care as long as I could close the bedroom door on it all. In truth I hated everything about this house. I felt like I was poor, which didn't match up with the sense of privilege I had grown up with. My sense of wealth was firmly rooted in material things, even though I was meant to know better. In the house. there was no proper shower. The bathroom was downstairs, beside the kitchen, and it was cold and I hated it, so I usually didn't wash. This was a big battle in our house. I just couldn't bear to wash there. It was hard because my father was so proud of the house and I was so proud of him. I felt I couldn't truly let my feelings be known, which only added to my misery. I missed my friends and felt disconnected from what I'd known until then. Dad would say things like 'Life changes, it's all about adapting', but I didn't like change one bit.

There was a green space across from the house and every now and then people gathered there, got down on their hands and knees and said the Rosary. Most likely this only happened on actual feast days, but the image of them praying really confused me: having inherited the philosophy of an atheistic father, I couldn't fathom why other people believed so fervently in God that they would embarrass themselves in public. The crowd was almost always made up of the older generation and the whole thing looked like an exercise in pointlessness to me. This confusion and sense of futility became even stranger when my mother would join them, which she sometimes did because she had great faith too. The only time I really liked being in church was for the choir in Milltown or St Patrick's Day Irish Mass in school, where everything was '*Suil, suil, suil le chroi*'. Choir was what got me through that massive change. Rehearsals on Thursday nights and songs on Sunday. My choir instructor said I was the best and could take over from her when she went to college, so I worked hard and went to Mass every week. The singing part of Mass I loved, but the kneeling in the cold, on the grass, in the middle of the town was beyond my comprehension.

Across the road from the house was an old style sweet shop with shelves lined with jars of liquorices, cushions, lemon drops and every imaginable taste and colour. The couple who owned the shop, Mr and Mrs Kearns, were in their late sixties and as ingrained in town life as the River Liffey that ran under the bridge the cars crossed to enter the main street. I went to their shop daily, buying quarter and half-bags of sweets. They would usually give me extra, too. My new friends, Karen and Jimmy, often came with me. We would buy our sweets and wander around the green area eating them, the other two chatting incessantly about movies I'd never heard of.

It was around that time that my stomach started to get funny. In the morning my cheese on toast would give me cramps and I'd refuse to go to school. My mom would eye me suspiciously. Was everything okay? It wasn't, but I was floating along nicely, not really noticing it chip away at me. I fell full-bodied into my Reading Log and spelling tests and every English poem I was given. But Irish was another thing. I just couldn't learn my tenses. I stared at the page for an hour at night, wrote them out over and over, but nothing worked. I felt terribly guilty about it and about the fact that I had very little interest in the geography of Ireland. I didn't mind reading about the Battle of Clontarf in History, but it all seemed a bit dull. They were my mother's favourite subjects though, and I wanted to be able to do well in them so we could talk about it.

The real problem at school was different. There were five of us at our table — three boys, another girl and me. And even though they messed and talked more than I did, they still seemed to understand more than me. The girl was a bit of a ring leader, and anytime I asked a question her head would shoot in the air and rotate around like an ostrich. 'Do you hear something?' she would ask and the boys would giggle. It was usually pretty easy to ignore her, but the incident with the crayon box was the final straw. On this day I had actually beat her in the spelling test again and she was rubbing out the mistakes in her copy so hard that the table shook. When it was time to hand up our copies, we placed them in the middle of our grey, rectangular table. She squared them up, as usual, but then she did something different. She took my copy and separated it from the rest. She didn't speak, just placed it under the crayon box and put everyone else's on top.

'At least now we don't have to have our copies touching Germs.'

Germs was what she called me. Germs when I sprinkled my enzymes on my food. Germ Girl when I coughed.

Something ruptured inside of me and I launched to my feet as our teacher was writing *as Gaeilge* on the board. 'What the hell is wrong with my copy? There's nothing wrong with it. *Nothing*!' I shouted. My insides froze as the room fell silent. 'Orla . . .' said the teacher, but I was already out the door. In the bathroom I shredded tissues trying to figure out what to do next. Outside the door I could hear voices. My teacher was negotiating something and when the bell rang for lunch, I came out.

That afternoon an assistant teacher took the class and the teacher brought our table of five outside to the carpeted P.E. hall. We sat in a circle and they all apologised to me. Afterwards the boys and I played chasing in the yard, but the girl was still the same. When I got home from school all I wanted to do was go to bed, but my mom caught me before I could creep up the stairs. It all just came pouring out and she said I should have told her I was being bullied. But 'bullied' was such a foreign word and I felt it had nothing to do with me.

When I think about it now, I would be so upset if I heard this was happening to a young child with CF anywhere. My condition was never discussed in the classroom and increasingly I hear of children, particularly girls in secondary school, taking it upon themselves to get teachers to explain it to a class so there's no room for misunderstanding and name-calling. While my own teacher was good when she finally noticed how the other children were treating me, there is so little support for children with CF in the education system. I would see this later in secondary school when arriving in late after doing home IVs and physio since 7.00am. I more often than not went back to sleep afterwards and then went in for 11.00 break. Some teachers thought I was lazy; a small few understood. Even though I had the ability and the vocabulary to explain my situation to them, sometimes it fell on deaf ears. I felt like it was my responsibility to defend myself, but they saw me as a mouthy drama queen.

While the main source of my cramps had been tackled, I was still having the problem with my stomach, which now began to jut out like a watermelon. My mother remembers seeing me standing with my cousin's friends at her birthday party, suddenly realising that my cramps were more than stress or the onset of menstruation, as she had first thought. She had read about this stuff before and she knew. She nearly always knew about me before me, so I always tried to learn more and know more than her. It was a constant competition. What she realised in that moment at the party was that the mucus in my bowels had gotten worse – not helped, I'm sure, by the new diet of curry chips every few nights. I had always been encouraged to eat anything I wanted, but now maybe it was catching up with me. When we got our photos developed from our summer holidays in Portugal, I marvelled at the difference between the flat-chested, long legged, tanned girl in the pictures, hair gently highlighted from the sun – and the girl sitting on the sofa with the ever-growing stomach. I knew that unless some sort of immaculate conception had occurred it probably had something to do with CF.

I spent four weeks in hospital trying to get it sorted out. They gave me a disgusting liquorice-tasting drink to glug in the hopes of washing out my bowels. They then changed my pancreatic enzymes from Creon to Nutrizyme, which they thought might help me digest food better. It was my first time on a new ward too, St Philomena's Ward in Temple Street Hospital. My parents had been trying to get me to move there for years, out of the public ward. They thought the semi-private would be better for me to study in, less distracting than 'Beirut'. My parents wanted me somewhere quieter, where there was a less chance of my toys being taken from my bed, and because there were fewer people on St Philomena's, they felt there would be more concentrated care.

St Philomena's ward had two rooms of four beds, one room with three beds and a baby ward surrounding the nurses' office. It was a big change for me, but it was closer to the school and the playroom. On my first day there I went for a stroll around and realised that if you followed the stairs off the ward and down a flight and through a secret corridor, you could get to Dr Murphy's private clinic which is where we went on Tuesdays. It was like popping up in an alternate universe. When you left the ward and walked up the stairs, past the Tellytubbies paintings, the door to the schoolroom was smack in front of you. And if you ventured down the corridor the furthest you could go, there was the fundraising office. This had always been my favourite place. I loved hanging out and tidying up leaflets, doing odd jobs to help out. It made me feel like I was doing something and not just wasting time. Everyone was always in a good mood in there and it was a welcome break from the screaming babies or someone wagging their finger at you while holding two litres of the most disgusting licorice drink you'd ever tasted. You had to drink it and not throw it up, or get a tube down that did it for you. There was no way I was getting any tubes up my nose and down into my stomach. I could drink it, I could drink anything.

When I came home from hospital my diet had to change. Dodgy bowels meant I was uncomfortable with some of the foods I had eaten with abandon before. I had bought bags of 'cough bottles' in Kearns' sweet shop, but now they just tasted like the litres of laxative I had had to drink in hospital. While in hospital I sometimes went on lunch break with the nurses when I was bored, if they weren't going to the smoking area of the canteen. One day, when my appetite was completely shot because of the laxatives, someone had offered me a cream cracker with Philadelphia cream cheese. From then on, I was hooked. Back at home again I had porridge for breakfast with the new low fat milk everyone in the house was now drinking, then Philadelphia on crackers for lunch.

Around this time my mom and I started training for the Lyons Cycle, a 10-mile cycle race through the town. We would get fit together, she said, and it made me less self-conscious about my stomach. It had shrunk when the poo was blasted out, but it was still much bigger than before and looked unusual on me. We trained every week for the race, and then most nights Dad and I went swimming in the River Liffey. While I was swimming I didn't think about my changing body or about the kids at school.

My bike was a purple Raleigh that we had bought in McLoughlin's bike shop in the middle of town. It was my first bike and I loved it. On the day of the race we set off from my primary school amid throngs of bikes and somewhere between the Newbridge and the Curragh I lost my mom and Dad. I kept going, cycling with my friend instead. It was then that I took a tumble into a bush. I was looking at her, talking away, instead of watching where I was going. For some reason an ambulance was nearby, I think maybe one trails behind every group. When I stood up, my knee was bleeding heavily. Then the battle began. 'Please get into the ambulance,' said a friendly looking man. 'No, I'm fine.' I had just scraped my knee and I had never been in an ambulance in my life. This hardly warranted it. I was holding a leaf over the wound and he looked at the now red-stained leg and back at me. I somehow convinced him to give me a patch of gauze, a white mepore bandage and jumped back on my bike before he knew what happened.

Afterwards there was a disco in a local hotel for all those who had completed the race. Karen and Jimmy went along to it as well. They danced in each other's arms all night and I just floated around, talking to random people. I looked pretty good in my black velvet dress with faded grey stripes across the top. Mom had bought if for me in London when we were over with my aunt Eilis, who I had nicknamed Stylish Eilis, a few months before. Eilis loved shopping, but it was my mother's idea of a headache. We divided time between shops I liked and shops Eilis liked, and I found a shop I hadn't heard of before – Miss Selfridge – a massive department store with wide-screen TVs on every wall. I remember watching, mouth open, a woman with pale skin and jet black hair twisting and turning on the screen. It was Madonna in her video for 'Frozen' and I had never seen anything more intriguing. My velvet dress went down a storm at the disco and even the girl who had called me Germs complimented me on it, but not before telling me to watch out for the corner near the bar 'because those guys will grab your ass and they're only looking for a ride'. I didn't know what ride meant, but I could guess.

When my bowels flared up again a few months later, my life seemed to get worse. I was eating the right food, I was exercising, but I was still getting cramps on and off. Sometimes I would sit in the classroom, desperately trying to focus on what was going on on the blackboard and clutching my stomach. Other times I successfully used The Power of The Mind Controls technique and the pain evaporated, but then it returned when I sat on the toilet and nothing except pea-sized poop came out. They brought me into hospital again and this time I had a chest infection too.

I was back in the same room, in St Phil's. After a week or two of watching it take three needles a day to get IV lines in to pump the heavy drugs into my system, my mother made a decision. She had heard about portacaths, a circular device made of titanium that could be placed, under anesthetic, beneath the skin to give permanent access to a vein so the patient could always get treatment. From the circular disk a cathether was threaded up through the superior vena cava to the heart. Years later I would be able to explain this off by heart, to draw diagrams for student doctors and to spent my time educating them on CF while I was stuck in hospital. At that time I don't remember knowing much about it, except that it would stop all the needles, which was fine with me. Even Eileen, the super cannula nurse, had spent an hour trying seven times to thread a long line up through my vein before leaving in tears.

When I woke up after surgery the next day, I felt an incredible heaviness in the right side of my chest, like it was weighed down with an anvil. Turning to lie on my right side felt odd, and my mother said it was because there was a 'foreign body' in my chest. I would get used to it, she promised. That afternoon my dad brought my brother up to visit me. They arrived with a box set of *Tom and Jerry* for him and *The Wizard of Oz* for me. My brother, who was three, was obsessed with Tom and Jerry. I became captivated by *The Wizard of Oz*. I watched it over and over, sometimes three times a day, blurring the lines between fantasy and reality. Dorothy was the most amazing person I had ever seen. It was a good distraction from the strangeness of life with a portacath.

During that stay, like every other, I loved to trail behind the Night Matron on her midnight rounds. I had lots of energy as a child and it got worse when I was cooped up in hospital. At nighttime there weren't that many people about and the rules didn't apply. If I was still awake when Matron was on rounds, she would take me with her. We would weave in and out of wards, I her assistant as we watched others sleep in six-bed rooms, in double rooms, in single rooms. The public ward was always buzzing at night. Children who refused to sleep ran up and down the corridors, sometimes driving a green play truck or a red and yellow car, bent on destruction. Usually you'd find someone with CF, or a teenage patient there long enough to know the drill, sitting in the office with the nurses, chatting or sometimes eating Chinese food.

From the public ward on the top floor we worked our way down to the baby wards. There was a wall of calm that hit you walking into Michael's B, the main baby ward. It was divided by doors with rectangular windows. Through the glass I could see little bundles lying peacefully. Sometimes the serenity would be broken by someone kicking their mini feet in the air or screaming at the top of their lungs, but it seemed so faint and faraway beyond the glass. The babies always struck me as so helpless and fragile, so unprepared.

I remember at the end of one night going back to the Night Matron's office with her instead of to my ward. She unlocked a brown door beside the payphones on the ground floor. It was as though it had just popped out of the wall; I had never noticed it before. It felt like we were doing something secret, something forbidden. Her office was along a corridor, behind the magic door, and it was not what I expected. It was small and dull, with tin blinds, the kind that get tangled easily and make a sharp noise when you pull them up. 'It's waiting to be repainted and it'll be waiting a while!', she said. 'Why?' I asked in my ignorance, as I marvelled at the toys on the ground. 'Ah, there's no money. There's never any money.' She was searching in her desk drawer.

'You can take something, whatever you like,' she said, sounding bored.

'Oh wow! No thank you,' I said, but secretly surveyed the pile out of the corner of my eye. Playdough – don't want that. Blonde doll. Barbie? No, Sindy. Horrible. What else?

She was talking and eyeing me with her sharp and cynical blue eyes. 'Cigarette?' she asked as she slid a brown stick from the red box without looking. Of course, she was joking, but I took it as a serious offer.

'No! No, God, I don't smoke.' I wanted to add that it's disgusting and bad for you, which is what I usually told people who attempted to smoke in front of me. I watched her as she flicked the lighter open and lit the end. I was in a 1940s mobster movie.

It was 3.00am and I was in her office, and I felt kind of cool being up so late. Eventually I said I was getting tired and she squashed her cigarette into the ashtray she had taken from the drawer. 'It's okay,' I said, and walked myself back up to the ward.

When I left the hospital after that admittance, I didn't go back to my dad's old house and Karen and Jimmy. We finally made our move down to Hawkfield, where I celebrated my tenth birthday. The morning of my birthday my mother was squealing about how proud she was that I had reached 'double digits' and I was trying to escape her poking tickles. Theses weren't just regular tickles, there was a lot of rib poking first and then tickling, which lead to out-of-control breathing and coughing. I couldn't really articulate why I hated it so much when I was ten, I just kept telling her to 'gerroff'. Tickling made me cough, which I didn't like to do unnecessarily. It also made me feel out of control. I was deeply serious at times and my mother always told me this made her sad. I don't know where it came from. I didn't like when she put suncream on my back or when she hugged me. I was just trying to get on with things. I was being strong, and hugs and tickles were a sign of weakness. Tears were also in this category. They were just pointless unless something serious had happened. I was hard on my mother, so she was hard on me. She cried, I didn't. She got emotional and I tried logic, which made her feel worse. She looked at it as me talking down to her; I looked at is as the most obvious way to solve things. She said things she didn't really mean when she was emotional and because I was serious and young, I took them on board. But I never cried like she did. I felt like I couldn't tell her things because she'd throw them back at me when we were arguing, so I just didn't let her in.

I'm sure it must have hurt her, but I didn't want to feel any of that stuff. I was dealing with stuff that was bigger than that and the me inside didn't have room for anyone else. By necessity, my parents controlled a lot of my life. If I needed home IVs, for example, they did them for me. Mom or Dad would insert a needle and administer drugs to me three times a day, eight hours apart; this entailed setting up a sterile field and took over thirty minutes each time. When I look at it now, I recognise how incredible it was for both my parents to do that, particularly my mother. She was a nurse in work and a nurse at home to her own daughter. And she knew so much more than me. But our relationship was blurred as a result: one minute she had her nurse's cap on, the next she had her mother cap on and then was trying to be my friend. I couldn't process them all, I didn't know how. I preferred having IVs in hospital because I didn't have to deal with my mom like that, but that in turn made me feel guilty: did I prefer hospital? Mom was tired, getting up at 6.00am to draw up drugs, because of me. Everyone was tense and angry, organising their day around me, and sometimes if I stepped out of line, they'd tell me that everything revolved around me and I'd feel awful. I can't imagine how disconnected my little brother must have felt. Hospital was somewhere I got to be the centre of attention without the long-term consequences. I always got to leave hospital, it was always temporary, but being the axis everyone revolved around at home was beginning to take its toll on me.

6.

When I was eleven years old I was hospitalised due to ongoing sinus problems. It was under investigation and Dr Russell was considering operating on me. I remember sitting on the windowsill in the nurses' office, just passing the time, when the nursing manager dashed in and said, 'Westside are upstairs, come on up!' The nurses swooned and elbowed each other. 'Orla can't go up to Top Flat because of cross-infection,' said another nurse.

Ah, cross-infection. It was 1998 and there were new guidelines everywhere in the hospital. The Rules had changed because there were new CF bugs in the country. There were now strict rules that no two CF patients, even with the same bug, could share the same room in case the recycled air went from one pair of lungs and was breathed into another. No longer was it as clean cut as the bacteria Pseudomonas Aeruginosa, the one I had, being an okay one and Pseudomonas Cepacia being the deadly one. There were now all these guys in between, these different strains and mutations that threatened people with CF. I imagined long lines of infection and particles rippling around my room, exchanging paths with other bugs and intertwining together, like cigarette smoke, looking for a vessel to float into.

The guidelines for drawing up drugs had changed, too. Now when I held up the tubular phials so that a nurse could stick the needle in at the right angle and draw the medication out from the bottom, we both wore gloves. The gloves were sterile and white, with a powder on the inside that made them easier to put on. Afterwards the powder made your skin shrivelled and itchy. If someone with CF was in at the same time as you, they got the schoolroom in the morning and you got it in the afternoon. Or if you had art class, which only happened once a week, then they got the playroom for that morning to compensate. Art class meant making decorations for the classroom, or learning how to sketch or make rainbows with colourful stones and stencils. In the playroom it could be anything from playing Sonic The Hedgehog on the Sega Mega Drive, painting on the double red-and-blue easel that stood beside the blackboard, or sometimes reading a book in the cushioned corner booth.

The reason I met Pat was because of the new guidelines. There were so many people with CF in at once, that time was divided up pretty thinly. One of the nurses marched him in to keep me company while everyone else was with Westlife. 'I'll bring you something back from the boy band. This is Pat,' she said, winked and left.

He was a blonde-haired boy with pale blue eyes and a little scar in the middle of his neck, where his windpipe was. 'Do you want to play cards?' he asked, in his thick Offaly accent. I looked at the nurse who was drawing up my IVs. She smiled. 'Off you go! I'll call you when they're ready.' So we went into his room, shook hands and he started shuffling the cards like my Uncle Frank, like he had worked in Vegas in a former life. I had never really played cards before, except Snap and Go Fish with Uncle Frank. He was my Godfather and cards and Xs and Os were his specialty. Pat and I were playing poker, for needles: orange was worth 10 points, green 20, blue 30 and pink 40.

I was well enough to be on home IVs at that stage of my infection, but I was waiting for surgery on my sinuses, which is why I was still there. I told Pat and then I felt kind of ashamed. He had five operations after his horse trampled him. He had a tracheotomy in for months and only in the past while was getting on without it. We became friends quickly. At nighttime we stalked the corridors together, visiting the places he had stayed. One night he introduced me to the nurses in ICU. It was a small ward with three or four cots. One baby was in an incubator, and just off the main part there was a single room with a bed in it. It had been his for the months he was there. The nurses told us to call back on Friday night. After my 11.00pm IVs on Friday we duly went up, ordered pizza and sat between the cots and the nurses watching *Sleepless in Seattle* and *While You Were Sleeping*. They were the sort of movies my dad would raise his eyebrows at and say he could have written it himself, but I was enjoying the pizza too much to care.

The day before my sinus surgery Pat and I helped the nun decorate the church for Christmas. We sat together, placing the pieces in the crib. I was sure the statue of Jesus could hear the unholy thoughts in my head. I was attracted to Pat, but it was confusing too. From a young age if I was talking to a boy on the ward, a nurse, ward attendant or kitchen lady would say, "Is that your boyfriend?' They'd laugh and tease. They weren't boyfriends, of course and it was always funny and good spirited, but it still confused me. I was hearing the word *boyfriend* at a young age from complete strangers. Even if I was just playing a game with someone, an adult would throw that line in and throw a quivering sensation into my gut. I didn't know. What did I know? Up until about eight years old it was funny, a case of ignorant giggling. But then it started to morph all by itself and I was suddenly more mature than girls my age. It made me angry, this assumption that just because I spoke to someone, I fancied him. I started to notice the differences: some people spent an awful lot of time there, others didn't. I wanted to be liked, but I didn't like being paired off with every boy I spoke to, especially when none of them were very exciting to me.

Pat's hair was dirty blonde and when he wrote, he joined his F's together in perfect, synchronised links. They started from the core of the F and rounded at the top, sailed down to the bottom and out in the middle to the next letter. It was on the napkin from the canteen that he wrote it, 'Forever Friends'. That's why I was thinking of the smoothness in his F's while I was placing the donkey in the crib, and the fact that the day before I had been resting on my bed and opened my eyes to find him sitting in a chair beside it. We sat there in the silence, then the nun came in and took a picture of us both. 'God would be grateful,' she said.

The night before we had gone on an adventure to the ward on the top floor, but one of my doctors on night shift saw me and said 'Orla Tinsley! Get to bed!' So I went to bed, for fear of getting in trouble and he went on without me. After I had done my nebulisers, I considered going to look for him, but I had no idea where he had gone. He could be in ICU; he was hardly in Top Flat. Maybe he'd be in the canteen? We both knew the codes and it was nice to eat there at nighttime. There were usually only one or two other people there on break, and we could take whatever we wanted. It was that way during the day, too. The dinner ladies were so used to me, they'd whoosh me up the line, give me whatever I wanted and tell me embarrassing stories in front of the whole line of visitors and patients about how they remembered me as 'a wee little one'. They never charged my dad either when he came after work and he used to have to go back in to the register area for butter and slip the money behind the Concern box.

At nighttime there were no dinner ladies and no register, but I couldn't go to the basement on my own. I sat in the giant lounge chair outside my the door to my ward, occasionally turning around to look in the wall-sized mirror behind the chair. Was I really sitting here waiting for a boy? Sometime later he arrived at the top of the stairs. 'Sorry about leaving you like that,' he said, stopping on the stairs just beside the life-size painting of the yellow Tellytubby. His pale blues eyes shone in the murky midnight light. He walked to the end of the steps and got down on one knee. I couldn't bring myself to move. He held up his hand and between his thumb and forefinger was a blue Roses sweet. "When I saw this, I thought of you,' he said. Of course he thought of me, I had eaten every single one of them in the nurses' station the other day waiting for my IVs to be drawn up. I don't remember what I said. I think my brain had stopped functioning along with my body.

The next morning we sat in his room and saw Bono on TV in his fedora and Jesus shades, riding in a car with various other people popping in and out of the frame. We decided that song, 'The Sweetest Thing', would always make us think of this time. I preferred the Corrs, but I let him have the Bono thing. Pat then took me to see a friend of his, who was in another room on our ward. Jim was paralysed from the waist down and could only communicate through clicking his tongue. 'One click for no, two for Yes,' Pat explained. I sat there trying to get in on the conversation, trying to understand that just a few months ago Pat had been in the same situation, clicking instead of talking. It was difficult.

Three hours later I went for surgery on my sinuses and woke up with two painful packs shoved in my nostrils. My head throbbed and I floated in and out of consciousness, staying in the recovery room for three hours. I woke up fully while they were tugging the packs out of my nose. They had gone up there to push two tubes in my sinuses together to make it easier to breathe and try and prevent so much post-nasal drip, which was enticing the various infections I was having that year. Blood dripped down my nose and my face ached when I woke up. My mom was there within minutes to help clean me up.

I never liked staying in the recovery room and always wanted to get back to the ward I was used to. The minute I woke up from any operation I would throw my legs over the side of the bed and make myself walk. I always prided myself on being able to beat the anaesthetic. Much to the nurses' horror. I would hobble across to the bathroom and back without calling them and then call them when I was confident enough to walk back to my original ward. I could do it on my own. I never threw up afterwards and I usually ate whatever lunch or dinner was put in front of me. Mind over matter was always what got me through challenging situations. This case was no exception. With my mother's arm around my waist and a nurse carrying my chart, I walked along the corridor, up the six steps and down the ten that got me back to my ward. I felt like I could relax properly once I was there because they knew my illness inside out. I slipped under the yellow blanket on my bed and conked out.

When I woke up it was 6.00pm and my mother wasn't there. She was in the cafeteria having dinner, according to my Uncle Frank and Aunt Frances, who were sitting at the end of my bed. They had some of their daughter's clothes for me. She didn't fit into them anymore and Frances was showing them to me, but saying I might be too big for them. Uncle Frank was drawing up an Xs and Os grid. The cream-coloured main door creaked open. Pat peered in. I could see half of his body. The pack of cards with red backs was in his hand and his glistening blue eyes stared. He was leaving tonight, I knew, but I couldn't be rude to my Aunt and Uncle and say I'd prefer his company to theirs.

An hour later I went to find him and saw him walking up the stairs with his dad. He was going to meet the President of Ireland for his bravery. I went back into my room and wrote him a letter. We were pen-pals for a while after that, but then we got lazy.

Just before Christmas I came out of hospital and when I got home a massive card made of multi-coloured paper was waiting for me. It was from my classmates. Each one had written a note on it, and at the back it said *Made By Oisin Productions*. My friend Jenny called me to tell me it was

Oisin's idea, that he got everyone to sign it and stuck it all together. And that wasn't the only thing. It was her duty to tell me he had gotten me a ring. He went to Dundalk with his parents and bought it a street near where the Corrs lived. How he knew this I did not know, but these were important details. He felt really bad about breaking up with me and wanted to make it right.

The thing with Oisin had happened just before I had gone into hospital. In the midst of a discussion on adverbs, he punched my arm and his face reddened: 'Will you go out with me sometime, maybe?' he asked. Sure. He had asked me in English class. It was impossibly romantic. Of course, I didn't quite comprehend what 'going out' with a boy entailed, but why not!? The word boyfriend was innocent in my mind: it was Power Rangers with Tommy and picnics in the park. So when a week later his best friend Aoife walked up to me and said, 'Oisin just can't do this anymore,' I was flabbergasted. What had I done wrong? Kelly, a girl who had recently transferred from America, was furious when she heard and marched over demanding an explanation from him. I was mortified. He said 'It wasn't going anywhere', apparently. To which she replied 'Where did you want it to go, Timbuktu?!'. Crestfallen at my inability to get 'going anywhere', I poured my thoughts into the gree-rimmed diary with the rabbit on front that my Nana had given me for my eleventh birthday.

Two nights after I arrived home from Temple Street, Oisin rang to ask if he could call over. It was early December and frosty outside. 'Does his mother drink wine? What does she like?' Mom asked. How would I know? Her question made me more nervous, and then I realised: I hadn't got him a present. My mother wasn't too gone on the idea. 'We're not made of money.' 'Please, please,' I begged her, 'please drive me into town to get him a present! Mom, please.' We ended up in a toyshop in town. I knew he collected Beanie Babies, so we got him one. My mom said he would be happy with the collector's item, but a crocodile full of beans felt so juvenile. We were serious young people.

I sat in front of the TV watching *The Sound of Music*, playing it cool. That's what Dad always said: Be Cool, Calm and Collected. When Oisin arrived I sat staring at the von Trapps dressed in curtains, trying not to be nervous. He asked how I was; fine, much better. He fumbled in his pocket and pulled out a gift. It was in silver wrapping paper and I opened it slowly. It was silver, with two small diamonds in the middle like either sides of a ying/yang symbol. It was beautiful, I told him, mildly ashamed at the squishy crocodile I was about to hand him. 'It's from Dundalk, you know,' he said. 'That's really great,' I said and handed him his gift. He twiddled the croc between his hands and smiled.

That summer all the gang came to my brother's Communion. He swanned around in his white suit and crutches after busting his leg some weeks earlier. Typically hilarious, he found a way to drag himself onto the bouncing castle, blue leg cast and all. We were the same type of creature. My friend and I were bouncing on the castle when she said 'Oisin really wants to kiss you.' I stared. 'But he wanted me to ask, can you catch it?' 'What?' 'CF?' CF. It sounded weird when my friends said it. When out of the mouth of this perky blonde girl on a bouncing castle tumbled something at once so private and yet so public. 'No!' I answered. It made me so angry. And unsure. Did I want to kiss someone who had to ask something like that? But then again how could he know, how could any of them know unless I told them?

I felt like I was extremely open all the time, but there were some things I just didn't have the tools yet to say. That I didn't know how to describe. Their lack of knowledge caught me off guard. Lucky for him I went for that walk down the bog. We walked over a rickety old bridge and kissed, washing-machine style, in an old timber shed that usually had nothing but turf in it. It didn't really matter that there was nothing afterwards but our friendship. I had gone somewhere.

7.

Every October my dad brought us swimming in the Irish Sea, and that was the sort of swimming I loved. And I needed some sort of regular sport to help combat my CF. My mom bought me a new swimsuit – a deep blue racerback Speedo – and white goggles. Then I decided I wanted to do something else. I begged my parents to let me try horse-riding. I started off in a place that was recommended. On one of my first visits the instructor took us up a hilly field and showed me and another girl how to ride a horse while hanging over one side, palms to the ground, and holding on with your legs. My parents took me out of there pretty quickly and I enrolled in another centre, nearer to home.

Horse riding was perfect for me, it gave me a cardiovascular workout and helped me move the mucus from my chest. My mother always marvelled when she came to pick me up after camp: 'If you only you could make your own room as clean as that, we'd be doing good!', she'd say. I loved shining the wheelbarrow and cleaning tack. The smell of the tack-room made me happy. From the cleaning to catching the horses in the field, it all made me happy. I went every single Sunday of my life between the ages of eight until eleven – apart from when I was in hospital – until one Summer Camp went wrong.

I had started off on Rusty, a beautiful, slim, auburn pony with a white diamond in her forehead. Later I moved to Spike, an overweight grey guy who plodded along, always sullen, as his stomach flopped beneath him. Rusty's jumps were smooth and lithe, whereas Spike's were clumsy and rocky. But when I was eleven I graduated to King, called thus because he was the King of the stables. He stood at 12 hands high and wore a shiny, chestnut coat. His hair was always plaited or done up in decorative buns – he was the King after all. Only a few weeks into riding him I won two rosettes and a third place trophy in a competition in our riding school.

That summer King and I moved up to the highest level of fences in our Pony Club Summer Camp. We had cleared the first three in the indoor arena and there was a sharp turn to the fourth, like the intersection between the stem of the letter L and the line at the bottom. We turned too sharply and the rhythm was out. He jumped, but I wasn't ready – and neither was he. We crashed down in the middle of the double-barrel white and yellow fences. He flung his hind legs in the air and all I could hear was a swarm of noise: 'Hold tight, Orla Tinsley!' I crashed in a heap over his right side, my left foot still in the stirrup. He started to canter, then gallop, gathering speed and dragging me, flopping, alongside him. My left foot in the stirrup was all that was keeping me from the ground, and possibly his feet, as two instructors ran behind, trying to catch and stop him without frightening him further. I managed to grab his mane and pull myself in a pile on top of him, as they cooled him to a stop. He shook his head at them and I coughed the floor sand out of my lungs.

I got off. They calmed him down. 'Are you hurt?' I wasn't really, just flustered.

'What?' Had I heard that right?

'Up you go,' Martha repeated. My mother, who was now in the arena, told me I didn't have to. Aideen said firmly, 'You have to get back on now, or you'll never get back on. You have to go back and jump the jump.'

There was an audience watching and I knew she was right. She gave me a leg-up and King shook his mane at me. I patted his neck and cantered once around to a brief applause and then headed to the fourth jump again. We cantered up softly and he stopped dead in front of it. I took him around again to shake it off and then with his neck perfectly elongated, he launched over it and we sailed through the rest.

A week later Aideen told me that Pat wanted to see me up at the house. Pat was the owner of the riding school and, like the Queen, she made few appearances. It was regarded as a privilege to be asked up to the house to see her. The back door was open when I arrived, so I called her name. The kitchen was small, with ornaments of horses on the mantelpiece and pictures of famous racehorses adorning the walls. Pat appeared after a minute. 'I didn't know you were sick,' she told me. 'I would have been more careful with you if I had known.'

'I'm okay, don't worry about being careful with me,' I said cheerily.

'Do you like Samson?' she asked. Samson was a light chestnut pony that had arrived a few weeks earlier. I had been riding him since the incident with King. 'I love him,' I said.

'Then he's yours,' she replied.

I stood in her kitchen, mouth gaping like a fish. Excuse me? Samson had been mistreated, she told me. They were going to send him to the meat factory because of a little problem he had when he was younger, but she had saved him. Now I could keep him, unless someone decided to buy him. I could take him to events, trek him out any day I wanted. 'Thank you!' I hugged her.

I smiled and left the house. I had a pony that I could take

out any time I wanted. I had private lessons for a while on Samson, to overcome my fear, but when I started secondary school there was no time for riding lessons. Samson stayed in the riding school and that was that.

I suppose it was kind of a funny situation that because of CF, I was given something extraordinary that I probably wouldn't have had otherwise. This was a familiar feeling to me, like when I was in hospital and someone dumped a load of toys on my bed and said I could take whatever I wanted. The truth is that these were the times when I liked CF, when I felt like I was lucky to have been born with it. But beneath those thoughts there always ran a deeper undercurrent of guilt. I was aware of the children in the hospital who had very little. Some were there all the time because they were sick, but some were there because of their socio-economic background. I didn't think CF meant that I deserved more toys or things than other children, but when I got them I felt happy, but also confused. The problem, if you want to look at it that way, was I loved attention, I loved performing, which made me a target for attention and special treatment. But I still didn't get why CF was a *carte blanche* to adoration and free toys. I was being rewarded for just living and I think that ended up making me feel entitled to things I probably wasn't entitled to at all.

My parents would have bought me anything in the world if I proved to them I wanted it enough, but they would not buy me a pony. They had once said that if I saved up enough money and proved I was responsible enough by taking care of myself, then they would consider it. But I was too dependent on them and never managed to meet that challenge. Sure, I saved pennies and tenpence pieces in a little pink beauty box, but it wasn't a real effort at proving myself to them. I just thought a horse made sense for me and still to this day I think that sort of thing is good for a child in the position I was in then. I think it would have taught me a lot more about responsibility. But my parents had their reasons. Perhaps they worried about who would mind it when I was in hospital. Or maybe a horse was just too expensive. I think the truth though, is my parents tried very hard to not over-indulge me, which was for the best. Unfortunately for them, there were so many other people all too willing to put me up on a pedestal. Unlike other children I had seen, I had everything, and yet people still treated me like I was a fragile miracle.

Primary school was drawing to a close for us now, and our final school trip was suitably memorable. It was not the usual tour around the Coca-Cola factory that we had endured for the previous three years. This time, it was a trip to Liverpool, by ferry, to see a Premier League soccer match. Soccer meant nothing to me. Despite messing around with GAA for a year in fourth class, I had no real interest in ball sports. Maybe watching people passionately roar at men kicking a ball around would be interesting in its own way, but that wasn't the draw. It was the prospect of sailing on a ship that had a McDonalds and a cinema on board that did if for me. I was one of the lucky twenty who got their names in on time, because not everyone in the class could go.

When the day of departure was near, I went along to the 11am break meeting with the other lucky nineteen and Mr Elstead looked at me and asked, 'What are you doing here?' He said I no longer had a place on the trip. 'What do you mean?' 'Well, because you were in hospital your mom said you weren't going to go.'

I stood on the hill overlooking the car park, fuming. Why would my mother do that? He obviously had it wrong. When she drove in the carpark I opened the door and asked her. She said she had gone and spoken to him about the trip because she thought I would still be in hospital. She was sorry.

The next day I knocked on Mr. Elstead's door, hoping to reason with him. He had had me as a pupil the year before, he knew I had CF, my mother had made a mistake. He apologised but explained that the place had gone to someone else now.

Back in the classroom, I sat angrily colouring in a Confirmation leaf. The leaf was part of our Confirmation tree, which would bloom with leaves showing our chosen names. It would be hung on the side of the altar in the church, to show God that we were growing and independently choosing names of our own. Why had my mother said that when she knew I would be out of hospital soon? Why wouldn't Mr Elsted listen? Behind me I heard my teacher's voice. 'Ceire-Angela?' That was the name I had picked for my Confirmation. My initials now spelled OP-CAT, which I thought was pretty cool. 'You can't really have two names, Orla.' Why couldn't I? Anne Marie had two, and just because that was a normal double-barrel name it was acceptable. What about Ceire-Angela, a hyphen makes it the exact same? She laughed at me and said if I could fit it all on the leaf, it would be okay. Oisin was impressed with my double-barrel name and as the news spread about the classroom, it seemed like a most interesting idea. By lunchtime the teacher was forced to announce that there would be no more name changing: 'Your name is what you wrote down yesterday, no more double-barrel names.' I got to keep mine though.

That year I entered a 'write a book' competition in school. My story was about discovering a secret world behind a boulder in a park. It didn't win anything. I thought it was brilliant, but it didn't win. The winning story was by a girl in my class who wrote a story about a girl from an orphanage coming to live with her and how her fictional characters' lives changed. I couldn't help but feel robbed because she was using her own experience, not actually anything she had thought up herself. The concept of *Write What You Know* hadn't been grasped by my eleven-year-old mind yet. Back then, writing was still a carefully crafted act of creative imagination.

The winners of the competition were going to be announced at a ceremony in Dublin, presided over by the well-known artist Don Conroy. He had a slot on *The Den* and all would-be artists in my class aspired to be like him. I had actually met him before in hospital and frankly his drawings of woodland creatures and multicolored birds did little for me. At the event there was a queue of children to get his signature, but I just hung back, waiting for my friends to finish. All of a sudden my Irish teacher took my carefully-preserved-in-a-cellophane-folder story out of my hands and handed it to Don, ushering me to the front.

'This is a very special girl,' she said, as his grey hair bobbed to the beat of his signature. 'She's in hospital an awful lot, just out the other day.'.

My jaw dropped to the ground. Oisin stared at me – he knew I wanted to kill her. I didn't know what to do, so I just stood there as Don Conroy drew a dolphin on the page for 'an extra-special girl'. When I got back to my friends, the boys who loved drawing were really jealous, but I couldn't bear to tell them why I got the 'extra-special' dolphin. It was mortifying that my teacher would treat me like that in front of Don Conroy, as if I had some sort of weakness that meant I deserved special treatment. I wasn't some vulnerable little girl to be minded. Looking back, I'd say my reaction was so strong because I had been meeting 'celebrities' since I was small. They felt accessible to me, so they weren't particularly overwhelming to be around. I didn't really care so much why they were famous, they were just people. And frankly, the minute I met one who told me I was inspirational, I zoned out. It was boring, superficial and stale. None of it felt real to me, they didn't actually care about me.

Four days before primary school finished for good and we embarked on our lives as secondary school teenagers, a girl from Ms Ryan's class knocked on our door and asked for me. She said Ms Ryan was in the yard and needed to speak to me. I walked out to find the teacher sitting on the kerb next to a girl in our uniform whom I didn't recognise. The teacher introduced this girl and said she was going into hospital tomorrow. She asked for me because she knew I could tell her all about hospital, that it was no big deal. The girl's eyes were red as she looked up at me, looking as lost as I was.

'Tell Orla why you're going into hospital.'

'Tonsils,' she whispered, on the verge of tears.

'What hospital are you going to? Crumlin. Okay, well I've never actually been there ...' Ms Ryan looked desperately at me, 'but....' I continued, '... you get to have lots of ice cream when you get your tonsils out, it's no big deal. I've seen kids get it done all the time. They just go in and whip 'em out, and it's fine.'

The girl kept her eyes to the ground and Ms. Ryan said I could go. I went back to my classroom feeling like I had failed something.

These four stories – Samson, the school trip I missed, Don Conroy, the crying girl – show the main effects of CF in my childhood. I was treated as special, which could be good, but I also missed out on a lot of things my friends enjoyed as normal. I was set apart from my peers as deserving special treatment, which made me feel like another species from them, but I was also expected to have greater maturity, greater empathy and a capacity for knowing the right thing to say, just because I had CF.

I had really started to notice all these adult expectations at that age and I really disliked it. I disliked their neediness and their desire to define me and use me to make themselves feel better – whether by making them feel their lives weren't so bad after all, or by feeling they had made me smile or laugh and had thereby helped me to forget my troubles. I knew I had a different life experience from other people and that, more often than not, this led people to call me 'an inspiration'. But my dad had always been very good at dispelling this notion, so it didn't ever become something I believed too much. He would talk philosophically about how different people think differently and interpret things differently. That was helpful to hear to put it into perspective, but even so it sometimes really overwhelmed me.

My mom sometimes took the other approach, particularly if we were arguing. She would say, 'If they only knew what you are really like.' This was the problem. What was I really like? I didn't know yet. Who knows at the age of eleven or twelve? I just knew what I was supposed to be like and, thanks to a background in performing, I was able to tolerate every single bad situation and every single compliment with a smile. Outwardly, I was every inch the brave, inspirational, strong fighter. But as I got older, these words became increasingly empty and valueless.

Everyone who met me saw one thing – CF – and defined me by it. But what about the rest of me? I was trying to grow beyond the strict parameters of my illness, but I kept getting crushed back into everyone else's perceptions of me and it. Teachers, adults, family members daily told me how great I was, and within seconds of meeting me strangers who heard I had CF said the same thing. Sometimes they said it with tears in their eyes. My dad always said that there's no such thing as 'normal' because normal is different for everyone; it's just a word. I started learning then that words are powerful. They can weigh on top of you until you can't breathe. Some adults would say things like, 'you make me strong' or 'when I feel low, you keep me going, you give me inspiration', so I ended up feeling trapped. How could I deviate from this pattern and grow if I was responsible in some way, small or big, for all of these people?

Of course, I was overestimating my own importance, but I didn't know that then. This was a child's mind trying to cope with adult concepts and emotions. I was left feeling that Spiderman thing: 'with great power comes great responsibility'. Except, unlike a superhero, I felt kind of powerless, but had a feeling of great responsibility. On top of that I also felt responsible for beating CF. I felt I *had* to do that. The idea of me was floating around, making everyone else happy, but the real me was underneath that, squashed and feeling like a phony.

One of the results of all this conflict was that I was kind

of hard on people. I have a vivid memory of my cousin Elaine falling off her bike outside her house on our lane. She grazed her knee and began to cry. I started laughing and told her to get back up on the saddle. She cried and screamed at me to stop laughing. This sort of thing happened a lot, and it probably really hurt the people I was with at the time, because it looked like I was laughing at them. But I didn't cry if I fell off my bike or stubbed my toe. That was small stuff, completely insignificant in my mind. I wasn't big on compassion for people who cried, it just annoyed me. I didn't understand why they couldn't just man up about these things. I now understand that my lack of compassion probably hurt people, but it was just my way of dealing with things that I couldn't fully articulate. My mother sometimes referred to me as a 'hard nut'. (And she still sometimes does!)

Now that I'm older, I know I can't control people's perceptions of me and that I'm not responsible for anyone except me. I understand, too, that people can only hurt you emotionally if you give them power to do so. We are all responsible for who we let into our hearts. When you're a child, though, you just don't know this stuff and it's really difficult to make sense of things. One therapist I visited in my late teens told me this has to do with boundaries and parents, and that my parents should have equipped me with better boundaries and ways of coping. I couldn't accept that. The truth is my parents did a fantastic job. I was away from them so much as a child that it was hard for them to be consistent – I was either not there, or I was there and everyone was trying to compensate for my absence. In our house, performance and creativity were valued higher than education, which some people might frown upon. But that was actually a good thing for me because it was dance and theatre and self-exploration that made me more open as a person, that made me able to gel with people more quickly and from a young age and that, in turn, gave me good instincts that I could rely on. It was the difference between being extremely lonely for weeks in hospital versus having good chats and learning experiences with the other parents and children. It meant being able to speak up at age seven to authority figures, such as doctors, when they were doing something wrong. It meant being able to protect myself. There is no perfect way to grow up, but I was lucky that my parents equipped me with ways of dealing with my unique situation. They made it so normal for me that when I was eleven I didn't think living a full life with CF was funny or unique, it was just me being me.

It was only when I reached my twenties that I started to realise how hard I was on the people around me – that ironic lack of compassion. I could never make excuses for myself, so if people around me were making excuses, I couldn't handle it. I felt disconnected from many of my peers in college because I didn't want to drink or go out partying all night. I didn't see the point. My mother always said to me, 'You never do something unless it benefits you.' This always grated on me and made me think that if it were true, I was a very bad person. Whenever she said it, I would wish I had been born somewhere like America because, through my TV show perception of America, it seemed people there didn't put others down for being focused and ambitious and wanting to achieve things.

The truth was not that I was completely selfish, it was that I had lost my sense of fun, or maybe I just had a different sense of it from my friends. I loved hanging out in the theatre back home and goofing around with scripts and accents and being naturally high from performing. I looked down on people who smoked and didn't understand all that drinking and the hangovers that wasted entire days. Likewise, some of my friends would apologise when they lit up a cigarette and complain that I made them feel guilty for enjoying a smoke. I've grown on from that now, too: people are who are they are and it's their business. When I was younger, I was over-involved, without even knowing it. I had seen so much in life that sometimes I was the bossy mom with my friends, trying to teach them a lesson they weren't ready to learn. I didn't really understand compassion then nor why you should just let people be.

Now, with hindsight, I'd say I couldn't let others be because people didn't really let me be. My life was full of rules and lessons and sacrificing things I enjoyed, like school and dance classes and Brownies. I felt like I was always behind, always striving to catch up and prove I was as good as or better than everybody else. When I was young, I wanted to be a famous actress or writer or popstar, or all three. I think having extreme dreams equated well with the double life I was living between home and hospital. I thought that, maybe, if I could be the best at what I wanted in life, then I would somehow get out of CF, that achieving my dreams would be my ticket out of illness. Even though I knew it was incurable, I think somewhere inside I thought that sometime, when I was older, it would just disappear and leave me free.

PART 2

'Courage is not a man with a gun in his hands. It's when you know you're licked before you begin, but you begin anyway and see it through no matter what.'

Harper Lee, *To Kill a Mockingbird*

8.

In March 1999 I turned twelve and that September I started secondary school. It's a milestone for most kids, and I was no different. There were two secondary schools to choose between in the town: a co-ed, fee-paying school or a public convent school. My mother had attended the convent school and she wanted me to go there. She thought it would be better to have no distractions from boys. I didn't know which one to choose. My friend from choir was in sixth year in the convent school and so were the girls from the *Joseph* musical, but most of my primary school friends were going to the co-ed. There was general consensus that the co-ed school was more sports-oriented while the convent was more about music and the arts. That's what made me a natural convent girl.

I soon realised that a roomful of girls could be a daunting thing. My favourite subject was English, and I threw myself into it wholeheartedly. One of my great loves was poetry. Our teacher's method of teaching poetry was to get us to learn it by rote, then recite it in class. At first, I loved doing this, but then I realised that some of the girls were laughing as I recited. To be fair, I was probably over-enunciating and really getting into it, drawing on all my theatre experience to make it as good as possible. This, to me, was completely normal. But hearing those sniggers affected me over time and in the end I lied to my English teacher, telling her I couldn't handle public speaking very well because of my cough. I had studied speech and drama as a child and was on stage every summer of my life until I was fifteen, so my sudden inability to speak in public was a blatant lie, but she let me away with it.

Sometimes she would forget and ask me to read Yeats' 'Wild Swans at Coole' or Plath's 'Child', but then she would say, 'Ah don't bother, sure I know you know it.' And that was the problem. I did know it, and the other girls knew I knew it, word perfect. There was only one other girl in the class at my level, and occasionally better than me; that was Isobel, but she was friends with the popular girls and we were quite competitive about essays and grades. Later, we would become friends of a sort ourselves, albeit for the wrong reasons, but back then she was in a circle I wasn't part of. She didn't really fit either, but for some reason she was accepted anyway. It was probably because she was easier to get on with; I was quite dramatic and tended to take things personally when I possibly shouldn't have. On top of that, English meant so much to me because it was what I was best at and what I loved. I felt like it was the *only* thing I was good at, so naturally it took on huge significance for me. That's why the laughter around the class when I recited ate away at my confidence.

My teacher was different, though. Whenever I read something out or made a suggestion, she would write it on the board immediately. I'd say a word like 'flippant' and there would be a moment's silence and then the class would burst out laughing. She'd keep steadily writing and say 'Girls!' in a warning tone. Each day her head would nod and nod and their eyes would roll and roll. She was a young teacher, new and enthusiastic. In first year I got a straight A in her class for an essay, 100%, even though it was said to be impossible in English. It was the first time I wrote about my own experience.

That was the year Mom, Dad, my brother and I had finally moved out to Hawkfield. Our house was at the very end of a narrow lane, just before the small surrounding towns of Milltown and Allen. We were a tiny satellite off a larger road: blink and you'd miss the little turn on the blind corner for our lane. I think that's why my parents liked it so much. Nature and fresh air were important for me, my mother would tell me. I wanted to appreciate it, I loved language and poetry and the essence of natural beauty, but I didn't always find beauty in the hawks that twittered in our garden or the blackberries that decorated the lane in summer. The colours delighted me, but I in truth missed the having my friends nearby and the external world of boys and drama and spontaneous popcorn-and-movie nights.

When I looked out my bedroom window, I could see the Hill of Allen on the left, now quarried away and barely surviving. The sea of fields to the right led to the Bog of Allen, which stretched across the horizon in a crooked line, like a painter had just swished his brush carelessly. We used to foot turf out there in the cool summer, although I usually weaseled my way out of it by helping to carry the refreshments. The one time we did help, my cousin Elaine got hit on the head by a sod of turf that was being thrown into the trailer. That got us out of it, and a few giggles, much to her dismay. We had no need to prove our strength by footing turf; we would go home to her house and prove our worth with the Ten Times Twister – a daring game in which we used rollerblades to skate in circles around the new tarmac patio at dizzying speeds. The Ten Times Twister wasn't just suave alliteration, it was also the amount of turns anyone could manage before the nausea set in and the dizziness threatened to knock us out.

Later, the bog would become something bigger in my mind when I studied 'The Tollund Man' in my first year at university, and Seamus Heaney became something far more significant to me than the man who wrote 'Mid-Term Break'. But when I was twelve the bog was just the bog, there were probably a few dead bodies down there, sure, but there was a lot of dumped furniture, too, which was less inspiring. We tried to minimise the dumping, of course. 'Quick! Run out there and get that registration!', Mom would say when an unidentified vehicle would brave the potholes and bump down our little lane to discharge its illegal cargo. I don't remember ever catching anyone.

That's all the bog was for me back then, which is why I was suspicious this particular day when my mother suggested we go for a walk there. It was 4.30pm – why wasn't I being forced to do my homework first? To be honest, I'd rather have been doing it because I hated walking. We were halfway down the bog when my mother said, 'Do you know Gerard Cronin?' Her voice was high, like a bird singing. She was nervous.

'I know his brother,' I said. I didn't really know Gerard because I wasn't allowed to, but it would have been hard not to have bumped into the boys – Gerard and his brother, Matthew – in Temple Street. It was a small hospital and Gerard was in a lot. We had different bugs growing in our lungs, so we couldn't be in a room together. I knew him only from shimmying past each other in corridors, *Mission Impossible*-style, avoiding all contact. Sometimes we would wave or salute one another as I went in one door of the playroom and he went out the door at the far end.

'We can't mix because of cross-infection, so I just see him when he's going in one door and out the other. That's how I know Gerard,' I said to my mother.

'He was very sick,' she replied. 'He's gone up to heaven with the angels.'

I wasn't actually upset. It was because she was struggling to say it that inflamed something in me, and the way she said it. Bloody angels. He's gone up to Heaven.

'He's dead, you mean?' I said coldly.

Mom started to sob and tried to hug me. So I ran. I ran

as fast as I could away from the dry, dessicated bog that was about as exciting as staring at your own piss. I ran in the back door and slammed through the kitchen door, bumping into Dad. 'Where are you going?' But my face was burning and he let me go to my room.

It's because Gerard died and Mom took me for a walk in the bog that I got that perfect A in English. I imagined I was at the funeral, watching from afar. I wrote, 'Here we are at the door to change, the hardest place for anyone to be.' My teacher placed the essay on my desk and leaned in as she pointed at the mark. 'It's as if I was there,' she said. And then I was embarrassed.

'Where? She was where?' asked Margaret, my best friend; our desks were attached to each other at the top of the classroom. I let her read it eventually and from then on she would ask me to do her homework for her, and I kept saying no. She was a maths genius and a runner and she argued that sometimes training got in the way of her English homework. But it was mainly because she hated English; she always had her Maths homework done.

For me, English wasn't just a subject in school like it was for the other girls – it was a lifeline. I read poetry obsessively, thought about poets' lives, read their words with a hunger I couldn't fully explain and invested 99% of my energy in reading and writing. It helped me to comprehend some of the things I had to deal with at that young age, like death. But I never really felt 'at a young age', so when adults were uncomfortable and unsure how to talk to me about death, I turned to the words of poets to find the clarity that I needed. When I was twelve I discovered Seamus Heaney and was deeply touched by the words of his poem, 'Mid-term Break'.

I read this poem again after meeting Seamus Heaney at a poetry reading in 2008, when I was twenty-one. I told him I had first read his poetry when I was twelve and I wanted to describe to him what a profound effect it had on me as a child, but I wasn't really sure how to explain it. When I was twelve, I recognised the innocence of the snowdrops and the cot and the purity that goes with the angelic image of 'a poppy bruise and no gaudy scars'. I recognised the fear of the aged shaking the hands of the now responsible youth, watching his father's tears and his mother's inconsolable grief.

At twelve, the main line that resonated with me was the final one: 'A four foot box, a foot for every year.' I didn't really understand what I was hearing when I was told 'they're no longer with us' or 'she passed away' or 'he's gone to the angels'. I hated the 'gone to the angels' line in particular. It sounded like complete baloney. People lived and died and I knew that much, but the way it was spoken of made dying seem like a romantic notion, a fuzzy thing with endless possibilities. Heaney's poem told me the honest truth in a way I could relate to and understand. 'A four foot box, a foot for every year.' That told me what I wanted to know. It was the fragility projected in those nine words that resonated with me and made me think of the eight years I had on this kid and how the older I got, the more difficult it would be to get a coffin to fit me. I thought about the power of those words and what they said about life, that it is fragile and short, but it can be calculated and powerful. That one sentence spoke volumes.

I didn't believe in Heaven or the subscribed notion of God, and I still don't. As far as I was concerned, when I died, I wasn't going to a paradise in the sky presided over by a man with a white beard. But I wasn't a realist either. I was drawn to non-Catholic notions of afterlife, like reincarnation and the living force of energy. I believed in magic, in energy and power in the universe, in the ability of those who have died being able to help the living in some way. I believed in witches and goblins and magic dust that Tinkerbell might flit around your garden. I believed that magic was within me too, that I had something special to offer. I just didn't know how to tap into it. From as early as I could remember, I had always felt I had a purpose in life.

My parents had imbued me with the sense that I was special, that I had been put on the Earth for a reason and that I had the strength and the power to fulfil that reason, whatever it was. I had a special path to follow. I just had to keep looking until I found it.

9.

My best friend in school, Margaret, was a dedicated runner and loved what exercise did for her body. I didn't understand her dedication, as she would frequently tell me. I didn't know what it was like to give that sort of commitment and to care so much about my body. 'You're lucky,' she once told me. 'You don't care about your appearance or your greasy hair. Maybe you should take some pride in it and wear some make-up. I mean, you actually have breasts.' She batted her eyes from beneath her light blue eyeliner as she delivered this compliment. The truth was, I never really cared about my appearance during secondary school.

I remember telling Marie this story one day while we sat on her bed, in the room beside mine, in Temple Street. 'It's so annoying,' she agreed. 'There are girls like that in my school, too. Those Little Ms Perfect types who just don't get it.'

'Yeah, they don't appreciate life like we do, but you can't expect them to. They don't know any better,' I reasoned.

By 'it' we meant life, as we knew it – that we were here for a bigger reason than clothes and trivialities.

Marie had progress muscle disorder, a slow, brutal illness that was similar in symptom and progression to MS. It was also extremely rare and pain management for it was not well developed at that time. Marie was one of the youngest people in Ireland with the illness and there just wasn't enough knowledge about it. She was only two years older than me, but we were both far too used to the inside of hospitals. She told me stories about her illness, like how one time a doctor had manipulated her sore foot and stuck sharp pins in it. He told her the pain she was screaming at him about wasn't real because it came and went and he kept going with the examination until she vomited all over him.

It was 2001 and we were the only two people of our age on our ward in the Children's Hospital – I was thirteen and Marie was fifteen. We bonded over our lack of faith in the medical profession, plus she was more glamorous than me, which was intriguing. The most regular gifts brought in by our visitors were cosmetics, like nail polish or eye-shadow palettes, but I wasn't interested in them at all. Marie was fascinated with them. At that point I didn't really feel like a girl. I felt like everything a girl was not – I didn't like make-up, I wasn't obsessed with boys and I didn't really care about my appearance, as Margaret had pointed out. I knew this set me apart from the girls in school, but in reality I was a bit depressed. I just didn't care about things like washing my hair, putting on lipstick, all those things. I felt like I knew too much. With Marie it was different, because we were inside the sealed environment of the hospital. I could try out these things without feeling self-conscious because it was easier to forget about the outside world.

During that stay, when Marie and I were roaming the corridors together, things got a little bit harder for me. I was now in second year, a time when I was supposed to be getting serious about study in preparation for the Junior Certificate exam, but as usual my body wasn't co-operating. I was by now used to getting my IV antibiotics through my portacath, but on this particular occasion the port had done something strange. While the antibiotic was being injected into my chest, a searing pain had ripped in a circular motion around the injection. I could feel the fluid swell in my chest and the stinging pain. The CF nurse and I laughed at the red swelling growing just below my collarbone, above my right breast. We dubbed it my 'third boob' and giggled about it. It was six years since I had had the device inserted and now the port was broken and needed to be replaced. Sometimes they lasted for the full eleven years that they were intended to work, other times they didn't.

The day after the searing pain I had a specialised x-ray, called a contrast study, done on the area. I stood at the door to the X-ray room and heard the light whip of the new sheet being placed on the narrow black stretcher below the machine. I climbed the two steps of the bedside stool and lay down on top of the bed. The large, square machine moved in clicking jerks above me. A whooshing surge came first, then a jerking click into place ... then silence. This could happen three or four times before the equipment was finally in place. I lay there, chatting to everyone around me. I was always happy, always smiling – it was like my trademark and kept me feeling happy when I wasn't. I lay there watching the grey screen and my insides illuminated across it. There I was, a xylophone of ribs and black matter. The thin line of the port's catheter ran from the needle site like a thread leading into my superior vena cava. The titanium circle was the size of a two euro piece and was buried under my skin. A faded pink scar was the only visible identification on the outside. The port was round and flat, with sloping sides and a spongy middle, like a baby's bottle if there was no top on the teat.

The doctor signalled and the square X-ray machine chugged again. I watched as the catheter illuminated with the dye they were injecting. It flew up the line, like coke being sucked through a straw. I watched the dye circle the titanium 'euro' and then abruptly my chest started stinging. It reminded me of one time when I was younger and my babysitter allowed me to stay up late. My parents came home early and before anything could be done I was hiding behind the couch, hoping to make it out the back door of our sitting room and up the stairs before they caught me, but then my squeal gave me away. I had landed right on top of a wasp when I hit the carpet. This was the same type of sting I was feeling now, but it was growing more intense and on the screen that area of my chest seemed to flood in circles. The doctor lay down the syringe gently, as it was still connected to my chest. She looked down before removing her gloves and all I could see was her bobbing blonde curly hair. 'It's gone,' she said, sounding genuinely peeved.

I sighed and forced a smile. 'That's okay. It had to go sometime.' I smiled and thanked everyone. My chest was heavy and the pain throbbed dull and steady, keeping irregular time with my heart. I walked out of the room to my waiting mother and told her it was gone. It had to happen sometime, no big deal. It was just lousy timing – the beginning of second year, the year where I had to get serious about study. My mother came towards me to hug me, but I put out my hand and nodded my head. 'I'm fine. Let's just go back to the ward. We can fix this.' If she had touched me, I would have crumbled.

The next few weeks were a jumble of events that are difficult to relate, like pieces of a jigsaw puzzle I can't fit together properly. The first time I went to surgery was in October and I was not scared. It was a simple in-and-out procedure. Professor Fitzgerald took out the defective titanium piece and popped in a new one. He used the word 'popped'; he wasn't worried. I woke up in the recovery room, my chest heavy, like lead was weighing on it. It had been six years, but the heaviness in the right side of my chest, where they had reopened the wound, was familiar. The morphine helped ease the pain and I held up my right shoulder, as though it was hanging from a clothes-hanger, to numb the pain.

The surgeons had put a needle into the port while I was

knocked out and a few hours later a nurse attached a syringe to my line. She pushed it to flush the saline through, but it wouldn't budge. I started to shake. I remember saying that they must need to change the needle – after all, there were three parts to it: the catheter, the titanium circle and the outside needle. The needle was not the easiest to solve and the line was burrowed in so tightly, and at a V angle, that the fluid could not get through. In spite of my protests, it wasn't as simple as a needle change. They would have to bring me to surgery again to fix it.

When I woke from the second surgery, my mom was beside me. I was just sipping water when the assistant surgeon came in to talk to us. He chortled and described the events that were unfolding as a 'black comedy'. This was humorous to him? I didn't feel like laughing. Did I know, he asked me, how special I was? How he went home and told all his friends about the special, brave girl he looks after? 'All of my friends know about you and they think you're remarkable.' So what, mister, so bloody what? What is that meant to mean to me? I'm so glad I've brightened up your life, made your work more challenging, given you something to talk about with your friends. I didn't say any of that, of course. I smiled a large, cut-watermelon smile. Smiling was the easiest defence.

He was not a bad doctor and he cared a great deal for me. His tactlessness was something familiar that I have observed in adults over the years. Children are different; their words tumble out like cascading butterflies. Like many adults, this doctor's words were recycled and layered: he wasn't being himself, he was being his idea of a doctor. As a child you get used to it, you take it. When you get older, it's much harder to accept that kind of disconnection from a doctor.

My line still wouldn't flush, which is why he had come down, to investigate. I had stopped sobbing by this stage because, despite the fact that I didn't trust the man, he said nice things to me, like how the large space between my big toe and the rest of my feet was a feature considered beautiful in his country. I didn't want to let my 'amazing girl' cloak slip. Just before he arrived I walked to the bathroom, placed the face-cloth flat across my face and sucked the water from it through my nose and mouth. I removed it and watched the water trickle from different angles of my hairline, across my cheek and along my nose. I smiled in the mirror and patted my face dry. Then I walked down the stairs to my room, placed my hand on my mother's back, took a sip of water and smiled at him.

He explained the situation. It wasn't that my portacath was broken, it was just that we couldn't be sure of its status yet, it was such a fragile device. I intervened. 'You can't get the syringe through the bung, but you can't put an orange needle in because you might put too much pressure on the line and blow it?'

He nodded. 'She is so intelligent,' he gushed.

I thought I understood everything that was going on around me. My mom wanted him to take out the cannula and replace it, but he kept saying that it would make Professor angry. He wanted me to lie down, but I stayed sitting up. My mother watched as he tried to open the bung. He was unsuccessful. Despite the fact that we had explained numerous times that a nurse had already attempted to flush it, he stretched over for some saline. I leaned with him, shocked at his stupidity. If I hadn't moved with him, he could have pulled the needle from my chest and I would have been going back to surgery anyway.

I watched the man intently, and waited. He screwed the syringe onto the green bung and lifted the tube up with the back of his hand. Mom shot me a dubious look and I smiled hard at him, hoping it would send him some sort of magical mumbo-jumbo that would make this work. He regained concentration and used the palm of his hand to try and push the saline through. I wrinkled my eyes closed and sucked air through the gaps in my clenched teeth. I was waiting for the pop, which had happened once before when there was a clot. That time, a male doctor had used his entire body weight to push the clot clear. I only found out afterwards that he could have snapped the long catheter from my port to my heart in half. When he had applied the pressure, the clot had shot through me and it was as though someone had pitched a baseball through my chest, straight for my heart, at Concorde speed. I looked at this doctor now, attempting to do the same thing, and told him to quit putting so much pressure on it. A trickle of sweat appeared on his forehead. He was mumbling something about 'The Professor'.

The Professor was Professor Fitzgerald, the wonderful surgeon who had saved my life as a child and performed all of my operations since then. When he did his Monday rounds, his presence inspired a kind of mania where all members of staff shook and reorganised until he arrived. 'It's the Prof! Code Red!' would be called along the corridors. I loved him. He spoke to me like an adult, sat on my bed, listened and responded. It was well-known that the Professor and I had a special bond, that we respected each other, which is why this doctor was nervous. He was afraid to call him and admit the problem. He had been given the responsibility of tightening the bung before I left surgery, and in his macho haste he had blundered. His job was what he was thinking about now as he squirmed.

He took my wrist in a sudden movement and his palms were slippy with sweat. 'I'll be back in a minute,' he said and looked at my mother, a trained nurse, who I felt knew more than he did.

'How far should we let him go, Mom?' My question hung in the air as he marched back in with a large green pliers. He opened a pack of sterile wipes and cleaned the implement. He clasped the bung and tried to twist it. With one wrong jerk, he could rip this line from my chest. There was no other official medic in the room. I could feel rings of sweat forming under my arms and I desperately wanted to tug the fabric loose, to cool myself down, but I dared not move. He sighed angrily and swung the light above my bed around, and now the spotlight glared on me. I was sweating, he was sweating, Mom didn't take her eyes off him for a second. The bung wouldn't budge.

He left the room again and returned once more, this time with a scissors. He cleaned it with a sterile wipe. Mom asked him what he thought he was doing. He looked at her dismissively. He opened the scissors and placed the two sides of it around the green bung, the simple little green bung that could have been twisted off so easily if it had not been for his stupidity. I began to feel anger. Why had he done this? Why was this happening? I felt delirious as the surreal events unfolded. Here was an assistant surgeon too afraid to call his superior to say that he had done something wrong, a man too afraid to admit that he couldn't correct the mistake he had made, an idiot who was now wearing a groove in my bung with an implement that I had used yesterday to make star shapes in the play dough. His wrist was jerking frantically, and then it happened. The lamp suddenly hit me smack on the head. It had fallen out of the wall and landed right on top of me. After a brief pause I began a giggle and then I couldn't stop. The doctor didn't find this funny, he lifted the lamp and looked me up and down as my mother's hands darted all over me, checking for problems. I laughed and laughed until I coughed. My belly ached and my head bobbed. The doctor smiled mildly and my mother laughed a little, but I could not stop.

The doctor called another member of his team, who arrived with a plaster-cutters from A&E. It was a large metal implement that looked like it belonged in a plumber's toolbox. I kept laughing. It's funny when you have to sit there and let someone do that to you, almost as though you're leaving your body. Eventually my doctor-tormentor gave up, and called the Professor.

Two days later they did another contrast test X-ray and discovered that the catheter had kinked inside my chest; no one knew how it had happened. They brought me down to surgery two days later to reopen the site again and tug the catheter in the superior vena cava back into its proper place.

One week later it stopped working again. I was brought back to surgery, this time with only a mild valium as sedation. I was awake as the Professor manipulated the site with his hands. I remember catching sight of myself in a mirror as I was being carried down from the recovery room. It was my fourth operation in two weeks and I was pale and wan. I looked in the mirror and saw this heap of a person. The surgery scars made me feel ugly and ruined. I was only thirteen, but my skin was already marked forever. Those thoughts took hold and I couldn't shake them off.

10.

After the fourth and final portacath surgery, I sat on the bed in St Philomena's ward eating mashed potato, chicken, gravy and peas. Toast was what you were meant to have after an operation, but I prided myself on being able to handle a normal dinner. Everything was a competition to prove I was the exception. Usually, about an hour after I woke up from recovery, I was hungry and ready to eat. Nurses always marvelled at it and I felt good that I could beat the anaesthetic. That's why when I suddenly said, 'Trish, I think I'm going to be sick,' the nurse looked startled, then rushed over with a blue bowl.

I couldn't keep anything down for the next two weeks and it was Trish who sat with me regularly, chatting about the x-rays and the tests and the possibility that it was reflux. Eventually, they moved me up to the top floor and that's when the dietician visited me for the first time. 'Orla, you've always been such a good girl. What's happening with your weight?'

Weight. It was the first time someone had used that word, and it was the first time I had thought about it. What had it to do with weight? Yet as soon as she mentioned that word,

I felt an immediate sense of guilt. My weight was something I was wholly responsible for and I had always fulfilled that responsibility. I was proud that it had never been a problem because as a general rule, it's a major issue for people with CF. To me, it felt like I was breaking another rule – the one that said I would not be able to maintain a healthy weight because of my illness. In spite of everyone's expectations and predictions, I had always managed to keep my weight at the right level. Achieving that made me feel separate from CF, like I was winning against it; once I started losing weight, it felt like CF was gaining the upper hand and I was the loser.

I had been transferred to one of the three single cubicles in the hospital, which were on a separate ward across from Top Flat, on the top floor. The doctors wanted me to stop running about the hospital with Marie and instead to rest completely. They were really concerned about the vomiting because they couldn't find a reason for it. The room wasn't as big a deal as I thought it would be, seeing as most people talked about it like it was Heaven itself. It was an oval shape and the windows were too high up for me to be able to see out. The walls were painted a cream colour, very calm in contrast to the Disney characters that danced garishly across the walls downstairs. I was constantly attached to a drip and was unable to leave my bed. I plaited my hair in boredom. In that room I had to relax, I had to focus and I had to think.

Spending long periods of time on my own wasn't a problem. I got to read magazines that told true stories about women who married murderers, sold their children or were able to eat the whole contents of a fridge in one sitting. I was able to watch MTV, a luxury we didn't have at home. Dad had always disparaged the 'type of people who would spend all day watching MTV', now I was one of them. It was a teenage rebellion against my parents, even though they weren't there to appreciate it. I could fry my brains all day watching MTV and no one would tell me what its base, crude shows were doing to me. I remember watching a fan programme where a girl who was obsessed with Sarah Michelle Gellar got to meet her. The girl was bullied in school and watching Buffy slay vampires made her feel strong. I watched it and I felt sorry for the sad, insecure girl. I tried to figure out which one of them I was more like: 'Buffy' or her fan.

As I lay in my bed trying to decipher what was going on, the light shifted and the door opened. It was Bernie, my favourite nurse from the other ward. She brought a glossy magazine and told me they missed me down there. I didn't really miss them because I was so wrapped up in the anger I was feeling. I was frustrated by everything and everyone. Things were falling apart inside me, but I was trying not to let it show. At least, I tried very hard not to let it show to my parents; it was easier to be more honest with the people in the hospital because they didn't care for me in the same way. I thought I was in control. I wasn't.

The fact that the doctors couldn't explain the nausea and vomiting made me feel like it had to be my fault. That somehow I must be doing something wrong to make it happen. I was really hard on myself and I couldn't explain my thoughts to anyone. I was afraid that if I said out loud that it might be my fault, it would be taken as an admission and then it definitely *would* be my fault. So I kept telling them over and over that I wasn't, as they suspected, making myself sick. At the same time, I could see all sides of it – I could see exactly why they would think I had an eating disorder. I became obsessed with these thoughts, with why the vomiting couldn't be fixed. I started to feel like I had no control at all. I was being told what I could eat and when to eat it. I had undergone so many surgeries that I felt as though my body was being routinely cut open and manipulated. I felt like I was losing myself and I didn't have any faith in how I would get out of it.

Eventually, my team sent a trainee psychologist to talk to me. Mom said she lacked experience of dealing with a child like me. I liked her though, because she was young. When I try and think of that time, I can't remember a lot of what we talked about. She asked why I wore black and told me some people wore black to look thin, but I didn't want to look thin. I just wanted to have some say in what was going on. She brought me down to a room in the psychology department and tried some art therapy with me. It felt ridiculous.

After several meetings, when they had moved me back downstairs to a shared ward because now they were concerned about me being on my own for too long, I finally opened up to her a bit about the things that were playing on my mind. We met in the playroom off the ward, amid the rocking horse and the Doll's house. I asked her, why do people die? Why did Gerard die? How did CF kill him? I wanted to know. She spoke for twenty minutes in a politically correct way, telling me death was a part of life, that CF was complicated. But *how? Why?* She lost her cool then, and it was shocking. She told me it was difficult for her, too, that she had been there with Gerard.

'One morning, around five am, we thought he was dying and I was the only one there. I had to call his parents and tell them.' I watched her, imagining my own parents and my brother getting woken up in the thick of night. He told her he wanted to be buried in his favorite football jersey. He had thought about what he wanted at thirteen.

I was obsessed with the human condition and what happened for someone with CF when they died. I wanted to know how it happened, what those last moments were like. I wanted her to tell me. I think it was because he was so young that it really resonated with me. It was like I wanted to hurt myself with the idea of it before it happened, so that I'd be prepared, so that I'd be in control of death. But in her PC expression of life and death, she left me empty-handed.

One day in the corridor I recognised a girl I knew from home and ducked into a doorway to hide from her. I felt guilty about my CF, felt responsible for it in some way. I had always been a 'good patient', as my dietician put it. I had gained weight steadily as a child, and maintained it at a healthy average. I swam to stay fit, in the River Liffey, in the sea – the more challenging, the better. Weight and muscle were good because the better my lung function, the stronger I was and the more able to fight infections. I knew that mantra off by heart, but it was like I was trying to input information into a faulty computer system. I was stuck in limbo, not going forward or back. I was still vomiting everyday and they were testing me for brain tumors and other exotic things. My consultant constantly told my parents that he believed in me, and I believed in him. I knew he would get me better, figure out what was wrong. But this was a frightening time for me – the first in my life when the doctors couldn't say definitively what was wrong with me. That's why the idea that I might be the cause couldn't be shaken off.

The thing about CF is that it is completely centered on food. People might think of lungs or even pancreas when it's mentioned, but the fact is that one of the cornerstones of life with CF is a constant awareness of food and eating. It's not something that feels strange as a child because it's all you've ever known. But gradually, throughout my youth, I began to notice the differences between my lunchboxes and other kids' and the fact that I ate anything I wanted, whenever I chose and was encouraged to do so. If you don't keep your weight up with CF, then you're less able to fight infection; more weight equals more ammunition. For most people with CF gaining and keeping weight is a massive struggle, but for me it had never been an issue because I loved food and was determined to beat CF on any front I could.

I was luckier than a lot of others with CF, in a few ways. First, because I focused on eating and maintaining a good weight, I didn't need a peg tube, so I was able to keep a healthy relationship with food – something that's very difficult for most sufferers. A peg tube is a tube that's inserted permanently into the stomach. You can hide it with your clothes, but it's always there. At nighttime it's hooked up to a bag of artificial feed, which provides all the nutrients the body needs, so the responsibility for eating is taken away from the person. Secondly, I was in hospital maybe four times a year, not every few weeks like others were. In fact, sometimes I didn't feel like I had CF at all. It wasn't that I thought they had made a mistake with the diagnosis, it's just that, I was invincible, wasn't I? I could do anything, so CF didn't fit in. Death didn't fit in. Then again, I had met a boy a few years earlier who had CF but had never been in hospital, had never used nebulisers or taken tablets or done physio. CF was just so complicated. It was a label that we tagged around and then sometimes it tagged all of us around with it. But then no two people had the same experience of CF, it affected us all differently: some of us with our chest, some only with chest, then some only bowel or bowel and chest together – the only predictable bit was that it would get worse.

There was just one thing all of us people with CF had in common: both of our parents were carriers of the gene, and it was just pure chance that they fell in love with each other and that they had a child with CF, something they didn't expect. And I felt guilty about that, that I couldn't be better for them, my parents. I wanted to be stronger, faster, more accomplished. Now, I was just a mess.

In order to combat the vomiting and weight loss, the doctors decided to feed me thorough a nasal gastric (NG) tube because I wasn't keeping enough nutrients down. My concentration span became diluted from the continuous drugs and half sleep. Thoughts jumped around my head, fighting for coherence, so I listened to music to drown them out – the Corrs, the *Heartbeat* soundtrack, Dusty Springfield, *Les Misérables*, anything by Andrew Lloyd Webber. At music summer camp when I was ten I had sung 'I Don't Know How To Love Him', from *Jesus Christ Superstar*, on stage. The words and the melody fused together like scent drifting from a fragrant candle. It moved me somewhere deep inside. I found songs that applied to what I was feeling, or an event that happened that day, or was going to happen later and I stuck myself inside the music, letting it seep through me and drag me into a subconscious plane. My eyes fell into a trance then, playing out scenarios and thinking and over-thinking. The best time to listen to music was at night. I used it to block out the feeling of the newly inserted NG feed plopping into my stomach through the tube in my nose.

When they took me out of the cubicle and sent me back to the ward, Marie was there for me again. I badly needed distraction from my own thoughts and feelings, and Marie could provide it. Neither of us wanted to be the one who went home first and left the other. Making the most of being in here was the fun part. Occasionally a nurse would come in and call 'Quiet Time' at us and make us separate and stay in our own beds for a few hours, but this particular night, we knew no one would be attempting to supervise our antics: it was the nurses' Christmas party. Once the day staff had trickled away, around 9pm, it was time for fun. Angela and Niamh were on duty that night, and Marie and I were going to have our Christmas 'Girlie Night' in with them. It was going to be better than the nurses' night out.

We started in the treatment room. The kitchen was tucked into a small space between it and the ward. I knew the combination to both. Someone had recorded two movies for the ward: *Clueless* and *My Girl*. We kept the tapes in Marie's room and watched them almost daily, fluctuating between the pain of losing Thomas J. to his bee allergy and the excitement and fear of High School. I wanted to be there, all at once: I wanted to be Vada and Cher and have both worlds. It would never be possible, I knew, but right here in our world it was. Here we could watch ourselves with the hopes, dreams and responsibilities of these roles and never have to play them. It was as though someone had built a house and trapped us in between the double-glazing. We understood what it was to be alive like

couldn't breathe properly or speak and he was in hospital a lot. He was about ten years old. My friend Matthew, who had CF too, had introduced me to him years earlier. Eddie was a lovely boy with light brown hair and piercing eyes. Eddie was dead.

'Eddie's dead, sorry,' I said, because it seemed like the only way to do it. Marie was like me, she didn't cry.

'The poor little mite, God rest him,' she said surprisingly fast and then she sat, mouth open, as though blowing an invisible bubble.

'Girls! Quiet. Time.' It was the other nurse, Niamh.

'Okay, just two minutes please, we've just—'

'No just. No buts. Bed!' I hated Niamh.

I lay in my bed, thinking about what I had told Marie and a shivering feeling throbbed in my chest. I felt it was my fault. I had said it wrong and I should have timed it better. I lay flat and felt a warm pool hover in my stomach, like a mini sea full of wrecked ships waiting to be fished out. I let them come up my oesophagus. Relief. I heaved the lumps into the blue bowl, brown against blue always showed up the contents starkly. Half-digested chicken curry. I had eaten the whole thing because I could, because there were no rules and there was no one to stop me.

Something different happened then. It felt like my insides were unhinging and rolling up and I started to gag. I was still being fed by NG tube and the tube had kinked into a V shape and was coming out my mouth. I couldn't catch my breath and fell into blind panic. I felt my insides coming out and I ran to the nurses' station with the blue bowl under my chin, looking for help because I was choking.

'Oh for God's sake, do that in the bathroom,' Niamh growled at me. I kept pointing my finger at the bowl and my neck to indicate that I needed help. The other nurse saw me. 'Okay, calm down,' she said gently, but then Niamh took over from her and brought me back to bed. 'Deep breaths,' she said and had me lie down flat. I strained my eyes down to try and see it without moving. I saw a shaking right hand, mine, as she tugged the tube from my nose gently and I felt it pull back in and straighten inside me. Then she pulled it out.

'Why did you take it out?' I snapped, gasping.

'It couldn't have been left there,' she explained, and said she would give me a half an hour before she put another one in.

'But that just went in yesterday and it took so long, I can skip one feed,' I pleaded. Waking up in the morning after an overnight feed made me feel like my body had been invaded. I usually burped a lot and it was usually the taste of the feed. My stomach felt bloated and heavy. I felt like I had no control over my own body. So the thought of waking up without that awful bloated feeling thrilled me.

Niamh consulted the doctor on call, but he wouldn't allow it. At 2am she called me to the treatment room to replace the tube. They had spent an hour putting it in the day before. She stood in front of me wearing white gloves and holding the thick plastic tube that always invited a circle of congealed snotty skin to hibernate under my nostril when it was in. As she dabbed the Vaseline on the tip of the tube, so it would slide down easier, I told her she should just leave me alone for the night. Some student doctors I had met before had told me they always tried medical procedures on themselves, within reason, before performing them on patients. I really respected that. Now I told Niamh that she should try inserting the NG tube up her own nose before subjecting me to it. The one I had in before – the one she had pulled out – was a soft one, easy to swallow, that's put in under x-ray. They used those because they lasted longer – they were left in for three weeks. The emergency one she was now going to insert was the thick white one that could only be used for a week. It was hard, like swallowing a large pencil. I was sick of it. I was sick of people making decisions about my body and not having a choice. I didn't want to swallow the stupid thing that night; I certainly didn't want her to put it in. But she did put it in.

We left the room and later I saw her leaning over the sink in the kitchen with her shoulders hunched. I thought she might be crying so I left quickly, annoyed at her weakness. I was really mean to her. I was trying to make her see that I was a person, not just a job to be ticked off on her nightly rounds, but in doing that I disregarded the fact that she did have a job to do.

I had thought my re-entry to the ward signaled a new chapter, but now it felt like nothing had changed. Yet again, I was being knocked back, trapped in my body. I felt increasingly disillusioned with life and disconnected from everything on 'the outside'. I had tremendous guilt because, on the one hand, I felt I had the power to fix it, but on the other I wasn't fixing it because I didn't know how. It was irrational, but it was how I felt and it made sense at that time, in that place. I was slowly becoming overwhelmed.

11.

One morning, a week after the NG tube incident, I woke up to Niamh poking me. 'Go on, get up! It's school time, come on, stop messing,' she scolded.

I wasn't messing. We didn't have school today. It was teacher's day off or something. Marie had left a few days before and I was becoming increasingly lazy and depressed. I had now been in for about two months and life outside the hospital was starting to recede into the distance. The day before, my team had introduced me to a psychiatrist. I had seen the psychologist before, but now my team wanted me to talk to this psychiatrist, just for a one-off assessment. We met in a cloakroom off the ward because there was no spare room for us. It was really cramped and small and we sat close together on two plastic seats. It was claustrophobic and intimidating. Not surprisingly, we didn't hit it off. Mom and Dad were wary of her too because they felt like I didn't need her; at that point they were 100% sure that I did not have an eating disorder.

The day after I talked to the psychiatrist a nurse approached me with a clear cup at drug time and I knew something was different. I didn't get meds at 6pm. 'What's this?' I asked. 'Just your vitamins,' was the answer I got. My mom was there too, so I just took it. I was on bed rest for the day anyway, so I did what I was told. The next morning I stood up to go to the bathroom and my legs buckled beneath me. I grabbed the iron bedsides before I hit the ground. I laughed and then fell into fits of giggles.

It transpired that the psychiatrist, who was top of her field, knew absolutely nothing about CF and had prescribed 10mgs of Valium a day to 'give me a rest'. My mother remembers it as though I had lost all cognitive control. She said on the second day I just sat there, staring into oblivion. My mother was a nurse and had seen drugged-up patients before, but she found it difficult to look at me.

At that time Mom was attending weekly meetings with the team about my care. The psychiatrist attended each week, too, along with the CF nurses, the schoolroom teachers, the ward sister and the dietician. At the next meeting the psychiatrist put forward the case that I had an eating disorder and needed to be transferred to St Patrick's Institute, the psychiatric hospital in Dublin, to be placed on a special program. Dr Murphy was deeply unsure about this idea. Mom told me he believed in me, he believed that I would get better. He did not think that I had an eating disorder, but rather that the vomiting was a behaviour brought on by a number of factors. The psychiatrist kept pushing and they kept saying no.

Looking back, I feel very lucky that Dr Murphy and his belief in me prevailed. The truth was that I didn't have an eating disorder as such, but rather had fallen into a pattern of disordered eating due to the circumstances I was in. I hated myself. Food had always been a stabiliser, something I didn't really have to give much thought to, in the sense that I just ate it all the time. I wasn't caught up in how much carbohydrates or protein or fats was in something. When they put me on the program to try and end the cycle of vomiting, I suddenly became hyper-aware of all these things that I hadn't even noticed before. I started to fear eating more than exactly what was on my schedule and to feel anxious about being weighed every morning. If I was down even just 0.2 of a kilogram, I was reprimanded for it.

If only I knew then what I know now about weight and how important it is for CF, but also how your weight is different at different times of the day, how you can be heavier just by drinking water. But I wasn't some sort of informed anorexic who knew these things; I was a naïve kid who didn't realise that what started out as something for which there was no medical explanation ended up as something that could have potentially killed me. The emptiness inside me was no longer filled with thoughts of getting better and getting back to normal life. Instead I filled it up with getting the weight thing right and then struggling with the desire to get it right for the people around me – my family and my team – and with what I wanted. I was addicted to the situation and couldn't see a way out of it. Outwardly, I talked about hope and appeared happy and gung-ho about getting better, but inside I was frozen and didn't know how to move forward. My emotions and self-worth had become wrapped up in food.

Maybe it all happened because my ability to keep weight on and eat all around me was one of the things my parents were most proud of and one of the things that I felt separated me from other people with CF, the really sick ones who needed to be fed by artificial means. I didn't understand then that there are so many very healthy people with CF who 'top up' their calories every night with an overnight feed and that they do it willingly. I hadn't accepted that we were all part of the same group. I thought I was beyond that and that, like my dad said, thinking outside the box was going to save me. Now in doing that, I had created my own box, and I had no idea how to escape from it. I knew in theory how to do it, but my inner self was suffocated with reasons not to comply.

On my fourth day of Valium they reduced my intake and said I was allowed go to the schoolroom again for lessons. I went to school everyday I was there when I wasn't on bed rest. It was part of the structure I had to have. Although the school in Temple Street was officially a primary school, they did their utmost to keep me on track with my own school. They brought in books that were on my curriculum and spent time researching them to keep me up to date. Weekly my mother would call my secondary school at home and ask them to put some work in an envelope for me. She would go to the school to pick it up, sometimes twice a week, and when she came to me there would be maybe one or two exercises in it. For my Junior Cert I did English, Maths, Irish, History, Science, Music and French. I used to get excited about the time of week when the envelope was due from my school, and then disheartened again by its contents because it would just be a few things from English, History and Music. The other teachers usually forgot or didn't bother, which made me feel even more disconnected.

There was an excellent vice principal at the time, who said decades of the rosary for me and constantly apologised that there wasn't more work being sent to me, but that didn't change anything. Losing touch with education was like stretching an invisible umbilical cord to its maximum, with me on one end and school life on the other. Get Well Soon cards meant very little considering the time taken to make them could have photocopied a week's worth of homework.

So the schoolroom in the hospital was my main academic support, as well as being a way of conversing with normality and weaning me back into the real world. I needed to develop, to occupy my mind with something other than food and weight. By now they were weighing me every morning and making me write a food diary. I was permitted to do light exercise on the treadmill, but I hated it because it was boring and pointless and my legs ached. But then, after about a week, I began to enjoy it and learn how to cope with it. It was only for five or ten minutes each time, but I did begin to get something from it. My enjoyment of it was seen as a symptom of an eating disorder, and I wasn't allowed to do any exercise for a week.

I don't know whether it was laziness or a genuine reaction to the Valium, but on that fourth day I didn't want to get out of bed. The ward sister came down and poked me when I wouldn't get up for the nurse. There was a Mass that morning and something had been rotting inside me regarding the whole compulsory religion teaching in our schools. It wasn't such a big deal at home because I was part of a choir and went to church to sing. I liked singing in Irish at St Patrick's Day Masses and the calming brilliance that came from the calculated arrangements of my secondary school choir. It had nothing to do with God, though. My mother went to Mass on Sundays and my father sometimes went. He didn't believe, but he went for our sake.

That day, I finally got up and arrived at the meeting point of the school room too early. After the effort it took to get me there, it was frustrating. I sat on the deep blue chair by the bookshelf with Moira, the teaching assistant. I told her I felt strange, there was something off. She told me to stay sitting and see how I was in a few minutes. The other children slowly filtered in from different wards and once all of us were there, we lined up to go to Mass.

The chapel was a small room in the middle level of the hospital that you had to pass to get to the school or any of the main wards. During each festivity there were drawings and artwork by the children who attended there, and at Christmas there was a Nativity. Sometimes it was held in the schoolroom, depending on how many people were due to arrive. I had been the Virgin Mary when I was seven. I remember being in the schoolroom with Mrs Dawson, the then Principal, when a girl came in from another ward and one of the teachers suggested that she should be Mary. Mrs Dawson said I had the golden locks for it and I got the part. There wasn't as long a dusty road for the Little Donkey to walk in the schoolroom, but we managed to make it to the manger for the final chorus. Some years earlier I had been in a choir and learned how to play the organ and when the sister in the hospital asked me to play at Mass once, I did. I was useful and, they kept telling me, there's no one quite like you.

That might have been what I was thinking about when I walked into the chapel with the children and sat down. They were all under ten and I was sitting there beside the teaching assistant, listening to the priest intone the Responsorial Psalm. It was the Thanks Be To God bit that lodged inside me. It sounded like empty words, people droning it without passion. The tabernacle started to shine and seemed to blind my eyes with mist. The mist was the tears coming hard and fast, and I didn't know how to stop them. This was so fake, all of this was so fake. Why were we listening to this priest? Who was he to tell us anything? We were being brainwashed. I was being violated. I didn't want to listen to this; I didn't want to be there. So I cried, large, grief-stricken cries that shook my body and forced the teaching assistant to half carry me out of the church. Something had broken inside me.

12.

Lying in bed afterwards, I was too ashamed to speak to anyone, but I wanted someone to come to me. I wanted to explain to someone what I had realised. I knew it was important. The ward sister came in and asked me what had happened.

'I don't know,' was all I could muster. I didn't feel like I could talk to her.

'Look, Orla, can you warn us the next time you're going to do that?'

'I told you, but you made me go anyway.'

'Well, we didn't know you were going to do that in the middle of mass!'

'I didn't mean to. I didn't know either.'

That episode, and her reaction to it, was the final straw for me. It was as though all the disconnections in my life had joined together to topple me from the Earth. I felt completely invisible and isolated from everyone.

It was a month later that I saw a book on Wicca, a form of modern witchcraft, during my hours out at the Jervis Street shopping centre with my mom. I couldn't stop thinking what the blurb said about inner powers, and a few days later I asked a nurse to buy it for me on her lunchbreak. It was a large purple book with spells and incantations in it. It had dedications to Goddesses and a list of what different herbs did. The most interesting aspect for me was the empowerment of women and the idea that you could create your own circle of worship and pull positive things towards you by sending out positivity.

I read the book from cover to cover and it made sense to me. I didn't want to follow any religion, but I had never realised how powerful a woman could be. This book told me I could do anything, as long as it didn't harm anyone. It was like a new set of rules that echoed what I was feeling inside me: the notion that we are essentially alone but the universe could help us out and guide us along our way. It was something I was learning for the first time: it's okay to be alone.

One Sunday artists from The Ark, a cultural center for children that was near the hospital, came in to create art with all of the patients. The artist I was matched with was a girl with long flowing auburn hair and a nose stud. Her clothes were loose and colourful. She saw the book on Wicca on my bedstand and we got talking about it. She believed in guardian angels and we decided to make a plaster cast of mine. We sat together and she showed me how to meditate. She told me to close my eyes and clear my mind of everything. I took deep breaths and gradually the noises of the children around me became increasingly muffled. Stephanie, it transpired, was my guardian angel's name. She had long brown hair. When I opened my eyes the artist told me to always remember that Stephanie was with me, whenever I needed her. We made a cast of her then and the next day painted her yellow, blue and purple.

Stephanie and my Tigger teddy bear were my saviours at that time. They anchored me when I was feeling raw and overwhelmed. Tigger slept with me most days, but then one morning, he was gone. There was a note on my bed: 'Leave 100,000 dollars in the Dollhouse in the playroom by 9am, or the Tig gets it!' I searched the playroom, but couldn't find him. It was very distressing. The next morning the student nurses came in and I got really angry when they told me it was they who had hidden him. I was serious and uptight and they were being childish. They reached up to get him from his plastic bag prison on top of my wardrobe and I heard a scrape and thud. They had knocked down Stephanie. She smashed into smithereens.

The playroom staff said I could make another one, that they would go out and buy me the ingredients, but I didn't want to. I was such a skeptical girl but Stephanie had gotten to me in a curious way. I didn't really need the plaster-cast Stephanie anyway, I felt like she was probably hanging around with me in spirit.

For the next while things continued the way they had been. I kept food diaries, got weighed, got sick and grappled with my sense of self until I felt exhausted. I was ashamed of my body. I didn't see how with all of these scars I could still be realistically beautiful. Logically, I knew that in the same way the word 'normal' didn't really mean anything, because it's all relative, that 'beauty' was subjective, too. But the problem was that while my head knew these things, my heart was weighed down with the idea of being a freak.

There was another, growing problem that was disturbing me at this time and that was the rapid demise of my family relationships. I didn't know how to function in the family unit anymore, or what my role in it was. I was at a time in my life where I was coming into my own, so naturally the relationship with my parents was tricky. For me, though, CF and hospitalisations complicated matters – a lot. I didn't always do my medications and as a result I argued with my mom. I felt she didn't understand me like my dad did. She was more scientific, whereas Dad was creative overload, with intense ideas and imagination and 'what if's'. I regarded my personality as being very different from my mother's because I valued creativity so highly, or at least what I perceived creativity to be. I snubbed almost everything else, including my mother.

I was obviously out of the house for long stretches while in hospital. I felt like I was the cause of a lot of arguments in the house when I was at home, that with me there things were so much worse than when I was out of the way. I don't understand it to this day. I look at that entire episode of vomiting and weight loss as a type of body panic. I started off with the operations and ended up a mess, not knowing what to do. It was like the vomiting – it started out as a possible gastroentiritis or bug that the doctors couldn't understand, but then became a pattern that I couldn't break. I never actually put my fingers down my throat, but I think the vomiting was psychosomatic. I didn't know then that I had such an addictive personality and that it could be so destructive. Now, that's essentially how I view what was happening then, but at the time no one suggested I was probably subconsciously searching for external relief for something that was gnawing away inside me.

In retrospect, it was part of an ongoing battle for control of my own life that I didn't realise was raging within me. I never saw CF as my enemy nor did I see my parents' nature as over-protective. I just didn't have the awareness, at thirteen, of my own ability to get myself out of situations or patterns of behaviour. The reality of true choice didn't dawn on me until much later in life. I went through stages of feeling like I was in control, but knowing that it was temporary. Our choices and what we know to be true evolve so much with age and I was on the brink of realising my choices as a teenager when this episode occurred. Instead of freeing myself, I ended up in a situation where I was infantilised. My parents monitored me closely, my team made decisions for me, everyone had an opinion on me. I hated it, but maybe in someway I felt I needed it, too? Maybe the real truth was that I wasn't ready for the responsibility of living in my own body, so I abrogated that responsibility through the 'disobedience' of vomiting and weight loss.

It took a while, but I did finally come face-to-face with that truth and suddenly understand what was happening to me. It happened during my Christmas holiday from the hospital, when I was allowed home for a couple of weeks. On one of the days I went into town with my mom. I wore a hat pulled down tightly over my head and kept a hand close to my face, ready to cover the NG tube if we bumped into anyone we knew. The tube was still there and embarrassed me down to my core. It was a symbol of my inability, of their control. I felt like a sub-creature from a Tim Burton movie.

Mom hated shopping, but she thought it might cheer me up, so we went into a small clothes store that was popular with teenage girls who wear brands like Diesel and Levi's. I didn't really want to look at the clothes in there, but I didn't want to argue with Mom. Standing beside the dressing room, rifling through clothes on a rack, I heard two voices I recognised and the before I could jump out of view, two girls from school walked past.

'Oh My God! Orla, Hi, how are you?'

I wanted to melt into the carpet. With my hand over my nose, I almost whispered, 'Oh, fine'. I felt like a rabbit caught in headlights. Why were these girls even talking to me?

'Are you out of hospital now for good? Coming back to school soon?'

I managed to shake my way thorough the answers.

'Well at least you're getting better, Margaret was filling us in.' They continued to tell me how Margaret told them she had visited me, that I was 'getting there'. That I wasn't, in fact, pregnant or had been raped or anything like that. 'There were all these rumours. I know you have CF, but you know, people don't really understand. Anyway you look really great.'

'Thanks,' I said. 'See you soon.'

When I got home I had to change because I had sweated right through my top. I spent the weekend looking up eating disorders on the internet. It was something I had thought about it, but I'd never been able to face up to it. As far as I was concerned, I was too sensible to have an eating disorder. But something about that meeting with those girls from school had triggered something in me and I needed to know more. I found pro-anorexia sites and pro-bulimia sites and prayers to Ana and Mia, the imaginary goddesses of strength who controlled the lives of these girls, who were devoted to being thin. The pictures of young women with their ribs sticking out and smiles on their faces made my insides tremble. I lay in bed, suddenly aware of the weight of flesh on my lungs and against my ribs as they dug into the mattress. I couldn't get comfortable and I was really conscious of it.

That visit home was difficult for everyone because I was so caught up in what was going on in my head. I went back to the hospital with a mixture of anxiety and relief – and I'm sure my family probably felt the same. Once back, I slipped into the routine again of timetables, medication and physio. I was doing physio everyday and I loved the physiotherapist I was working with at the time. We would sing songs from *The Sound of Music* as we walked along the corridor and she would tell me tall tales about her adventures, like mountain climbing in a country I had never heard of. On this day, not long after my Christmas 'holiday' and internet searching, we sat side by side in the treatment room, watching the red fence spikes rise up towards the apartment windows, creating a jagged little border from which to view the people in the flats.

'Dee?'

'Yes, Ms Tinsley?'

'Do I have bulimia?'

The question surprised both of us, I think. I took a deep breath and launched in, and it went something like this: 'It's just, I was looking on the internet, trying to figure out what was wrong with me, and I know the team have tried everything and last month they checked for a brain tumour. And I was in the bathroom when Dr Murphy came on rounds. I was hanging over the toilet bowl throwing up the coleslaw I had eaten in the canteen. He walked in with a furrowed brow, his moustache wrinkling under his nose. 'Good girl, don't worry. We'll figure this out. We'll fix this.' And it occurred to me last week, maybe I could fix this. Maybe there was a reason why all of those tests and x-rays and specialists didn't have an answer. Maybe I can get myself better.'

Her cheeks were rosy and tears were glistening in her eyes. 'Yes. You've done it. Good girl.'

I laughed nervously. 'Right. Identifying the problem. That's the first step.'

For almost three months the team had been searching for other possible causes for the vomiting. A new suggestion would be mooted and they'd dutifully check it out. All through this Dr Murphy had continued to hold fast in his belief in me. Now, finally, it seemed that belief would pay off. After talking to the physio and saying my fears out loud, the vomiting stopped. A week later, I hadn't been sick once. I can't explain this, but it wasn't a big epiphany moment, it was quieter than that. For some reason, I had simply reached the end of this way of thinking, and I stopped.

The next week the team came in and told me I could go home. Yet again, there was no simple emotion for this – I was caught between relief and apprehension. Separating myself from the hospital world, the place I had been hiding out in for five months, was hard; reality was hard. That's something I feel isn't really talked about much: the feeling of safety in a hospital that is unique to long-term patients. It's something that didn't feel strange or unusual when I was a child, but as I got older, it became something I felt guilty about because logic told me that I shouldn't feel this way about a hospital. I know other people with long-term illnesses, some with CF, who have reiterated the same feeling to me about their hospital experiences. It stands to reason that if you spend a prolonged time in a certain place as a very young child, where you feel safe and loved, that place is going to feel somewhat like a home, even if that thought defies logic. Hospital, like many things in my life, wasn't stereotypical.

Like safety and love, food was another factor in the hospital setting that felt normal to me as a child. I had to consume large amounts of calories and fats, so I was eating substantially more than my peers, but as a child I never felt strange about that. In fact, I felt lucky that my parents never restricted me in any way. I couldn't foresee what would happen when I hit puberty. Now I can see the difficulties that started in the teenage years, when I got very distressed about my relationship with food. I know that a lot of girls with and without CF go through a tough time like this at some point in their teenage years. The situation is you're being told you have to eat large amounts of calories to stay well. But the world around you often reflects a very different reality, especially the mainstream media images of what a woman is. So no matter what way you go, you feel alienated in some way. It was around this time that I began to feel alienated from myself, and my image as a young woman.

While logically I knew the most important thing is to stay well as long as possible, and to eat to stay well, I had no idea how emotional patterns can affect behaviour. I knew that not having a positive mental attitude was a bad idea, but I didn't know that too much of that kind of thinking was equally bad. No one is truly invincible, and it's not a weakness to acknowledge that. They kept saying it was an emotional problem made physical, but I couldn't understand that phrase. The phrase I clung onto was what Dr Murphy said: 'She's a strong girl. I have every faith that she'll grow out of it'. So I wove my way through the exhaustion and the confusion and found a way out of it. But I wasn't free yet.

While in hospital I found out my Uncle's neighbour worked as a roadie with the Corrs. Earlier in the year my uncle had appeared with a tin whistle and a pass from The Brit Awards for me. Authentic Corrs' memorabilia. It was unthinkable. I listened to their music over and over on my Discman during that time. 'Queen of Hollywood' was my song. I read once that it was written while the band were driving through the slums of LA and that Marilyn Monroe was an inspiration for it. I had read her unauthorised autobiography on my summer in Wexford the year before. These women made me feel less alone. In retrospect, as a 24-year-old feminist I know having your role model as Marilyn is probably not the best thing. But with the culture I grew up with back then it made complete sense. I wrote to Andrea to say how much their music touched me and to thank her for the stuff. Their albums were like my lifeline, they were the one familiar thing in my volatile environment and for that I was so grateful.

I had gone into the hospital in late 2000, now it was February 2001 and I was rejoining my home and family for the first time in months. It was a difficult transition. I was taking on some responsibility for me, but also handing some to my parents as well because they would be taking up where the team had left off. I would still have to be weighed, once a week for the first while, then once a fortnight. It meant there was still an intense focus on my body and what it was doing and my parents were naturally part of that monitoring process.

At first, living together again was like holding onto pieces of precious Delft, all of us holding our breath, waiting for a jolt to come and smash it all to pieces. It was as though we were a family introduced for the first time. The hardest part was the suspicion, rows and anger. We needed to regain each other's trust, but first I had to believe I could trust myself. I had been so consumed by what was happening with the operations that my emotions had taken control of my logic and I had no way of combating it. I was using all my energies to physically recover. Sometimes I slipped, I threw up and then crumbled on the bathroom floor, crying at my own lack of strength. It wasn't about weight, I had been brought up to believe that I could always do something about CF. It was about the port operations making me feel helpless. Through all that time my body hadn't belonged to me and now it had been given back to me, scarred, and I had to work with it. How could I be an actress now? How could I move ahead? In a world that was so rooted in body-image perfection, these thoughts consumed me.

My parents struggled, too, in the beginning. Time and again I would walk out of the downstairs bathroom to find Mom at the freezer in the utility room next to it. She'd swear she wasn't listening, she was just taking some meat out to defrost, and we'd stand there, sometimes silent, sometimes screaming at each other. Our trust had been so broken and somehow we had to get it back. Except I couldn't remember what it was like to see my mother as Mom and not as some disciplinarian figure on medicine and what's best. I felt she had transformed on me and I never felt relaxed around her. I couldn't remember what it was like before.

My brother had gone five months as an eight-year-old without a sister and I hadn't really thought about it. Except when my mom would scream at me for not eating in front of him or for causing a food-related scene. I would pass on my problems to him, she said. But I knew he was smarter than me. He took in so much and held it there. He was incredible. Nothing in those five months was about my family, it was all about me: my reactions, my food, my wants, my needs, my body. I know now that what was underlying all of these behaviours and insecurities and private rebellions was that basic question of human life: death. Mine, specifically. As well as being a teenager, with all the angst and self-questioning that brings, I also had to contend with an ever-present awareness of my own mortality. And I wanted to do things immediately, I wanted to write and sing and work, there was no time for this childhood lark. I didn't want to waste time, and yet I tied myself in a knot so that I had to stay stuck there.

I think Sylvia Plath, John Lennon, all of those shakers who died young appealed to me because while I was determined to squeeze everything out of life. I felt like 30 was my expiration date – and maybe it is. You can't be dreamy about CF, it is what it is. But for a long time I shrouded it over with hippie skepticism, Wicca, energy vibes and anything else I could bring my mind to. I was brought up a liberal, and I was forever changing. It was my way of dealing with it, by trying to experience as much as possible, and not regretting a second of it. But my life became so increasingly bizarre that I forgot where and why it started. But my real problem wasn't that, it was that I had been trying to escape in the first place. What I had to get to grips with was an understanding that accepting the reality of CF wasn't going to make me weaker. Instead, it was going to give me the power to move forward into whatever I wanted. For a long time, I just didn't want the reality. Now I was ready to ask myself, what did I own? What was mine? What did I want for me?

13.

On my 15th birthday, on 22 March 2001, my Nana, brother, Dad and Mom watched me blow out the candles on my cake. My mom had asked if I wanted to invite any friends over, but I didn't. People hated getting lifts out from the town and apart from that, I didn't know if I had any friends left. I had been back at school for two weeks, but I seemed to have been left behind in every way. Margaret, my best friend, was different when I came back and had made a new friend. I had a strange moment in Music class when two other girls told me all about how Margaret had described her visit to Temple Street to see me. She told them that I had been pale, but in good form and that I said Hi. I think Vivaldi was playing in the background while they told me because I remember it feeling extra-dramatic when I told them it was all lies. She had never been to see me and hadn't even rung me, apart from one phone call, over the five months. Deirdre Coates had come to see me though. 'Who,' they asked?

Deirdre had been my best friend back in primary school. We still saw each other now and then, usually when we were both auditioning for school musicals or any type of singing competition. We didn't hang out anymore though. Except that day, she called my parents and asked could she come to the hospital to see me. She hated car journeys – I knew that – but she made it up to me. We sat in the ward, but I don't remember what we talked about. I felt something familiar, something that made me feel less isolated. She was the only person from school who had made the effort, and that hurt.

Just after my birthday, my mom found herself in the principal's office at my school, asking for help. We needed to find out what could be done to help me with the work I had missed. A conversation had already started before she arrived between the board of education representative and the principal, so when Mom sat down they had a strategy ready. It would be easier for me, for everyone, if I moved from my current class into the remedial class. It would be less taxing for all parties involved. My mother remembers an angry exchange. They had come to this meeting either not understanding what cystic fibrosis was or looking for the easy way out, she accused them. She then informed them in no uncertain terms that there was nothing wrong with my mind, learning ability or adaptability in the classroom. Exasperated, she explained CF to my principal of two years and to the board of education representative. Eventually it was agreed that the board would aid me in grinds and that I might have to take some pass subjects for my Junior and Leaving Cert exams.

Secondary school was a difficult jungle to navigate. I did poorly in subjects like Maths and Science that weren't my natural forté anyway. They were also the ones that had given me nothing throughout my time in hospital. Ironically, although I wasn't one of her pupils, the teacher who taught honors Maths had sent me some work-sheets once. I hadn't a clue what to do with them, but I did try out some of the problems with the teachers in the hospital. The English teacher was the only one who had sent me work regularly and actually helped keep me on track with the class. The problem was that there was no system in place for absent children. If there was a Junior Cert in creative writing and drama, I would have sailed through, but this was not the case.

That September I started in third year, and that's when I started writing again. I hadn't written throughout my whole hospitalisation and for a long while afterwards. It started with English homework and then I just kept going. Every night I wrote poems, three or four a night, and it was better than any psychologist I had seen in the hospital. I was baring my soul onto paper and the more I did it, the better I felt. Constructing with words, feeling the rhythm, writing music to go with it – it all came together. We learned about Sylvia Plath and Emily Dickinson in English class, and both women offered me a kind of camaraderie in my recovering year. Hope was the thing with feathers that perched in the soul. I could drown in those girls. Dissecting poems made me feel warm and happy inside. It was familiar and vital. I loved figuring them out, the endless possibilities.

When it came to literature I received great encouragement from my aunt Breda, my mother's sister. Breda was a book-obsessed banker. She was my godmother too and the copy of *The Bell Jar* she had given me at Christmas was the best present that year. Although she also knew how obsessed I was with Plath and worried about whether I should broaden my reading a tad. I was a fast reader when I was young, but after the long stints in hospital at the beginning of second year, my ability to concentrate had gradually worsened; now it usually took me up to two weeks or more to read a book. It depended on whether it was 'unputdownable' or not.

I didn't always have time to read, particularly novels. I had to sacrifice reading so I had time to write. I felt that in order to do something fully and with proper intensity I needed to have something else raging against it demanding attention too. Now that I think of it, it could be the whole CF raging against life aspect and me in the middle trying to sort them both out. I worked better with self-imposed competition, otherwise I just got bored. Poetry was always my favourite: quick and melodic and sometimes so perfectly formed. It gave me a rush though my body just to read Edna St. Vincent Millay's 'What lips my lips have kissed', or Yeats's 'An Irish Airman Foresees His Death'. I read *Ariel* cover to cover until it was tattered and I had to buy a new edition. *Johnny Panic and The Bible of Dreams* did little for me, but then, I was never enamoured with Plath's short stories. I loved the tragedy, that teetering-on-the-edge-of-reality vibe. Dickinson did it for me, too, and the story of her life was fascinating. English taught me important things. For our English Junior Cert mocks, for example, one of the visuals was of Lego figures standing in lines all along the page. It was a campaign for the UN and the slogan said, 'What's wrong here?' What was wrong was the conformity, the suggestion that these people could be cattled together and that like Lego figures, they were all the same. I was obsessed with the idea of individuality, of what made people independent and how they stayed like that and what beat them down again and how, and if, they fought back.

Over the course of third year I had three infections that required me to do home IVs. Difficult as it was for both of us, Mom had to administer them. I resented her waking me up at 7.00am when I was exhausted, and at the same time I felt guilty for being the reason she had to get up so early. Sometimes it was fine, other times she said I didn't appreciate her; she was right, at times I definitely didn't appreciate her. It was hard to strike a balance and I often wonder if she had been a parent whose profession wasn't in medicine, would it have been easier for both of us? She had medicine at work and at home, and it took me years to even begin to imagine how difficult that must have been for her.

Home IVs were tough in terms of school, too. It meant I didn't get to school until 11.00am, which some teachers found hard to understand, particularly if they'd seen me at choir practice the evening before. A lot of the time, I felt like a big faker. If I could have turned myself inside-out to show them the other side of me – my mucus-filled lungs and my stressed-out teenage brain – I would have. Then I didn't realise the effect of the dusty room and lack of air on me, and I berated myself for my lack of concentration and motivation. But there was more to it than laziness – it was the effect of the environment on my condition.

Then, I unexpectedly found someone who did understand. At our school PE was compulsory, except for me and Delia. I didn't do PE because I felt uncomfortable running around with all those competitive girls – I got breathless quickly and I chickened out a lot. Delia had osteoporosis, so she was free to opt out too. Every PE class we sat together on the sidelines, and gradually we would sneak away from the pitch to the nearby sixth-year social room to chat. Delia was one of the cool girls, so at first I didn't think we had anything in common. But then we started talking and realised we shared some experiences. She told me about her osteoporosis and her anaemia and over time I pieced together what had happened to her. She had had an eating disorder, but was now recovered. We sat and talked, and I told her parts of what had gone on with me. It was an intense friendship, but in the end not a very healthy one for either of us. We bonded over a mutual obsession with English and body image. We consoled each other when doctors or parents told us things we didn't want to hear. We had both experienced people being critical of our bodies and our choices and taking control from us. We couldn't have said all this to our other friends, but we could be honest with each other.

Near the end of third year we had a stand-in English teacher who told me one day that she had been able to recite all of Shakespeare's sililoquys by the time she was eight years old. She didn't take any prisoners in class. She insisted on a full week of *The Merchant of Venice*, and it was exactly what I needed to catch up. It was Easter time and at the end of our last class with her, as we left the classroom she gave us each a Creme egg. Delia looked at me, terrified.

I opened mine and just ate it and then she did the same. We made a pact that that summer we would get healthy properly and exercise properly, together, somewhere where no one could see us sweat, or fall over and break a bone.

The best part of third year was the end of it. We had an end of-year awards ceremony, but even though everyone predicted I would win for English, I knew I wouldn't. I was right. It was embarrassing, but then I heard my name called out. I had shown some of the poetry I was writing to my English teacher and as a result I won the schools junior poetry cup. I felt like I was on the right track. After that I sent letters and poetry to publishing houses with youthful gusto, but only got back one reply. Gallery Press were kind enough to send a rejection slip that said I wasn't ready yet, but to keep up the good work and try again soon. It wasn't too bad to hear at fifteen and it reinforced what I already knew: I had to be a writer.

14.

I planned to do transition, or fourth, year, but I was sick on
the day they took the applications from the third years and
when I returned I was simply told I had missed out. So
instead I would go straight into fifth year. In the summer
before fifth year started, Mom and I went to Lourdes with
the CF association, which brought a group of people with
CF and their carers every year. I wasn't religious and the
word 'shrine' made me purse my lips and squint my eyes;
my mother would say wryly, 'You better hope the wind
doesn't change or you'll be stuck like that.' I didn't want to
go to Lourdes, but I liked the idea that I would get to meet
other people with CF. I started calling it 'France' to my
friends and using phrases like 'our free holiday to France' in
front of my mother. I tried not to be too cruel. I knew it was
important to her. The heavy hand of religion would just
have to be endured for a few days and, besides, it could even
be interesting.

The people with CF on the trip ranged from their late
teens to thirties. It was an interesting experiment on my
mother's part: having just emerged from my battle with
food and vomiting, she felt it would be good for me to find

some positive role models. So that's why we were in Lourdes, hanging out with a group of people who had CF. It was madness, really, when I think about the cross-infection risk. At the time everyone who signed up for the trip had to get their sputum tested up to two weeks before they left to check what type of bug, or Pseudomonas, they had. Only those with no resistant P. aureginosa could go. The risk/choice was your own.

At that time I didn't realise what a big deal this was. I was just so glad to meet older people with CF. I'd been having a type of mid-life crisis, so meeting older people who were living, succeeding and working with CF was fantastic. One guy in particular was memorable. He was going out with a girl who also had CF and on the way back from the Grotto at two o'clock one morning, we started chatting about how he got to the age he was – he was in his late twenties. Exercise was the key, he said. He ran, he swam, he did everything he could. It was visible: he was stockier than the other boys; they looked thinner and smaller next to him. He made it sound like exercise was a secret medicine that was waiting to be tapped into. I told him what I did, swimming and all that, but that I wasn't serious about it. I did it for my parents. I didn't really do it for me. In the cool breeze of the early morning the ease with which he explained how he fit all this into his life and went to college really struck me. It was probably what my mom had wanted me to hear. It was what I needed to hear.

It wasn't all holy water and inspirational chats, though. There was also some debauchery that wouldn't normally be associated with Lourdes – people kissing in corridors, collapsing from hangovers in church and being taken away in ambulances, laughter, love and a great support network. All the extremes of CF were there, including those who were fulltime wheelchair-users and those who could only walk short distances and needed piggy-backs home from Mass. It was the first time I got so lazy that when someone offered me a wheelchair, I took it. It was a free ride and a bit of a laugh to be wheeled. Now, the idea of it horrifies me. Lots of things seemed funny then that I would question now. There was one boy who only ate chips, literally that was his entire diet, and he got away with it. It was strange to hear people claim they understood me more than anyone else ever could because we shared an illness. I remember coughing one night in the pub when one guy was telling a story and he said to me, 'For example, I know when you cough, to stop talking until you finish. Not like ignorant people who just keep getting louder. That's the kinda stuff that happens when people don't have CF.' It was funny because I had never looked at it like that before. I had never considered that we had different behaviour or that there were allowances to be made. I didn't see my life quite like that. I didn't divide the world into 'them' and 'us'.

When I arrived back home, I hooked up with Delia and we embarked on our summer of healthy eating and exercising. We decided to start going to a gym on the opposite side of town. We soon had a routine of sorts worked out: walk on the treadmill for twenty minutes, then the Stairmaster, then sit-ups. We had no idea what we were doing, quite obviously, but we felt good about ourselves. Delia spent longer on the treadmill than I did, so I would go for a swim while she did that. By the time the sit-ups came around, we did them together.

The grey-haired man who guarded the desk in the exercise room would sometimes walk through and we would make funny faces at him. He wasn't the sort of gym instructor you'd expect to find playing 'Macho, Macho man, I want to be a macho man' on continuous loop on the sound system. We sized up his hunched shoulders beneath his grey jumper and the sagging belly that hung over his trousers and ignored him. That is, until the day he decided to come over and tell us we were doing our sit-ups wrong and showed us how to do them properly. While showing us he said to Delia, 'You don't need any work,' and then he turned to me and eyeing my stomach said, 'but you, you need a lot of work'. I went for three more sessions and then left, but what he said to me kept playing on my mind.

Since I had stopped horse-riding I hadn't taken up any sports, much to my parents' dismay. I just wanted to write, go to school, do theatre, read magazines and poetry. I never considered the effects lack of exercise would have on my health. As I exhibited no desire to exercise, my parents let me join a stage school in an effort to get me moving. The classes were on Monday nights, from six to seven pm. After choir, which was from 4.30 to 5.20, we drove the mile-and-a-half home so I could shovel down dinner and be out again in time for class at six. Contemporary Hip Hop was held in the wooden hall of the Patrician School downtown. Our teacher was a small, spry blonde woman with lightly muscular arms and a penchant for bending backwards until her head poked out through her legs. With enough training, she assured us, we too could do this too. After one year of classes we would be allowed to showcase our work to our parents, but not before that.

Dancing made me feel good, but when my friend remarked one day, 'Ew, gross, SWEAT' I was in a puddle of salty misery. Of course I was sweating, the kids from *Fame* sweated all the time. I, however, dripped after three minutes of hardcore warm-up because of my overactive CF salt glands. The other girls didn't. We marched on the spot and teased ourselves into the splits – a kind of gradual thing that we worked on every week and were applauded each time we got down further to the ground. Dance class was exhilarating, but the sweating was not. So one weekend I searched my mother's closet for a long-sleeved, black T-shirt and found a black lycra onesie to match. I wore it under my garish yellow PK T-shirt and after warm-ups the dots of sweat were faint, and sometimes non-existent. It was exhausting having to rush to the toilet just before practice and strip my entire top half to be able to pee, but it was worth it.

Our dance instructor brought agents to come and see us

work and told us that what they were looking for was an entertainer. They wanted dedication, organisation and someone who would always try. 'It doesn't matter if you can't do something, don't ever say that to a casting director. Tell them you can try and then try your hardest.' She said that if we were really serious about dancing, we would have to make sacrifices, prioritise it. I knew I wasn't the best dancer and that, unless there was a dramatic plot line to go with it, my singing was mediocre. Acting and writing were my strengths, so I tried to improve the weaker points.

I started ballet in fifth year, despite my mother insisting I was too old. Nonetheless, she had heard from her friend that when her daughter started ballet it had improved her concentration and discipline in school and other areas, and my mother hoped this would translate for me. The ballet was affiliated with the Stage School and held in the small, carpeted hall in the same building as Hip Hop. After four weeks of attempting to prance across a room horizontally while posing like a peacock, the ballet teacher pulled me aside and said I was wasting my time. I knew this, of course, but I stayed another month just to prove to myself that I could. When I left, much to my mother's dismay, I switched over to drama which was more me anyway.

The drama classes were small and focused, but there was an emptiness about them. Our teacher was a man in his twenties who told us what we should do rather than let us do it. One day he gave us an improvisation to do, where we each had to tell a story and the others had to guess whether or not it was true. I sat on the carpet and told him something like: 'One day I was in hospital with my friend, he had the same thing wrong with him as I did, which is how we knew each other. We were sick of the ward and school was over so we decided to go on an adventure. Underneath my ward was a stairs to the basement, where the ghost of an old matron nun roamed, so naturally we headed for the basement. The stairs creaked at every turn and as we crept deeper down into the abyss, a light breeze stole over me, escaping from an open door near by. *Bam!* A noise, I scream, he jumps and hits his head off the groove under the stairs. We run quickly back to the ward so that no one catches us. True or False?'

The teacher smiles at me. 'False, false, who hangs around hospitals?'

'True,' I said. After class he called me aside and told me about a youth theatre company nearby that I should join. 'You'd do better there,' he said.

For Leaving Cert English I got a new teacher. On her first day she read out our new reading list and my heart sank: *Amongst Women*, *Dancing at Lughnasa*, and our movie was the film adaptation of *The Dead* by James Joyce. Obviously a wave of Irishness was going to wash over our final two years of secondary school. I didn't have anything against Ireland, I just preferred American – anything that wasn't based here and wasn't filled with drudge and resentment. I asked if we'd be doing *The Bell Jar*? Definitely not, was the curt reply. I didn't want to be a typical teenager, but I was chin-deep in Plath and St Vincent Millay.

In early February I started dating a boy. He was the first boy I went out with in secondary school. It wasn't that I didn't like boys, but I just didn't rate a lot of them. Most were content with making eejits of themselves, joking around and obsessed with alcohol and sports. I wanted the perfect guy, but didn't think I'd have any luck finding him. I wanted the boy who wanted to stay in and read poetry rather than go out and get lashed, the one who thought nature was more beautiful than *Playboy* magazine and that words were more important than cars. In fact, I was a hopeless romantic, but I liked to think my head was firmly out of the clouds. I wanted to date someone perfect, who probably didn't exist. And then I found Vince.

When I met him, I was engrossed in writing and analysing poetry. He felt the same passion for literature as I did. He wanted to be a poet, a writer and an actor. He also wanted to be a vampire. On our first date we went to see

Sylvia, the much-maligned movie of Plath's life starring Daniel Craig and Gwyneth Paltrow. We kissed behind the cinema after the movie. It felt so dangerous and bad – in a good way. For the next few months we wallowed in our own perception of aesthetic beauty and the boy was so hungry for words and prose and the damn hard slog of sweating them all out. We had similar attitudes and, it turned out, similar tempers, but we had different ideas about the world. After two months – which at sixteen seemed like a lifetime – we broke up. I was pretty devastated at the time because I didn't realise that he was breaking up with me. He just stopped replying to my texts and I had to figure it out for myself. It was the stuff of great romances.

15.

After parading around in Penney's finest Japanese-style pajamas with at least one hundred other girls in the school musical, *The King and I*, I joined Kildare Youth Theatre, a group of about fifteen players that had set up in the town's arts centre, the Riverbank Theatre. It was a life-changing decision. I felt safe prancing around on stage, illuminated by the electricity of the audience. I got to escape and yet I had to think on my toes; hyper-awareness was the key. Being part of a collaborative attempt at make-believe made me happy, the sheer strength and serenity of it made me feel alive again. The first part I got was in the showcase of new talent in the inaugural year of what is now called the Wyeth Festival of Youth Drama, sponsored by Wyeth, the medical pharmaceutical company that has a factory in Newbridge. The scene I was acting in was an extract from *Antigone*, by Sophocles. I played Antigone, in conversation with Persephone, my sister. We've just killed our father, Creon, which I found funny because Creon is the brand name of my daily pancreatic enzymes.

It was my first real test as an actor for the theatre group. Our scene opened the festival and I was the very first person on stage. The direction was to walk on, pondering the death of my father while waiting for my sister. The director of our piece was a renowned actor but had never directed before. We were nervous, and so was she. As we stood in the wings and the hum of the audience faded, she quickly ushered me on stage. I began walking and pondering, and then the intercom bellowed, 'Welcome to the Riverbank Arts Centre', before an arm shot out from the wings to pull me backstage again. I wanted to sink into the ground and never return. I wanted to kill her. Five minutes later, after the announcements about the fire escape and mobile phones were finished, I walked back on stage again, a little sweatier, and a lot more nervous. I felt much more confident after it, though.

In a theatrical atmosphere there is an extraordinary amount of energy exchange, openness and a sense of liberation. There were some nights when, exhausted from rehearsal, many of us would have gladly slept on the Riverbank's hard floor. On those exquisite nights when I told the overall theatre director I didn't ever want to leave he cried, 'Stay! Stay in the theatre, forget about school – you can learn that all here anyway.' And I knew life was too short and I electrified myself with that thought any time I felt I was slacking, but I couldn't really give up school for theatre and writing. I knew that, somewhere beneath all my melodramatic teenage layers, there was a good writer waiting to be released. Writing was tough, though, a succession of stops and starts as I struggled to get it 'perfect'. But theatre was in the moment. Our director constantly told us, 'Be present. Be present. Always be in the moment' and I could do it on stage and I was working on it in life.

When you can create that sort of energy between people and expose yourself freely, to get the essence of you out and into the character, boundaries shift and there is this sort of free-flowing energy and incredible camaraderie. One girl in the troupe was different from the rest, though, she was angry, abrasive and gutsy. But she also had an astounding amount of knowledge and that allowed her to get away with it. It was the way that she could recite quotes from any play, expand her imagination in a flash and paint you a story so that you could smell it. She also talked about lesbianism constantly, and made jokes about it. My natural instinct was to hate her for her exhibitionism, but there was something so charming about it. When I was sixteen, I loved it, and then I thought that maybe I loved her. She did everything I didn't, like smoke cigarettes, sleep with boys, kiss girls and talk back to teachers. She slouched when she walked, and she just didn't care. It was intoxicating.

That year we put together an adaptation of *Totally Over You* by Mark Ravenhill for Shell Connections, The National Theatre project. This was a drama competition in which youth groups took on plays specially commissioned for young people from famous playwrights and competed to be declared the best and win a slot to perform at The National Theatre in London. We rehearsed three times a week and did our first public performance in our own theatre, The Riverbank in Newbridge. After that we rehearsed for our competition performance in Belfast. The girl and I, I'll call her Anneka, started having serious chats about how girls understand girls more; she was angry at her boyfriend. One day I just told her out straight that I was attracted to her. By this stage I was lovesick and didn't know any other way to resolve it. And I knew that I was attracted to girls as well as boys – and didn't think much of it. My dad had always explained that sexuality was fluid, and shifting between one attraction and another so this seemed natural to me. She told me she liked me too and that she wanted to kiss me, but it would have to be in Belfast, and we would have to be drunk. We had watched too many *Friends* episodes: another country doesn't count and if we were drunk, she wouldn't be cheating on her boyfriend.

The problem with this plan was that I didn't drink. I hated alcohol and the stupid way people behaved when they had too much of it. I had enough problems with my body; I didn't want to add alcohol consumption to the mix. And yet everyone my age did it and they were intelligent people. They got drunk, they smoked, sometimes hash, and I couldn't understand it. Most of them – especially her – would apologise to me after they smoked, or if they were going to smoke, or they'd spray themselves with deodorant, which only made it more obvious. I had at some stage explained to them about CF and why I didn't smoke and how I thought people who did were wasting perfectly good lungs and that it pissed me off. I had a lot of anger about it.

The other way I vented about this was with my parents. This was a tough time for us. But I felt that my parents couldn't understand the ways I was changing and, in my self-focused way, I hated them for not understanding. My dad could talk openly enough about things, but when I tried to talk about some things with my mom, often her reaction was to take things personally. Sometimes we argued so fiercely I wouldn't speak to her for days afterwards. She would argue with me when I didn't do my medication, but sometimes I was just too tired, although other times I just couldn't be bothered. When I felt really well and there was no sputum in my chest, I didn't see the point in doing it. But the biggest cause or our arguments was when I needed lifts in and out of rehearsals because times could change with very little notice and sometimes there was the pub afterwards. She said I could throw it all away if I wanted, she didn't care if I ended up working in a dead-end job all my life; she knew that idea made me want to jump off a cliff. I wanted to be a writer, that was all. Why couldn't she just let me do that? She replied that she would happy if I got an actual job out of it in the end and all the sheets I'd ruined from falling asleep writing in bed would then be worth it. I told her nighttime was the best time for writing – I loved the feeling of being awake, creating when everyone else was asleep, like Jo in *Little Women*.

'Except it's not for the people sleeping in the room beneath you while you snore and your hardback copies fall out of your bed onto the wooden floor. And my sheets, Orla! You're only getting the ink-stained ones from now on.'

'Fine! I do not snore!'

At this time I had started to take care over my appearance, wanting to blend in with the other girls and look the part. She would tell me that the fake tan I had taken to wearing made me look like a hooker; I would tell her what she thought of me didn't matter to me at all. She would tell me I should care what people thought of me. I did. Somewhere inside I cared way too much, but I still thought I did what I wanted. If I was going to get the most out of life, setting my own rules was the only way. We'd stand in our kitchen after school and I just didn't want to talk to her about how the day was. I wanted to go to my room and write, or phone my friend and talk. It might be classic mother–teenage daughter dialogue, but it feels like an abyss when you're in it.

I had an older friend who taught me how to put on fake tan, straighten my hair and apply make-up. My mother didn't approve of her. What she didn't understand was that covering up my body made it easier to live in. But even that wasn't straightforward because at the same time I hated conformity, hated people who followed convention, but I was trapped in this habit of 'fitting in' physically and I couldn't break it. If I took out the blonde hair dye, I would look the way I looked when I was cut open and threw up every time I ate. I did not want to be that girl again. The truth was that I wasn't really rebelling against my parents at all; I was just rebelling against myself.

My mother rarely wore make-up and my dad did not like too much make-up on women either. One morning Dad was driving me to school and it was the day after I had applied progressive fake tan. I was now the deep orange of an Oompa Loompa. Dad told me that I looked ridiculous, that people would laugh at me and that he was only saying it out of love. He said I had to ask him permission the next time I did that to myself. So I kept doing it – without his permission.

Fake tan was the least of my troubles, though. Somehow the whole story about my wanting to kiss Anneka had gotten through the school grapevine and some girls in the class would hiss 'lessssbian' whenever I walked by. I had always hated labels – stupid, man-made traps to make everyone feel safe about being able to put people in a box. So in my head, kissing girls was completely fine. But on a deeper level, I felt a sense of shame. I didn't want to be different. I wanted to be unique, and individual, yes, just not different. Those words had various meanings. My dad was always encouraging me to be myself, but there was only so much of myself I felt I could be within the confines of a small town secondary school. I wanted to fit in and stand out at the same time, but not for the wrong reasons. So I kind of swung like a pendulum between being what I felt and what I felt others wanted me to be and every time I thought I found a happy medium, something would happen to throw it off-balance again. I thought I understood the 'just be yourself' line, but I was far from living it.

The departure day for the Belfast trip arrived and I remember the whole thing now as a haze of hormones. We stayed in Queen's University Halls and I gave Anneka all my sterling to buy alcohol. I was so nervous about the whole thing I ended up in someone else's dorm, being handed shots of something blue and something a murky brown. I happily downed them. I wanted to forget I was there, forget about the desperate desire for kissing, forget about the feelings. I just remember being handed shots and taking them, and after four someone saying, 'that's enough for now', so I headed to another room.

The next flash of memory is of standing over a toilet bowl, with Anneka holding back my hair and telling me to stick my fingers down my throat. 'Come on, you've done it before. If you don't, I will.' The thing is, I hadn't done it before. I had never been bulimic. But she always reminded me of this, always felt like she had to look after me. I wanted to prove that I was stronger than that, I didn't need to be minded. I could be kissed and I could be independent and I wasn't fragile. But no matter how hard I tried I was still someone to 'watch', to 'keep an eye on'. The director said I was like some Marilyn Monroe fairy. I did try to explain that episode after the surgeries to her one time, but it came out sounding like bulimia. It was so unreal it was almost funny. I had been a pioneer since the age of ten, now here I was, throwing my alcohol-sodden guts up in a student dorm. It was against what I believed in, but I was changing to try and get what I wanted.

The next memory is of someone making tea for me and telling me to Drink! Drink! Drink! 'I hate tea,' I told her. 'Can't I have something else? I never drink tea. Tea reminds me of my Nana's. It's all my Nana had.' I drank three cups of tea that night and felt sick. I woke up in another dorm, in one of the boy's beds, alone and fully clothed; my own key had gotten lost somewhere. That morning another girl in the group pulled me aside and told me she would love to kiss me, if I wanted to try it out. She'd done it before. The thought was mortifying. I felt like I was rolling around at the bottom of a barrel waiting for a signal of what to do next. Anneka had yelled at me that night and the next morning she said sorry but we couldn't look at each other. My girl feelings were just wrapped up in fantasy, they obviously were meant to stay there. And it hurt.

On the way home on the bus we found out that we had in fact won the drama competition and we would be going to England for the international finals. Later, back in Kildare, she roared at me in rehearsals one day about how they had all thought I was going to die that night, they all thought I was going to die. And there it was – they saw me as this little creature who needed to be minded, and it drove me crazy. I was not a victim. I was not some poor sick girl who needed sympathy. It was the same old picture and I was sick of looking at it.

16.

After Belfast, a friend invited me to take a role in a play she was in, *Many Young Men of Twenty* by John B. Keane. I knew I didn't really have time to fit it in, but I was doing mostly home IVs at the time, so in the end I decided I would be able to work it all out and I agreed to it. In rehearsals we all stood around, shooting the breeze, going out for drinks or food and I fit in well, even though I was the youngest. It was easy to be myself with them. In school, things were totally different. The truth was I was barely connecting with my classmates at this stage. I didn't get them and they didn't get me. It was easier to focus on plays and choir and older people who understood my ridiculous need to talk about how much I loved the word *supercilious* and why, rather than someone who laughed at me.

Around the end of May, near exam time, I dyed my hair jet black, much to my parents' dismay. Our school tour that summer was to Italy and none of the girls wanted to share a room with me. I didn't feel the need to tell them I was not, in fact, gay, so I found the only room that had a spare bed and ended up staying with girls I barely knew. This all went well until I forgot that there was no lock on the bathroom door. I yanked it open, only to reveal a screaming room mate who scrambled frantically to cover her naked body with a towel. I left, apologising over and over as she screamed the room down.

When I got downstairs I bumped into two of the girls who were in the same stage school as me. They did ballet, though, which definitely wasn't for me. They were shooting the breeze with an Italian man who worked there. Everything was fine for a few minutes until he said, 'Wait, *you* are Irish, too?' He looked theatrically shocked and said he thought all Irishwomen were small. 'But you, you're ...' and he made a gesture with his arms that looked like he was holding a massive Swiss ball. I was standing beside the two ballerinas, who were both ballerina thin, of course. And I wasn't. Here I was in Rome, and I was fat. Of course I didn't know then that a lot of Roman women were praised for their curves, right then I was just plain too big.

I remembered that comment when I came home, couldn't scrub it out of my memory, and I played it over and over in my mind like a broken record. It was one of those things that reminded me that my body wasn't good enough, that I wasn't good enough. It made me angry and I lashed out a lot as a result. My poor mother tried to help by asking what was wrong, but that just made me worse. I felt suffocated in school and at home. The only things I really enjoyed were writing and theatre. I wanted life to start now. I think, subconsciously, I was walking around filled with fear, but I called it ambition. I convinced myself I was better than my own environment because I still struggled with the idea that this was it. This was me, in total: I was seventeen, had a Leaving Cert to do, had a family I fought with a lot and I had CF. I would probably die before my classmates. Was that it?

I wouldn't have said then that I was someone who went around thinking about death. I wouldn't have said that chronic depression was a big factor in many patients with CF. I wouldn't have said that I was out of control – after all,

I was a teenager and I had a positive mental attitude. I was praised for how much I smiled, and sometimes I was laughed at too. But I was, in fact, all of those things. I was driven by fear and not by love, and that's why I never really got anywhere. In school I was afraid of failing, so I didn't work as hard as I should and I beat myself up about it. Theatre offered an escape because I couldn't really fail there. My family was more about creativity than academia and so I felt it was inbuilt in me to do drama. I was naturally good at it.

I still found school a bit of a trial. I was just very competitive continuously. I worked hard at extra-curricular things like choir and theatre, but not so much when it came to the subjects I was meant to be studying. I didn't know how to focus and then there'd be these moments in religion class where we'd watch a programme about a child being fed with an NG tube or the Karen Carpenter Story was rolled out again (about three times in total throughout school) and I just disconnected. If I didn't I would suffocate. I found friendships difficult, although I managed to maintain some. By now, my friends were dispersed between different years, so I didn't necessarily have them in most of my classes. I had two main friends at the time, Jenn and Anna, and they stuck by me through most things, even though I wasn't always the easiest to get along with. I'm sure I must have bored them silly with my incessant talk of plays and writers. Even though I was sixteen, I still didn't care about going out or boys and I had zero interest in getting drunk.

Mine was a nice class to be in, but we had our scrapes. So much of it is funny to me now, but at the time it all seemed deadly serious, like what my peers thought of me was the most important thing in the world. The problem was that even though I craved to be part of everything, the things that were important to them weren't at all important to me. I think if I had thrown myself into some team sport and just tried harder overall, I would have had a happier time of it, but my priorities and their priorities felt infinitely at odds. I wanted to succeed as an actor and a writer. I also wanted to have the perfect body. I knew I shouldn't obsess about hair and make-up and fashion over other things, like furthering my writing, but I couldn't snap out of it. I felt like time spent partying or drinking or just 'hanging out' was a waste of precious time when I could be improving myself, so I just stayed away from all that.

We reprised *Many Young Men of Twenty* for a run of a few nights at the Moat Theatre in Naas. My part as an Irish emigrant was very small, but it was important enough that I needed to be at rehearsals. After our first-night performance in Naas, we all headed to the pub to toast our success. One of the older men announced that he had compiled a backstage view of rehearsals, and he showed his 'mockumentary' on a screen to entertain us. It was the local downtown pub, and there were about eighty people in the room, mostly us but also some regular punters who had nothing to do with the show.

When the tape rolled it was relatively inoffensive, but even so when my image flashed up on the screen, I cringed a little inside. I looked okay though – until the tape rolled further. That night at the Moat I had gone straight from study to choir rehearsals to the theatre. I had only had a Diet Coke and fizzy jellies for fuel, so when I hit the theatre I went looking for food. The screen showed my search for food: picking up sandwiches and putting them into my mouth, chewing them, eating a cake, catching crumbs with a tissue, drinking diet coke, examining the cheese platter – all shown in slow motion and magnified to make me look like a food monster. The camera zoomed in on the food in my hand and the food in my mouth. I actually hadn't had that much, but the way it was edited made it seem so much more. Everyone laughed and someone elbowed me as I smiled and turned my head from side to side in some attempt at laughter. I don't know how I was still sitting in the chair. My insides quivered. This is a joke, obviously this is a joke, this is not important. This is just a stupid tape. I smiled through it. I did say, at one point, how embarrassed I was, but I don't think anyone knew just how much it affected me. This would be what my mother called 'my true self' that was affected: on the outside I was happy and bubbly; on the inside I was serious and took things to heart. I hadn't found a way to get the two sides of me to meet yet. And so no one really knew how upset I was to see that image of myself projected for everyone to laugh at. It wasn't intentionally cruel, I knew that, but it also wasn't an image any teenage girl wants to see of herself.

Of course, I was doing other things at this time rather than just hanging around and hating myself. I presented a talent competition in the youth theatre one night and got to flex my MC skills. I also took part in a fashion show fundraiser for the theatre group, although that did lead to more awkward body examination. First, the electric pink dress that was assigned to me was too tight, as in it wouldn't zip up. When they eventually got me a new one – black, sheer and strappy – my portacath was on show. This, to me, was the most embarrassing prospect, worse than busting a zip. In the dressing rooms when the girls all stripped off and got dressed, elbows and boobs were everywhere, and everyone looked better than me. But they all told me I looked beautiful. They were all so supportive, but I just couldn't accept the idea that I was perfectly lovely as I was – port, scars and all. One girl suggested I leave my hair down to cover the portacath, but not being a mermaid, my hair wasn't long enough. Another suggested a shawl, which the fashion director vetoed while we were lined up back stage, waiting to go on. My friend quickly explained to the director why it was important to me and she was so kind, she paused everything and pinned on a shawl around my shoulders, partially covering my chest. I felt so embarrassed to inconvenience everyone, but I just couldn't handle that exposure. Now, I think nothing of parading around in my bikini on a beach or wearing a low-cut dress at a party, or being naked in the gym changing room. But back then it was the worst fate imaginable.

Shawl in place, I resumed my position in the line-up and waited nervously with the rest of the 'models. The PA system boomed out the song 'Roxanne' from *Moulin Rouge*, a tango-style beat infused with passion and drama. I pushed up my chin, threw back my shoulders, tried to think confident thoughts and stepped out onto the catwalk, ready to strut my stuff. Just as I started sashaying down the ramp ... the music stopped. Silence. The tango beat was suddenly replaced by the *click-clack* of the too-high heels I could barely walk in. I could hear my own heart beating. I managed to get to the end of the catwalk without falling down, laughing or crying – how, I don't know. As soon as I hit the wings, the song picked up again and the other girls got to walk in time to the rhythm.

17.

When my aunt Breda was diagnosed with cancer when I was
in sixth year, the walls around our house started to crumble.
Mom was a nurse, so she took charge. She was the efficient
one, the one who could instantly smooth things over and
make everyone feel like things were under control. But
cancer was different. It hung over our house like a shadow,
threatening to engulf us all. I loved Breda and I was shaken
to the core to see her diminished and scared.

One morning I stood at the window of the sitting room
in Nana's house, waving at Breda through the glass. She was
wearing her bandana and glasses and I wasn't allowed to
pass the protective barrier of the window. I wasn't allowed
in because the pseudomonas in my chest could hop into hers
and kill her. Standing there, feeling like an invading army
that could destroy my unsuspecting aunt, a new feeling
started to well up inside me. I began to feel sick at the
realisation that for the past few years I had been so
consumed with my body and appearance. I had been
trapped in a cage of my own making, always focused
inwards, self-absorbed and now it was like someone had
rattled the bars and shown me what a selfish fool I'd been.

It ate away at me when I saw the fake tan in the bathroom, or when our hip-hop dance instructor told us to keep smiling, keep waving and put the fat girls in the back line. How had we all been taken in by this silly way of thinking?

In early 2003 the youth theatre director offered me my own one-woman play. He thought it would be easier for me both in terms of managing my health and study for the looming Leaving Cert. I could rehearse on my own terms and take breaks when I needed to. It was the ultimate opportunity – not only could I show what I could really do but he wanted to tour it around Ireland and the UK, so I would be connecting with a wide audience. It would be taking part in the same competition that our group had won the previous year, but that meant the regional heats would take place just before the exams. He secured an understudy for me to make it work, but I knew I couldn't do the one-woman play, hip hop dancing (which I was still doing once a week), study, drama workshops and stay well. I was also – unknown to me – experiencing glucose intolerance for the first time, which meant I was randomly exhausted but didn't know why.

I didn't fully understand what was happening to my body at this time. Most nights I couldn't sleep and during the day my moods swung in tandem with my blood sugars: I was cranky and irritable, subdued and numb. I wasn't hungry all day, but I'd wake up thirsty and starving in the middle of the night. Plus, as everyone in my family seemed to notice, I was losing weight. No one thought to put this all down to glucose intolerance; the general consensus was that I was majorly stressed about the Leaving Cert. and about my aunt Breda. In class I sometimes found myself with a heavy head, wanting to nod off; at other times so jittery and irritable, I didn't want to sit down. Now I know that this is what happens if I don't take my insulin, but I hadn't been diagnosed with diabetes yet and I didn't know it was a complication in CF. I had started drinking Diet Coke like my dietician suggested in order to avoid it, but I still ate ridiculous amounts of fizzy jellies from the shop beside the school. I was all over the place and felt completely stressed and crazy. So I gave up my incredible one-woman play opportunity to the understudy and when I saw her perform it at the first festival in Newbridge, I was so jealous.

One Monday evening Jenn and I sat on the wooden floor in recovery position at the end of Hip Hop, listening as our instructor called out who was ready to move up to the next level and the Tuesday night class. I smiled quietly when she called out my name. A Tuesday night class would be easier to manage, there would be more time for choir and study and theatre group. Our instructor got down on the floor and did ten push-ups, then flipped over and started doing sit-ups. If we were serious about this, if we were moving to the next class, we had to be body aware. There was no room for things jiggling or hanging out. 'You're selling a product, you have to be your best. Cut down on sweets and practice for half an hour every night. Professional dancers work out every day.'

Something inside me started to tug. This was bullshit, this was enslavement. If I started thinking like that, like she wanted me to, I wasn't sure what it would do to me. It might be okay, but it might not. The smell of fake tan from my own body suddenly suffocated me. I got up and walked out. For good.

I think this was the start of me becoming me. I was standing up for what I believed, I was refusing to accept other people's ways of thinking or doing things. I had found a new maturity that demanded I live for me alone, not taking on other's standards or principles. I was learning that being true to oneself is the best way to live, that honesty is a life-saver and that I had a brain that was as good as anyone else's and I could trust it to make my own decisions for me.

The plan to kiss a girl in Belfast hadn't worked out at all, but I still wanted to do it. Maybe it was that competitive girl thing again, that I wanted to show I was over the Belfast incident, whatever it was, I was open to the idea of seeing what kissing a girl felt like. The opportunity came about after I walked in on the younger girls of the theatre group playing spin the bottle and daring each other to snog other girls. I was laughing with a fellow actor, Amber, about it on the way to the Arts Center, and she said she'd like to try it. 'Me too.' 'Have you kissed a girl before?' 'Oh yeah,' I lied, 'it's no big deal.' The lie popped out before I thought about it. It was a stab at cool nonchalance: if you want to kiss me, go ahead because I'm a consummate expert. As it happened, she did want to, but not in the street, obviously.

I think it was the play that tipped us over. Backstage during the interval she drank wine and we skipped outside and started kissing. I stopped and asked her if she was sure, was it just the wine? She grabbed me again and it felt like the most normal thing in the world.

The second half of the play went well and after the curtain came down, I didn't look for her because I don't want to appear uncool. My dad rang to say he was waiting for me in the car park, so I headed outside. There she was, up against the bonnet of a car, kissing one of the guys. I wasn't angry, but I was confused and hurt. Was I that bad at kissing? I threw myself into the car and didn't say a word all the way home, just stared into the night like it was a comforting thing.

The next morning there was an apologetic text. She wanted to be with me. Be with me? That was a little dramatic. I didn't like that sort of thing. I hated people my age using the word 'love', for example. My dad said no one knew what love was at 17 and I thought he was right. I was all for lust and longing and obsessive over-analysing, but not 'love', not anything that suggested I didn't know exactly what was going on. Love was beyond me, I knew that. I always tried to take the approach my dad advised and be calm, cool, collected and in total control. With her, though, it was different.

Over the next few weeks we saw each other a lot. We told no one. She would come over to my house and we would stay just long enough to make a picnic to take down the bog with us. We sat on the high bog, with damp grass and bugs beneath us, and kissed and fumbled and kissed some more. Then we ate the ham and cheese sandwiches my mother had made. The days meshed together: we picnicked, we went to the movies and at some stage, she told me she loved me. This was too much for me. It signalled something else and I wasn't ready for it. When we broke up it was easy to just go back to the way things were. It wasn't as challenging as the whole 'love' idea. Love was too complicated.

One night not long after this, Mom and I were on the way home from a visit to Temple Street and we detoured to Loughlinstown Hospital to visit aunt Breda. I was allowed in for a few minutes. She lay in the bed, pale and weak, but still laughing her squeaky through-the-nose laugh at my story about leaving Hip Hop.

In May, when Breda was dying, we were taken in twos to say goodbye to her, but because Mom was going in again, I got to go in twice. I robed up in plastic apron for the ICU ward, but Mom said it didn't really matter anymore. It was too late now. When I kissed Breda on the forehead she gazed at me and said to my mom, 'She's beautiful, isn't she? So beautiful' and the words pulled at some string deep inside. The string that was holding the 'strong' me together. I sat on a bench in a corridor in St James's with my mom, uncles and cousins scattered around, talking in low tones. 'Eternal Flame' by The Bangles played on a radio behind the counter. I knew I would never feel the same way about that song again.

After Breda died she was laid out in my Nana's house for the wake. I walked around talking to the younger kids, making sure they were okay, so I didn't have to think about how I felt. I had never seen a dead body up close before. When I touched her brow she was cold, but she was still so beautiful. She looked just like herself, but empty. While we sat around her saying the rosary over and over, the string inside me unravelled and I started crying and crying and crying. Like a line of dominoes, the younger girls followed suit and eventually I had to leave the room.

On the morning of the funeral my other aunt pulled me aside and said, 'Now, none of that like last night. You need to be strong for your mother.' I got through the ceremony until the walk-out. I was strong. I could withstand any thing. At the back of the church I saw my two best friends from school standing in solidarity. The tears came again and I couldn't help it. I hadn't cried in so long. Crying was for sissies. I had rarely cried as a child, because it made more sense to be diplomatic and solve the problem rather than to waste time crying over it. My inability to cry meant I didn't do very well when other people cried. But it was just that crying seemed such a redundant thing to me, plus it made people treat you even more like a child. Now here I was, seventeen, and I couldn't stop myself. It was like two plates had collided inside me and this volcano of tears just erupted from the very bottom of my insides. They were grief-stricken tears belonging to so many different moments I had held inside me. I let it all out.

18.

When I was seventeen I had sex for the first time. I wasn't particularly excited about the idea, but I was curious. Movies and TV programmes made it look so saucy and explosive. The kids on *Dawson's Creek* and *The O.C.* were doing it. I wasn't naïve enough to do it just because someone else was, but I did find myself caught up with the idea of it. My curiosity wasn't helped by a close friend's questionable encouragement: 'Just get it over with, and then you'll be flying. So you do it once, it hurts, you'll probably bleed and then you're sorted.' Sex is kind of presented like that on TV: it's virginal, then it's a bargaining tool, then it's a power play, then it's a selling point, and somewhere in between it all it's also used for creating other human beings. I was at once unamused by it and totally enthralled, so I set about trying to make it happen with my boyfriend of six months, a boy I'd met in the theatre. In the beginning, he wasn't quite as enthusiastic as me. We planned it, but it didn't happen because of location issues. This is one of the biggest problems as a teenager: the where. Obviously it had to be a bed. There was not going to be any of this back seat/dark alleyway/roll-in-hay situation. When we could find ourselves in possession of a bed minus our parents was the real issue.

The time finally came on an unexpected occasion. His Grandfather had just died. We had lunch in the local coffee shop before going back to his house to see if we could help his mom sort things out. I wasn't exactly fazed by the death of older people, so it didn't affect me so badly. I just felt sad for him. We were sitting in the computer room, addressing mass cards to the numerous people who had sent cards of condolence, when his mom popped in to say she was going out for a spot of shopping, would we continue to do the cards for her? We agreed, and saw our chance.

He said we couldn't use his room. One look in the door at the strewn clothes and unmade bed showed why. So we chose another room, down the hall. It was all very deep and serious, which kind of made me want to laugh. But I was also slightly petrified. In retrospect, if you're too afraid to be taking off your clothes in front of your chosen partner, you probably shouldn't be getting naked in the first place. But there I was, taking off my clothes under the covers, like an expert. There was fumbling, some oohing and ahhing. I was uncomfortable. It was sore. We did our best. Afterwards, alone in the bathroom, I looked in the mirror and contemplated the fact that I was 'a woman' now. It didn't feel like any great shakes – in fact, no shakes at all.

When my Leaving Cert results came out a few weeks later, in August 2004, I sat looking at the yellow slip of paper. I shouldn't really have been surprised, but seeing my future surmised on that piece of recycled tree made me slump in fear. The Leaving Cert was ridiculous anyway, but I had wanted to do better than this. I hadn't gotten enough points for English in Trinity. It wasn't enough points for any of my top three choices. I just wanted to write and stupidly I had let that take over the 'most important year of my life'. I moped around the house, barely speaking to anyone.

My parents wanted me to go to NUI Maynooth because it was close to home. They weren't keen on my plans to

move to Dublin, or anywhere else for that matter. But I
wanted to start again. I wanted a new town, new faces, new
buildings and sights. The monthly call to the same chemist,
the tired streets and the way the post office hung in the
middle of the town weighed in on me. To the left was the
area where we used to live, where the Liffey was and the
Arts Centre. To the right were the shopping centres and the
McDonalds that had been so fiercely opposed by residents
some years before. I couldn't be a writer here. I needed
independence. I needed to be on my own.

I was offered a place on the Journalism course at Griffith
College in Dublin, but my parents had already explored the
idea of me going back to repeat the Leaving Cert. I quite
liked the idea of repeating at Leinster Senior College, the
new grind school in the courtyard in town. You could wear
whatever you wanted and only people actually committed
to school and passing the exams went there. But Journalism
made sense too, it made an awful lot of sense. My parents
figured the best thing was to get a good degree first, maybe
do a H. Dip. so I could teach if the whole writing thing
didn't work out.

I couldn't see myself teaching and I couldn't see writing
not working out, but at the same time I was terrified. I
wanted to take control of the situation, but I also didn't
want fear to guide me. In the end, I forfeited journalism and
went to the grind school. The lecturers talked fast, expected
the best and I took on Classics and Economics to jazz up my
schedule.

After one month of 8am to 8pm days I landed back in
Temple Street with another bowel blockage and a chest
infection. I was in for two weeks and each day I spent in the
four-bed room, the idea of studying would present itself, but
then fade before I could muster the energy to reach for a
book. The IVs misted my brain and made it impossible to
concentrate. If I really cared, I'd do this. But I do care, don't
I? Isn't this what I want?

Hospital was tough at that time. I had lost weight and

changed my diet. I was trying to eat healthier to fit into my Debs dress, but unfortunately this was perceived as a relapse into disordered eating. This perception wasn't helped by the fact that I was having mood swings and bouts of exhaustion and that my new consultant knew my history and didn't trust me. There was a doctor who was running a study on glucose intolerance and diabetes in CF, and he asserted that that was my problem and that insulin would solve it – take care of the mood swings and the exhaustion and make me put on weight. For anyone to take this diagnosis seriously, it would have been helpful if I hadn't been a wannabe actress, stressed out, with less-than-stellar exam results and a preoccupation with fashion and appearance. It looked too much like a classic eating disorder for his hunch to win over the doubters.

Nonetheless, the consultant eventually agreed to a glucose test. When the results came back, it revealed that my HbA1c was sky high. I felt so much better – I had proof that I wasn't crazy, that I wasn't killing myself. I was just trying to eat less junk and more healthy food. I was worried about putting on too much weight because I didn't want to balloon out, not because I wanted to be a size zero. I knew that with CF I needed to maintain a healthy weight, but I was also a seventeen-year-old girl with normal preoccupations about myself. Problem solved, I thought to myself. Phew!

It wasn't that simple, however. They retested and the consultant came back and asked me if I had peed out Lucozade. Pardon? Had I gone to the toilet between drinking the Lucozade and getting my bloods done because if I had, the test wouldn't work because I had cheated.

Cheated. Now there was a word I hated. My new consultant had informed my father that I had a problem and recommended psychiatric assessment to prove there was nothing wrong with me. I agreed and went along and the psychiatrist told me I was fine and that if I had any type of eating problem, it was an atypical one, but that because of having CF losing too much weight was a big deal because it could irreversibly damage my health. She didn't know much about CF, but she had devised a plan with my consultant. She asked me to sign a contract agreeing to be admitted to St Patrick's Insititution if I deteriorated suddenly. We probably wouldn't need it, but it would be a 'safety net'. Deterioration could happen with CF, she understood, and it was only provisional. It's just that the waiting lists were so long and, besides, I could always refuse when the time came. I trusted her, but I didn't trust my new consultant. I refused to sign it.

As a result, every Wednesday I had to go back and get weighed. I felt like a criminal. Weight, weight, weight, all over again. The threat of a psychiatric hospital, all over again. The dietician said, off the record, that she didn't think I had an eating disorder, that it was ridiculous and that I should probably just sign the form to get them off my back. It's just late teens stuff, she tells me, and it only happens to extremely intelligent people and when you are in your twenties, you stop caring about body image and it gets so much easier. I clung to that advice and started eating what they wanted me to – over 4,000 calories a day. My weight was not down by that much in reality, but in CF world, 2 kilograms is an awful lot.

My bowels started acting up for the first time in years, too. I was getting daily cramps and my regular laxatives weren't solving it. Sometimes I strained so badly on the toilet the water was stained with blood afterwards. It was the random mucus thickening and causing blockage, but it made the current situation so much worse. They increased my laxatives, but when I was home I had to be 'watched' to make sure I was taking them properly. That was the problem: I was constantly being treated like a bold child. My mother would say, 'We'll stop treating you like one when you stop acting like one', and sometimes I wondered if it was easier for everyone to focus on me being the problem so they didn't have to look at themselves.

When I left hospital I went back to the grind school and couldn't sleep properly at night. I had so much energy and I couldn't regulate back into normal sleeping time. A doctor put me on Zimovane to help me sleep and each morning I woke up with a headache. The unnatural sleep was the only way to have enough energy to get up every morning for the course. One evening, after Saturday morning study, I met one of the girls from the youth theatre group and we walked to the Arts Centre to watch rehearsals. It turned out to be an open call for *The Importance of Being Earnest* and I watched people prance around the space auditioning, wishing I was up there with them. The next night the director texted me and offered me the part of Gwendolyn Fairfax: 'You *are* her, darling.' I told him I couldn't do it, not with school taking up all my energy. That night I hid under my covers, trying not to feel the itch. The next morning my phone displayed a message – we could rehearse on Sundays so that it would fit in with school, although nearer showtime we might need an hour or two during the week. I knew it was wrong, but I said yes anyway.

Each moment I spent on the black floor of the auditorium was like an injection of adrenalin. Nothing was more important than developing character and letting the words consume me. Gwendolyn was a myriad of ideas. Her rigid beliefs weren't her own, they were her mother's, and out of fear she repeated and repeated them. She cared so much what other people thought that she aimed to follow the straight and narrow, but there was this undeniably rebellious nature about her, this desire for mischief that ultimately led her in ruthless pursuit of the perfect husband.

Our costumes were made by a woman called Wilma, who made dramatic skeletons of the undergarments of Wilde's ladies' dresses. My costume consisted of two hulahoops, one at my feet and the other hanging at my thighs, tied from the waist. Over that a handkerchief-shaped, velvet red bib enclosed my body tightly on the sides, but the dress was loose on the chest and back. I wore white gloves and a dainty red hat also. A week before the show my friend Rachel and I were getting ready in the dressing room when Wilma marched in, clearly frustrated. 'You keep shrinking,' she said to me. 'Every time I check your costume, the line gets tighter and tighter. You have a problem.' I was shrinking and I was under too much pressure, but I couldn't pull out now. After rehearsals Wilma came up to me, 'I'm so sorry, I didn't realise you had Cystic Fibrosis'. Thanks, I told her. I just wanted to finish. Finish the week, and then get IVs. School would have to wait – again.

Mom was gearing up for a well-earned holiday with my aunt Eilis and my Nana, the first since Breda had died, but I didn't want to know about that. I cared only about the performance, where it was going and where it would end. As performance week moved on, my cough got worse and between scenes I ran backstage for someone to adjust my bustier. The hoops hung like rocks from my waist. Gwendolyn stood like a lady, at all times perfectly poised. There was no room for slouching, except for a nice release in the proposal scene and again in Act three, where she sits for long periods of time. I made a conscious decision to leave school after classes at five and then eat, sleep and do my Ventolin and physio, which gave half an hour until show time to get in and warm up. Cecily, Prism and I would then start warming up our vocals with a little singing, vowel stretching and some jumping up and down.

I was managing okay, but usually started coughing when I hit side-stage and needed those few minutes to clear sputum. If Gwendolyn coughed on stage it was a ladylike 'ahem', with a cupped hand and a flutter of her eyelashes. Gwendolyn had never seen sticky green sputum. After the third night the director said in our cast meeting that we had to do something about the coughing. 'It's not her fault, Peter!' Lady Bracknell yelled. But he was right. It was ridiculous. We devised a plan to combat it.

Between each scene break I ran out the soundproofed backstage door and coughed my guts up, leaving a puddle of sputum on the ground. Smokers who didn't know me looked alarmed, but one of the stagehands would stand behind me, signalling them to sod off, while the other waited side-stage until my cue was near and came to get me a few seconds beforehand. Sometimes my transition from breathless coughing to poised Gwendolyn made the guys convulse with laughter side-stage. On stage, I saw nothing except the scene, everything else was a haze of space.

I had to keep going. I just had to keep going until I finished. On the final night I lay in the dressing room before the performance with Rachel. 'Baby, this is nuts,' she said gently. 'I'm fine, I'm just resting!' I wasn't fine, but as long as I kept saying I was, I would get through the next two hours and could cart myself off to hospital in the morning. Gwendolyn was like a release, she was so calculating and shrewd but vulnerable and precocious at the same time. After the final performance an examiner from London appeared and we spent an hour closeted in a room, explaining where the heightened sexuality and innuendo of the performance came from. I drank two bottles of water, sipping slowly, trying to feel better, but I didn't. All the while my cough was quiet, easier to manage. This was either good territory or bad territory, only sleep would tell.

The next morning I woke when Mom was leaving to go to the airport. I wasn't feeling well. I heard the front door slam and rolled over, back to sleep. When I awoke later in the day, my lungs were filled with what felt like cobwebs. They were filled to the brim and all I could do was throw up into the toilet. This was my own fault, of course. I called Dad and then the CF nurse, who told me to go to A&E.

When we arrived at Temple Street I was feeling a bit stupid and a bit embarrassed. My body felt light and exhausted. I should have just slept all day, stayed hydrated and taken some laxatives for my bowel. It was probably all okay and I was just over-reacting. They brought me straight into A&E and four nurses appeared around me. My oxygen saturations were 80. Seriously? The nurses spoke in soft rushed tones. 'Okay, we're just going to put some O_2 on.' My head couldn't get past those sats of 80. How had it gotten so bad? 'I don't need O_2,' I protested weakly.

My dad went to get some liquids for me and the CF nurse arrived. 'Orla Tinsley, you Drama Queen, sure you're fine. You don't need O_2, sats are 97, take them off there.' After a minute the monitor alarmed and she put the prongs back on my nose. The doctor arrived, listened to my chest and sent me for a chest x-ray. 'You have to go in a wheelchair.'

'I can walk.'

'You really can't.'

I got in the wheelchair and my dad pushed me the five-minute walk to the X-ray room, with the oxygen cylinder on the back of the chair. I sat waiting and for the first time I was scared. What the hell had I been doing?

19.

I was in Temple Street for a number of weeks on that visit and when I got home, I faced into a difficult three months, from December 2004 to February 2005. I had left the grind school in the midst of all the craziness with the play and my health, and now I began to feel directionless and raw emotionally. This dark period was like a winter hibernation – I curled up tight inside myself, waiting for the spring to arrive so I could breathe again and feel sun on my skin.

I slowly began to emerge and feel hopeful, but then in March my chest got bad again and I went into hospital for a week to pre-empt it and make sure it didn't get as bad as last time. It felt like a knock-back, but then it turned out to be a blessing in disguise. While I was there, World Book Day was celebrated, on 3 March. That morning, Ciara from the schoolroom came down to tell me that the authors Marita Conlon-McKenna, Sarah Webb and Marissa Mackle would be coming in to talk to us about books. The schoolroom teachers smiled at me and said I should bring my poetry to show to the writers. I don't know Marissa and Sarah, but I sure as hell know *Under the Hawthorn Tree* by Marita Conlon-McKenna. I couldn't show a brilliant writer like her my poetry. Ciara, assuming this was modesty and not sheer terror, whipped out my poem 'What I Want To Be When I Grow up' and dangled the white sheet in her hand. 'Will I? Won't I? I will, right?' Fiiiiine. Of course I want to know what they think, but still.

Marita read it and smiled at me. 'You want to be a writer?'

'Yes. I want to be a poet and maybe a novelist later.'

'Well, it's a very good poem. But there's not much money in poetry.'

I tell her I don't care about money. I just want to write.

'Well you'll care about it when you get older, most writers have two jobs,' she said. Her presence shone from where she was sitting. 'You know, you could write children's books, if you developed this more.' She told me I should send the poem into a children's magazine and placed it back down on the counter so that it hovered a little before finally coming to rest. 'It has a good grasp of rhythm, children would love it.' Her validation made me run downstairs to my bed to get the rest of my poems.

The nurse caught me. 'IV time!'

'It's not, just two seconds!'

'It is! Look, I have them ready.' I sat on the bed while she pushed the IVs in through my port and I re-read my poems. There was no paper on the ward so I had used a flip-up Crayola book in which each page was a different colour. The blue pen on the dark blue sheet is hard to make out, but the blue on yellow and maroon is okay. After fifteen minutes of IVs I ran back upstairs. Phew. They were still there.

The Crayola book was passed around the circle. Real, published, female authors were reading my words. Marissa told me that it was only much later in her life that she realised she wanted to be a writer. She wished she'd known when she was younger. Sarah loved them, too: 'I can see the real emotions in them, the feelings of being trapped by your illness.' Was I trapped by my illness? Is that what I was saying? In one poem I use the phrase 'barricaded lioness'.

She loved that. I liked it too, but I had never considered that I was writing about CF. My writing was compulsive and blind; learning to structure or anticipating a theme before I started annoyed me. Sarah gave me her address and told me to send her more work when I did it and she could help me out. I walked back to the ward on a cloud. I would write my book of poetry, I would write my novel and then I would go to college.

A few days later I was feeling better and my consultant decided to do a bronchoscopy. This involved putting a camera down into my lungs and taking samples of the bacteria. While I was under the anaesthetic, they decided to clean out my lungs too. When I was lying on the operating table I could see the consultant hold her hand to a tube that looked like it was going into my lungs. She asked someone to check the suction. I was scared but she said it would be okay, they would just take a quick look and then I would wake up and be back to the ward.

When I woke up in recovery I was groggy and the taste of gas mask anaesthetic made me want to throw up, which I eventually did, into one of the fabulous blue bowls. An hour or two later the consultant came around and said it was no wonder I had been so breathless, there was so much stuff down there. But they got a lot of it. I realised that the minute they 'got it' and sucked it out, it had just started multiplying again. Which I always knew, but it was strange to think of.

On 22 March 2005 I would turn eighteen and become an adult. I told my parents I wanted a big party. I wanted a caterer and hot food and when Mom suggested a marquee, the dream was sealed. My soul was minimalist and rooted in lying in the grass and tasting the dew, but my teenage brain was hungry for a bit of indulgence. I was leaving childhood and I wanted to enter adulthood in style. I thought of what the boy with CF in Lourdes had said, 'Eighteen is our thirty', and I didn't believe it, but I was still afraid, which I didn't say.

On the night of my birthday, I sat in my bedroom with my cousin Elaine and friend Sophie, and put on my new, silver, mermaid-style shoes from Office. The heels were skinny and the material bunched at the toe like perfectly shaped sea-shells.

'Just try and walk in them, Tinsley.'

'I'm not actually going to wear them down the stairs. I'll just walk around the house in them.'

'But you have to wear them dancing, Orls! I can't believe you still can't walk in heels.'

I felt awkward and stupid. Heels weren't me, but I was trying so hard to be a 'girl'! Besides, the dress was too good not to have the shoes to set it off. I buckled the final buckle and threw a hook eye at her. 'I can if I want to, watch this!' Jumping up, I did my best saunter. Right, left, right, left … jam! The heel lodged in a crevice in the wooden floor and I fell forward, crashing into the shower frame. The roars of laughter were worth it and I decided to hold firmly to the banisters, unashamedly, and make my way down to greet my guests. A friend had brought a mix CD of George Harrison, Destiny's Child, The Beatles and Cyndi Lauper and my mother suggested we put it on the sound system upstairs to get maximum affect. The music filtered into the hall, lingered on top of the booze counter, but failed to turn right into the sitting room and into the Marquee.

Band On An Island, a group that played songs about Taking you to The Master Bedroom, were sitting under the blue and white canopy of the marquee, preparing to perform. The lead singer called me over and gave me a signed CD as a present. An hour later three friends arrived from town – they couldn't find their way to our little lane and were bearing a giant Toblerone as an apology and peace offering. But at least they're there. The actors huddled together and the musicians smoked outside. There was a mix of people from school, not sure where they fit, and an older friend or two keeping watch over the soiree. My parents and relatives stayed out of the way. I threw Dad looks when he sauntered into the room, trying to make conversation.

At around 11pm, it was time for the second part of the night – the foray out to the nightclub for all those under the age of twenty. I hated nightclubs. I hated loud music, well *bad* loud music, the music that seemed to follow me around in my nightclub experience – the type that bangs and thuds and has no words or melody. But there was nothing else to do in Newbridge and Sundays were 1980s nights and I was eighteen, so it was part of the rite of passage. I knew I'd smell like cigarettes and sweaty fake tan in the morning, but I accepted it in honour of my eighteenth year. It was so good to see how much better this landmark birthday was and how much happier I was compared to four years ago. I was really looking forward to getting out of Newbridge and starting my new life, whatever that was going to be.

Back then, I believed anything was possible and had notions of going to LA and pursuing an acting/dancing/ singing career, even though my voice wasn't that good. I wanted to do something great. Something that was worthy so that when it did all stop, I would have something to show for it. My main mission was to be free of my past and the labels that people had put on me. I hated the idea of spending my life being 'an inspiration'. I didn't want to spend my life serving others. I wanted to be free to let my life happen the way it was meant to, without the responsibility of propping up other people or feeling like my failures reflected on them, too. My parents had so much love and admiration for me, but with all of that – the idea that I was so great and that I could do anything – came the self-induced pressure that I was responsible for so much. I had CF forever, I hated when people lauded me for it. At that time my CF wasn't that bad, so it made even less sense to be praised for it. It was kind of like a shadow that flashed over me at times. It was creeping up on me and although I always managed to seem positive and to urge people on when they felt like they couldn't do something, it was burning me out. I wanted a life where I could start from scratch and be considered 'good' because of genuine steps I made in whatever community I was in – a community that had nothing to do with my past failures, or with CF.

Perhaps CF gave me a sense of urgency that my friends and peers didn't have. My parents always told me to just do my best and that was all they wanted of me, but at the same time I felt a pressure from them, like they were pushing me constantly to achieve. Now, I wonder if CF gave them a sense of urgency, too. They understood things about CF that maybe I didn't know yet; I found out years later that my mother had a penpal, a young woman with CF, and they corresponded until she died. It was a double-edged sword: my parents said I could only do my best, but they also said I was very special and could be anything I wanted to be. This made me confident and ambitious, but it also made me fearful and burdened – saddled with the idea of being 'special' and fearing that I would never fulfil that expectation.

As I left my childhood, I was very aware of how much I hated being lauded just for having an illness, which had been a hallmark of my life to that point. According to most people I was great and inspirational for just getting on with life – something I obviously had no control over or choice in. That in itself made me angry and determined to prove I was more than just this inspirational person with an illness. I don't think people realised how ridiculous that amount of adoration was, but at the same time, I don't know how I would have coped as a child without it. After all, there is no perfect way to raise a child.

Now, for better or worse, I was setting my face to the world as an adult. I was going to have to take responsibility for my own feelings, my own actions and my own thoughts. It was daunting, but it was also intoxicating and I was anxious to get going and find my way beyond CF, to my real self.

PART 3

'In the sky, there is no distinction of east and west; people create distinctions out of their own minds and then believe them to be true.'
Hindu Prince Gautama Siddharta, the founder of Buddhism, 563-483 B.C.

20.

A month after my eighteenth birthday party I was sitting in our little sitting room at home, sucking a lozenge. My throat felt like someone had ripped a razor along it. When my mom returned from doing her regular stint with Meals on Wheels, she found me plonked in front of the TV watching *Dynasty*. She pointed out angrily that when she was there, I was in my room, writing, day-dreaming or listening to music; when she wasn't there, I emerged and watched television. I didn't have the energy for an argument.

'My throat is extremely sore.'

She looked at it with her nurse's pen-light and said my tonsils were up, big time. We tried to soothe them with her Bach flower remedy, but by the next morning sputum was dripping down the back of my throat, it was hard to breathe and coughing was dry and raw. We got into the car and made the journey to Temple Street, for what would be my last visit to the hospital I'd known since birth.

When we got there, tonsillitis was confirmed and I was admitted immediately. Technically, I'd changed over to St Vincent's, but we decided to go back to Temple Street this one last time. We knew them, they knew me and the world of adult health services was too uncertain. I also knew there was ice cream after the tonsillectomy in Temple Street. I still felt a bit foolish, though: I had said my farewells to Temple Street and now I was back, at the grand old age of eighteen, with the most childlike of illnesses.

The frustrating thing was that the following day was my first cross-over appointment in St Vincent's. For the cross-over, the Temple Street consultant had sent a letter outlining my case to the St Vincent's consultant, after which I was to go in to meet my new CF team. Instead of my parents bringing me, I was accompanied by one of the ward attendants. One of the nurses said it was better that way: 'sure, shouldn't you be doing these things on your own now?' That was my parents' greatest fear, I think: me in charge and cutting them out of the loop, then abusing that responsibility by not being compliant. Truthfully, the idea of being completely in control of my own medications and life both excited and terrified me. Sometimes I wished I could live far away from them and from everyone. But I couldn't, of course, and now, as an adult, the illness was mine and I could take it or leave it.

We arrived at St Vincent's by taxi and sat in the outpatients area, waiting to see the CF team. I noticed a boy talking loudly; he looked like someone I had met before. 'I called the fella from the Star about it, it's fucking ridiculous. He was screaming all night,' he was saying and I felt my insides knot. I prayed to the Universe or whoever was listening that this place wasn't as bad as I'd heard. I felt like the room was rotating around me. Would I really be coming here forever? My old team had warned me about responsibility: 'People put in their own cytocans, people draw up and give their own IVs, unless they're very, very sick.' It terrified me. It sounded so isolated. I would be the youngest, the newbie, and I would have to share with older people.

Finally, we were called into the meeting and it went well. Afterwards, there was another wait to see the consultant.

The nurse apologised for the delay, but said he liked to see new people individually. The consultant arrived and he was taller than me, with grey hair, and when he shook my hand he indicated that he had used hand-sanitiser. He talked to me about my CF and asked what I was doing at the moment and what my goals were. I told him I wanted to go to college, that it was my ultimate goal. He looked me in the eye and smiled, 'We will help you reach your goal.' In that instant, I felt good about it. We were team players, on equal footing.

Before I left Temple Street on that admission, the consultant told me they had found a rare bug, with a name that sounds like Xylophone, in my system along with the Pseudomonas I already had. I had had Pseudomonas bacteria since I was about five years old. My mother was convinced she could remember when I contracted it and who gave it to me. She found me playing with him while the nurses were not watching one day and everyone was angry. But when you're so young, it's so hard to understand that stuff. The consultant told me they didn't know much about the Xylophone stuff: it might do nothing, but it might do something, but probably not. It was a relatively new fungus. I thought of it right down at the bottom of my alveoli when I was doing my physio that night, and focused on blitzing it.

That cross-over trip was my second visit to St Vincent's. I had gone once before with my mother, on a kind of reconnaissance mission. I was nervous, wondering, would they like me? Would I like them? Mom and I walked along the corridor and towards the chapel, which seemed to intone the older hospital's purpose: 'We will pray for your life here until you die', it seemed to say. I shuddered, then banged straight into a colossal figure of Jesus on the cross that was mounted on the wall. We both giggled nervously. That was the thing about 'crossing over' – this would technically be the last hospital I attended. It was a conscious leap to that 'other', adult chapter of my life, which is why I had put it off as long as possible. At the age of eighteen, there was no longer any way to avoid it. I had heard horror stories about the place from other health workers and older CF patients, but I tried to remain logical and unemotional. If change would happen, it would happen here first. It took me a long time to see I got this ability to emotionally detach from my mom, this soldier-like mentality. It was how she had to be, dealing in health crises all the time. Strong.

We met a nurse who talked to us about CF care and showed us the wards. Our walk-through visit was quick, to avoid cross-infection. Then we quizzed her: did everyone get their own single room? *No*. Would I be separated from other CF patients? *As much as possible*. How often is it not possible? *It depends who's in at the same time as you*. We have private health insurance, can we use that to get a private room? *The consultant's policy is to keep as many patients on the same ward as possible so that the team can reach them quickly. The nurses on St Paul's ward are specially trained in* CF. Okay. *There's no mixing with other CF patients, but if there are no other options we'll put two patients with the same bugs in the same room, and you can mix with them and no one else*. Some weeks later, when I had my first inpatient admission to St Vincent's Hospital, I would see exactly how these policies worked in practice.

At the end of our visit that day, the nurse showed us the CF sitting room. It was a small room with two couches and a bookcase donated by someone who had since died and whose name and lifespan was recounted on the glass in gold lettering. Depressing. On the wall was a picture of an airplane on a runway with cat's-eye lights lit on either side of it. It had been donated by Dublin Airport. Above the fridge was a newspaper article from the *Irish Independent* entitled, 'Learning that death must never stand in the way of life'.

'It's a quiet place to go, for a break from the ward,' the nurse piped up.

I was listening, but I was also staring at the picture of the mother who wrote the article and the picture of her dead daughter under it. When I read it I realised that one of her daughters who had passed away was called Colette. I wondered if it was the same Colette whom I had met when I was very young, who had died in Children's Hospital. The timeline was the same. Maybe this, among so many other things, was a sign that I should choose here.

At the back of the room, an ironing board was folded away between the bookcase and one of the couches. There were two fridges, a freezer and numerous games consoles. There was also an exercise bike facing the only window. You could live here comfortably for a week or two, I remember thinking. My head started to make stupid metaphors out of the situation: this room was adulthood and I was stepping into it. This was growing up. This was real. There was nothing but this, no other option. It was a bridge I had to cross. Coping mechanisms!

Then I saw the curtains, colourful and bright. For some reason, that alone gave me a small sense of relief. I grabbed at this little shot of optimism. This was the national referral centre for adults, I reminded myself as I watched the sun seep through the window and illuminate the curtains. Mom called me and I stepped out onto the ward again, then into the narrow corridor. It was to be the hottest summer on record, but if I had to spend any of it in hospital, this place looked easiest. A few helium-filled balloons and some flowers would work wonders with my bed space and it wouldn't be so bad. I had made my decision, and it would be okay.

21.

The first time I was admitted to St Vincent's Hospital as an inpatient was in May 2005 after waiting at home for a bed for three days. On my last night there I hung out in my friend Anna's house with our friend Jenn. They listened to me talk of my fears about the place and we watched *Sex and The City*. I couldn't really eat the Chinese we ordered so ended up drinking ridiculous amounts of diluted lemon juice Anna's mother had. We were always eating her out of house and home. They were such great friends and stood by me, even when I was being a Diva. That night we said our goodbye's, they said they'd visit and I prepared myself for a bed the next day. This is what the nurse had said when I called – there will probably be on tomorrow. Hopefully. The next day I was in Clontarf with my dad. I was helping out on the *Spokeout* magazine, his company's publication for people with physical disabilities, writing articles on the challenges facing young wheelchair users. I sat in the office, feeling like my lungs were hanging out of my chest, but energetically anxious at the same time. It was the funny, irritated mood I got when I was unwell, and I knew I had a chest infection and needed IVs. I called the hospital for the third time on the third day and asked if there was a bed available. No. The options were to wait at home until they called me, or to go in through A&E and hope I was given a bed relatively quickly.

The nurse at the end of the line said, 'You didn't hear it from me, but your best bet is to go to A&E. There won't be a bed.'

'Why didn't I hear it from you?'

'Well, it's just that bed management don't like people with CF going in through A&E.'

'But where else would we go if there's no bed and we need IVs?'

'Yeah, I know. Look, we'll see if a bed pops up, but sure, make your way in anyway and bleep us when you get to A&E.'

I put down the phone and told the two women in the office what was happening. The editor erupted. 'This is *insane*! No one with CF should go to an A&E department, they're so dangerous.' I called my dad, told him what the nurse had said and he drove me over an hour later amidst angry mutterings.

I remember sitting on a trolley opposite the swinging doors that led to the ambulance area. The breeze whooshed my face every time someone walked in or an emergency got whizzed through, which was pretty frequently. After a while Dad had to go back to work and I convinced him I'd be okay. I was there on my own for an hour before the CF nurse was able to come down to put in my IV access. I was used to the emela cream being applied first, which anaesthetises the skin in about twenty minutes, and when I asked about it the nurse said: 'Oh, you use that? Most people don't.' I felt so embarrassed that I didn't protest. I followed her to what I presumed was a room with a door that shut; I would have to partially expose myself. It turned out to be only a curtained area.

'Can I stay here now?'

'No, sorry, we'll try and get you a curtained area, but this is just so I can put in the needle.' I could hear a man shouting at medical workers as I unbuttoned my top.

'I've had five port operations, my port is very precious,' I told her while sitting in the curtained area on an equally narrow trolley. I didn't want to insult her, but I was on new ground here. And I was pretty worked up. Some people were excellent at inserting cytocans; others should never be allowed near a needle. She looked like she knew what she was doing, but she didn't take out a cytocan. Instead she whipped out a 'gripper', which is a different brand of needle, a cheaper one than the cytocan brand, as it happens. I was a cytocan girl, though, used to that clear circle pushing up on my skin as the needle sailed into my chest. I had gotten used to its bizarre bulge underneath my tops over the years. Gripper. It was green and flimsy looking, like a butterfly needle. Actually, it looked pretty smooth under my top, I realised afterwards. It was an interesting change, but it had still taken me ten minutes of interrogation to allow her to insert it. Was she absolutely, 100 per cent sure it was the same? It was definitely compatible?

'Yes, of course. Sure we wouldn't put it in if it wasn't!' she said, playfully frustrated. I smiled. I needed to relax, but it was hard in the constantly rowdy atmosphere. After the needle went in smoothly I got an ABG (arterial blood gas), which is routine for all A&E patients. You know that lovely, tender, soft spot of skin on the palm side of your wrist? The place where a vampire, if he couldn't get at your neck, would probably drink from? That's where they stick the needle for your ABG. It's like someone punching you deep in the gut. It's so internal that it forces you to be completely still, or else you might vomit all over the offending doctor. I found out that it stings for a few days afterwards, too.

I sat on my trolley, minus pillow, for an hour or so after that, digesting the silly nauseous feeling of my first ABG. Things were different here. I never felt this stuff, needles never bothered me, but I was being super-sensitive in my new environment. No nurse came near me as people elbowed past each other and relatives huddled around beds. Some held up newspapers and stared at their loved ones from behind them, and with a flick of a corner occasionally peered over to ogle other patients on trolleys, and sometimes me. There were so many slow-limbed, grey-haired people lying around. The room rumbled with bodies, but was zapped of colour. My mind kept saying, 'This is like a war zone, like some sort of field camp hospital.' It is also said, 'How unoriginal, Orla.' But it was true. The smells of body, sweat and excrement hung in the air and there was no real oxygen to breathe in. It was a heavy sort of dankness that enveloped the place. I got up and walked to the shop to buy some trashy magazines. When I returned, no one had been looking for me. Moments later my father arrived and we began our negotiations.

Some patients were lying in curtained areas, while others lay exposed on trolleys, like me. What I would have given for a curtain, a tiny way to hide myself from the infections and the gazes. Some people were topless, some were sitting up fully dressed and there was a mixture of shouting and rattling from some place nearby. My father called the nurse, as I had done some minutes earlier. It was 7.00pm and when she arrived he said something along the lines of, 'You have to understand, she's eighteen. She's a young girl. I can't just leave her on this trolley tonight.'

Her face was deadpan. 'I understand, but . . .'

'She has cystic fibrosis and we heard someone over there has MRSA,' he said, more forcibly.

Her guard shot up. 'Well we certainly can't confirm that . . .' she said. We weren't trying to attack her; we did appreciate her position. It wasn't easy for anyone. But if there was no bed, could she please try and get me a curtained area for sleeping that night? An hour later, as my father was getting ready to leave, she arrived back. There was a bed available; the staff would call me when it was ready. It was on a ward that had nothing to do with CF, but it would be okay. My father left and I felt more relaxed. At

9.30pm a night nurse who had just come on duty told me the bed was gone. *Gone?* This 'your bed is gone' business was a new phenomenon to me back then. Could a bed sprout legs and walk? Hardly. How could it be *gone?* She didn't know; it was bed management's decision; she was very busy.

'Can you please try and get me a curtained bed to sleep in?' I asked.

'We'll see what we can do,' she replied.

'Look, it's my first time here. Please, some sleep would be great.'

The next two-and-a-half hours passed like an eternity as I read about Katie Holmes and Tom Cruise in *Heat* magazine. There was a picture of him jumping on Oprah Winfrey's couch. I fried my brain trying to block out the reality. At 11.00pm, finally, they moved me to a curtained area. I had now been at the hospital seven hours and I still hadn't been given my first dose of IVs. Two hours would have been my maximum waiting time in Temple Street. They sure did things differently around here and I knew I was destined to compare and contrast. I knew it would be my pitfall too, unless I kept reminding myself to step back and think 'outside the box', as Dad always said. I had been treated like a princess in Temple Street, and I always felt safe there. I needed to figure this place out and start with a clean slate. This was just one bad experience.

Around midnight, I was moved again. My bed on St Lawrence's ward was deep and warm compared to the blanketless trolley. I was tucked between two others, near another door. The draft trickled in softly from the corridor. The woman beside me turned in her bed on average every three minutes and every time she moved, she called out a gabble of meaningless sounds. I made some notes on the yellow paper my friend Anna had given me. I liked it because it looked journalistic and American, and I was a stationery fiend. When a male nurse came to give me my IVs at 2am, I was exhausted. It was my first night in A&E and

I hadn't closed my eyes once. I watched him prepare the tray on the wooden desk at the foot of my bed. The light was dim and the guttural moaning that ebbed from behind the curtain that surrounded me made me feel like I was in a horror movie.

This feeling was magnified as the nurse sat on the end of the bed, as he cleaned the bung on my portacath. Something glistened on the silver tray as he held my bung in one hand and fished in his pocket with the other. He extracted a piece of paper and handed it to me, saying it was from a boy. I had seen this boy earlier, also on a trolley, and he had looked about my age, so I said Hi. I'd talk to anyone. It turned out he had CF, too. 'I think he likes you,' the nurse said, an excited smile on his face. 'He is nice boy.' I stared at the phone number scribbled on the piece of paper. I felt angry and vulnerable and not at all flattered, and then I saw it. The silver tray my IV antibiotics were on was glistening in the faded light. The area around it had a dark red stain. Old, congealed blood – and it wasn't mine. I was in a twilight zone.

In Temple Street, that tray would have been white, plastic and sterile. In Temple Street, he would have been wearing sterile gloves. He would have worn sterile gloves to draw up the meds and then changed them again before he gave them to me. I told him to go and draw it up again, that I wouldn't accept it with that blood. I shook as I said it to him. He sat for a moment and stared at me.

'Whose is that anyway? That's disgusting,' I plucked up the courage to say, unsure of my territory.

He sighed and looked agitated, and then he left to draw it up again. Two hours later the nurse came back and apologised for the delay. My eyes rolled back in my head from tiredness, but I was a manic kind of awake. If I reached out, I could touch the elderly lady sleeping restlessly in the bed parallel to mine. On my right I could reach out and touch the toes of a man in his late fifties. Across from him was another elderly woman. We were strewn here, like half-people. The dim light had a curious heaviness; with my curtains fully closed, it was almost completely dark. The elderly woman's intermittent cries kept a type of beat throughout the night – just as I would start to feel that warm glow of relaxation in my chest, she would start again.

By the early grey hours before dawn, I felt helpless. This was insane. Who could I talk to about this? Surely they knew I had CF? The boy who had couriered his number via the A&E nurse had come in after me, but he had got a bed before me. It made me angry. Why did he get a bed first? Well, he was a man and there was a male bed available, I was told. I didn't even know the basics of how it worked back then. All I knew was that it didn't really work at all. All through that long night I wrote notes, meaningless words, little poems. It distracted from the smell that crept to my nose, the noise in my ears and my own desire to vomit from coughing so much. *I would get a bed on the ward, the CF doctor would see me, everything would be okay* was my mantra. *This is just one night, and I'll say it to someone in the morning or I'll write a letter to a newspaper, like Dad's friend suggested. This couldn't be the norm.*

When I opened my eyes was 6.30am. The last time I had checked my watch it was 5.00am. A person-shaped dent in my curtain appeared and a whispering voice grew increasingly louder. Then the smell hit me. The woman beside me had soiled her bed and was being cleaned. The next few hours were like watching paint dry on a drab-coloured canvas. The lights made me blink, resisting the 7am reality. A version of breakfast was offered to me by a woman who looked like she wanted someone to shoot her. The department clanked and rumbled into life and by 8.30 doctors had started to appear. My mom arrived at 10.00, with my Nana. My incredible, 80-year-old Nana who sat on a small, uncomfortable stool beside my bed, ready to cheer me up, amongst women her own age who were incontinent and senile and alone. My mom asked had the doctors been down yet? Nope. Had I had my morning meds yet? Nope.

But they weren't due until ten. They finally came at 12.30, after the CF nurse had visited and reminded the staff to give them to me.

My mother brought me a pair of pyjamas. She hates shopping, but wanted to cheer me up. The trousers were mid-calf-length with green, red and white stripes and yellow laces at the end to pull them up, like three-quarter lengths, and there was a lime green camisole top with chiffon around the top. In short, the colours were hideous, but the kind thought and the fact that smelled and felt new really brightened me up. Seeing Nana helped, too. She sat there asking how I was, what she could do – a question she would repeat again and again over the next few months. Was it a matter of money? My eighty-year-old Nana wanted to give her own money to get me a bed. She would pay anything. It made me feel physically sick inside. It wasn't about money. It was something more convoluted than that. It was May 2005, the Celtic Tiger was roaring and there the sick were being treated like this – what was going on?

At 5.00pm, hours after they forgot to give me lunch and I had walked to the shop and bought my own, a nurse came and told me there was a bed for me in another ward. 'I'll be back to check your property list.' My what . . .? She arrived back at around 6.00 or 7.00 and I had to list my property for her so she had a record of what I owned. Apparently this was meant to have happened when I first arrived in the department. iRiver. Phone. Charger. Bag. Pjs. Sometime later a group of three nurses arrived at my bedside. None of them was Irish. One, who was holding a chart, started talking to me and I couldn't quite make out what she was saying. The other pushed a wheelchair right up to my bed. 'We had to wait for portable oxygen,' was all I could make out as she reached to put the prongs around my nose. Whoa! I bucked back.

'I don't need oxygen, thanks! My sats are fine.' They were having none of it.

'Please sit in the chair.'

'Really, I can walk'.

It went on for ten minutes until I climbed in, prongs up my nose and the end of them attached to the portable oxygen tank. I remember sitting in the lift with the three around me as they spoke Filipino over the wheelchair. I had been attending hospital since I was born, literally, and I had never felt so alienated. In that lift I felt like I had never been in a hospital before. I didn't understand the environment, the oxygen, the wheelchair or the rapid nuances of the language. In Temple Street I had been an old pro, able to understand every little thing; here, I was cast back into maddeningly unknown territory, feeling completely overwhelmed, like facing a deadly adversary who had weapons I'd never even heard of.

When the three nurses wheeled me into the orthopaedic ward and to my middle bed in a room of six beds, I felt I was running up against a brick wall. By now it was late and I still hadn't gotten hep. sailine to flush my portacath, which needed to happen straight after my IV dose hours earlier.. The nurse checked my blood pressure and sats. She decided to keep me on the O_2, 'in case'. I knew I didn't need it. 'It has been charted,' she said. I told her if the admitting doctor, or any doctor for that matter, just saw me, they would know I didn't need it. She didn't listen and she wouldn't give me hep. sailine.

'I've had big hassle with my port before, I really don't want it to block,' I told her honestly. If it had been Temple Street, someone would have just given it to me, even if it wasn't charted. There, they knew what a port was, what it needed and why it needed it. Okay, she was following the rules, but she didn't know my history and in this instance it was at the patient's expense. At 9.00pm I was still arguing with her and as she peeled back my top to stare at my chest, I started to feel she didn't really know what was going on at all. I curled into bed that night and closed my eyes tightly, though not really sleeping because the two ladies across from me started a sort of sympathetic wailing to one another. My insides jumped each time I heard it. It was like the noise a whale makes, or an animal in pain. I felt so sad for her, and I closed up inside, steely and cold.

The next morning my mother and my aunt Eilis came to see me. They brought what I wanted – raw carrot batons and lemon ribena to mix with water. I had been drinking it in my friend Anna's house the night before I came in. It made me feel comforted, like I didn't want to throw up. The night before I came into Vincent's, three of us had sat in Anna's kitchen. Jenn was preparing for her college exams and Anna for her repeat Leaving Cert – the one we were meant to be repeating together. They were going to college and I was coming here, to hospital. I felt like my soul was dying, like the childlike, happy part of me was being smothered out of existence. My mother watched me, concern all over her face. I didn't want to eat. I wanted to sleep, but I had to stay hyper alert. I still hadn't seen the CF team. I was in some sort of culture-shock bubble that rendered me paralyzed. The crackling wheeze of the woman beside me was alarming. What did these people have? What sort of respiratory infection was in this room? And at 11.00am, after over 24 hours without it, I was still no closer to getting hep. sailine.

My mother asked the nurse to bleep my doctor and point us to the nearest shower room. There was no shower on the ward, she was told, but there was a washroom. The washroom was a row of three sinks with a pulley shower curtain between them. I took a look and then went back to get my mom so she could stand guard. We stared at the faded salmon curtain and the foul-smelling brown stains on it. The small black hairs smudged on curtain number three were pretty disgusting, too, and more was gathered at the plughole. I slowly peeled off my top at sink number two and ran the tap. My mother pushed in front of me and started to scrub the sink clean with tissues. 'I'll bring disinfectant tomorrow,' she said. I cleaned my top half and bottom half while she stood guarding the door. Did three people really get naked in here together? With merely a flimsy curtain between them? I dried quickly, brushed my teeth, dressed and we left to once again put our case for hep. sailine to the nurse. In Children's Hospital, there had been a big emphasis on privacy as I became a teenager. I had the use of a private bathroom, and the sister even had a word with me about wearing short pyjamas around. They were watchdogs, but like family. Here I felt disconnected.

My room had five ladies in it. To my left, a curtain was pulled across and a girl was cursing behind it, making someone else laugh. To my right, an elderly woman lay under her covers reciting the rosary for most of the day. She had brown hair and glasses and reminded me of my Granny Tinsley. I don't remember who was on the left or the right across the room, but I do remember who was in the middle. She was slumped over in the chair, like a blob of pink. Her grey hair hung over her face in weedy curls, but her eyes were clear and piercing. She stared at me for hours. Occasionally she talked. She told me that she had nothing to clean herself with.

'Does no one come and visit you?'

'No. I have no facecloth.'

'Will the nurses not give you one? Surely the nurses will get you one.'

'No. They were stolen from my locker.'

Throughout the evening I poured her water from her grey jug, identical to the ones we all had. I did the same for whoever else asked me. As the woman stared, I wrote a poem about her. I had been writing my feelings out all day, and now was the perfect time to escape the weight of her stares.

That night I got into bed and tried to sleep, but I couldn't. The lady with the piercing eyes moaned throughout the night. When no one came to her aid, she yelled. This had a domino effect and the lady next to her, who had previously been quiet, now emitted small grunts, slowly and steadily. They were like a bizarre double act. The nurse offered me a sleeping tablet, which I refused. Sleeping tablet? Why should I put that into my system? My mother always said they affected breathing. My resolve would weaken over the coming days, but as I lay awake that night, I tried to make sense of it all. Both of the women had been speaking coherently during the day, so why were they making this noise now? If they were in pain, why weren't they given painkillers? In reality, I knew it wasn't a conventional pain. I was annoyed that I couldn't get some badly needed sleep, but at the same time I felt so sorry for them. They seemed to have no one in the world to take care of them. How did some elderly people end up sprightly and independent like my nana, while others were condemned like this? It was a crazy lottery.

The whole experience was a complete shock to me, like I had fallen down the rabbit-hole and was residing in some parallel universe. I knew that I couldn't do this for the rest of my life, stay in a room like this when unwell. It felt like some sort of surreal punishment for the sins of a former life. The women weren't vibrant and energetic like other elderly people I had met, they were on their way to death and it echoed inside me. The longer I stayed with them, the more I feared it would rub off on me.

22.

Three days later I was finally moved to St Paul's, the CF ward, which had twenty-five beds in total, six in my room. It was the Holy Grail of CF treatment and I called my mother to tell her. In the bed next to mine was a girl who was a little older than me. I offered her some jellies and we got talking. I told her I was surprised that someone else with CF was sharing a room with me and she told me to get used to it. Indeed in the boys' room, there were more than two people with CF. After a week, I began to understand how it all worked. This was called 'the CF ward', but it wasn't really. It was a respiratory ward, which meant a mix of patients with CF and elderly patients with respiratory ailments. I had thought a CF ward meant quietness and strict infection control, but that turned out to be wishful thinking. The CF patients were thrown in together with the respiratory patients, which didn't benefit either camp.

Opposite my ward were two single rooms, one of which had a nurse stationed outside it all the time. Another patient with CF, a boy in a room down the corridor from mine, told me it was because the guy in that room was 'on his way out'. Over the next while I met the mother of the young man. She was one of the most inspirational women I have ever met, her strength astounded me. Her son was in his twenties and had to sleep sitting up because of the pain. I had never heard of that before.

I treated myself to a new notebook and started writing down thoughts and feelings and things I saw. Sometimes I wrote nothing and it was just a comfort to look at the purple hardback and know I could escape inside its covers. The girl in the bed next to mine made the screaming ladies easier to handle. There were four elderly ladies in our room and they were constantly calling out, 'Help, Help, Help,' non-stop, like a record stuck on repeat. It was unnerving, but somehow easier with this other girl there. Her name was Martha and she had been doing art in NCAD until she fell behind in her work and the college refused to give further extensions. She had tried everything, even brought her mom in, but they wouldn't listen and so now she had her own studio. It was small, but it worked. How did she afford it? Rent allowance. Apparently I was entitled to it as well. I could have my own apartment by virtue of the fact that I couldn't work full-time with CF. I never knew that. And it sounded brilliant.

It was good to discover these positive things alongside the bad discoveries: I was told I had osteoporosis and such severe glucose intolerance that I needed insulin immediately. I texted my old dietician about it and she told me to try and hold off as long as possible. She had always maintained that CF diabetes was not like normal diabetes and that taking insulin too early made the pancreas lazy. It was hard to know who to trust when I was been given different opinions. Martha told me she had full-blown diabetes and wished she had taken better care of it when she was first diagnosed. My attempts to figure out the best course of action were trial and error. I had to take the insulin after meals because when I took it beforehand and then didn't eat enough, I'd get a hypo and shake as my blood-sugar levels took a nose-dive. If I took too little and they went too high,

I'd get woozy. My mother constantly scared me with stories of people who didn't look after their diabetes and woke up one morning with a toe that had fallen off. Lovely.

Martha and I talked about our ambitions for the future and how some people we knew with CF didn't want anything other than hospital, where they felt safe. It was interesting to finally talk about it with someone – the way our illness tugged us frequently from our 'normal' lives and into hospital land, where we got taken care of by others. It was a relief to finally break the taboo and admit that hospital life can suck you in and make you lose motivation to leave. If you were 'inside' too long, you could begin to feel safe, and that was the real danger. Some people got too attached and forgot there was a life outside. It was good to just say it without feeling weird. I had thought that way of thinking was just me. It was like a big dirty secret I had carried around from when I was fourteen and had the eating problem. But it turned out that a lot of people had felt like that at different times. Unfortunately, there were some people who never realised it and therefore never got free. That sort of attachment shouldn't happen, because it's a hospital, but growing up somewhere where there is love and warmth equal to that at home eliminates conventional thought on it. I no longer coped like that, but was terrified of encountering it or seeing it in other people. I hadn't quite made peace with myself yet about it, but talking with Martha helped put it in perspective. We talked about when we were first diagnosed with CF. We both had *meconeum ileus* scars – the first time I'd met another girl with one.

Martha didn't eat very much – just rice pudding and organic food – which made me feel better. I described the eating problem I'd had and how it had been treated in Temple Street and she was horrified. In fact, the more people with CF I met, the more I realised that not everyone actually adhered to the insane recommended daily calorie intake. But then, when I looked at the boy across the hall who slept sitting up, I was willing to devote my life to eating. What had I been doing before? I hadn't been trying to shrink my body, I had just wanted to feel beautiful, but there are people in here with peg tubes and they are happy and I felt stupid about my insecurities. Being alive is enough god, just being here on earth.

The patients' sitting-room was located just off the ward and there is only meant to be one CF patient in there at a time. After five days in a stressful room, Martha and I decide to head to the sitting-room for a break. In spite of the rule, it was where most of the CF patients hung out. At the time, I wasn't worried about cross-infection because I was so off my head with tiredness and anger. The window remained open. The Pollock Report had just been published and it said we would die younger than our European counterparts because of Ireland's poor treatment facilities. There were six of us sitting in the room and I listened to the boys talk about how some of them had been on Sky News, or in newspapers, talking about the gap between what we needed and what we were getting. This was not new news; it was just a report that proved what had long been known. The boys do different things in their 'outside' lives: one is relatively fit, coaches football, another delivers pizza and one had a job in a factory but got fired because he was in hospital too much. I asked him why he didn't do something about it and he shrugged and said he couldn't be bothered, there was no point.

When Martha went home to attend her grandmother's funeral, I was alone in the madness. My parents bought me an MP3 player and I listened to the Corrs over and over, trying to block out the noise and the inhumanity of the whole scene contained in that room. It did bring something good, though. A woman had occupied an orthopedic bed while I had been up there and she was so lovely. She noticed me scribbling in my notebook, asked me why I was writing and I told her about it and what it meant to me. She said her daughter was a journalist working with *The Irish Times* and that I should talk to her about my writing ambitions. I said sure, I would love to, but to be honest, I didn't think anything would come of it. I was wrong. One day the woman's daughter, Róisín Ingle, arrived at my bedside, introduced herself and we talked about books, writing, life and CF. At the end of it, she suggested that I write an article for the *Times*. She was warm and funny and despite some of my friends warning me to 'be careful of how manipulative journalists can be', I decided to go for it. Surely, once people read about what was happening here, the government would do something about it and things would improve for patients with CF? How could they ignore the Pollock Report? They had to listen. Our lives depended on it.

I decided I would write the piece and discussed it with Martha and a few other people. I figured that if I just told it as it was, clearly and honestly, it would be okay. I didn't know if it would really achieve anything, but I was hopeful. It was a scandalous situation, but it was also hard to describe it from the inside looking out. The prospect of having my work published in a national broadsheet was exciting and terrifying in equal measure. On the one hand, this was what writers dreamed of, on the other, I didn't have any desire to be known for having CF. I was so much more than that. However, Róisín reassured me that getting the message out there was the best way to make a difference. My piece was going to appear in the *Teen Times*' section on teenagers' alternative life experiences.

I wasn't scared of what would happen as a result of speaking out. While I didn't want to offend anyone, I knew it was too important an issue to ignore. I also figured it would be okay because, having listened to the chat in the sitting-room, a lot of other CF patients appeared to have been doing it as well, in different media. At the time I felt like I could sort it out. I felt like no human being with a conscience, who had a choice, could allow people, particularly young people, to remain in a situation that threatened their lives like this. Especially when young people with the same condition in other countries had much more positive outcomes and experiences. My dad thought the article was a great idea and encouraged me. My mom was supportive too, but she warned that it could be hard because as a nurse herself, she knew how tough it could be to see things written about the hospital you worked in. They were both right: it was a great idea, but some people would find it difficult to accept the truth written bluntly. (For article, see Appendix 1.)

23.

I seemed to be on a never-ending run of intraveneous antibiotics and Martha was in again too. Our bugs meant that we weren't at risk to each other sharing a room. The summer of 2005 was the hottest in years, and during those hazy days we lay out on the grass, picked daisies, listened to Gemma Hayes' songs about hanging around and talked about boyfriends and peer pressure. Each night we watched a movie, things like *Fame* and *Leon*. *Fame* was great – we had both watched the 1980s TV show and loved it. The evening usually ended with us rolling around laughing or stretching like lunatics, in the day room, showing off just how low we could go in the splits or how high we could kick our legs. Silly stuff, but just what we needed to keep us going.

It was nice to find someone like me in there, someone who wanted more than the label of CF and continued on against the odds. Martha had done Ancient Greek and Roman in school, too, and we talked about her art and my writing and it was great that we had so much to discuss that had nothing to do with our illness. It was a real lifeline. So many people with CF were so focused on it – they talked about CF and who they hated or loved on the CF team and eventually it went around in ever-decreasing circles in your mind and made you feel brainless.

When I had first arrived in Vincent's, Martha had told me to always be alert and not to trust anyone. I had nodded, but decided she was probably delusional and must have been in too long herself. After spending some time there, my opinion had changed. I slept a maximum of three hours a night; five hours was an extremely good night. This was not because of my cough – which could keep me awake at the beginning of infections – but because of the constant noise in the room. The lack of sleep made it very difficult to gauge whether I was getting better – was I plateauing, or was I improving but unable to feel it because of exhaustion? Is this an infection or exhaustion? I was tired of opening toilet doors to find unassisted elderly patients struggling to use the facilities on their own. I was tired of cleaning toilets that were poo-smeared or pee-dotted. I was tired of trying to get someone to clean the shower so that I could use it. I was so very tired.

After two weeks the consultant changed my IVs and the new drug proved to be amazing. My sputum just shot out and I was getting better and I was telling everyone that Azactam was a miracle drug. One day the registrar came down to my bed while my mom was there and her face was grim. 'I need to tell you something important.' She closed the curtain. I told Mom she could stay and as the registrar sank down onto the bed, with a very serious expression, flanked by the Senior House Officer (SHO), I was more than a little concerned. 'There is a problem with your drug.' Oh shit. I knew it was too good to be true. 'It's being recalled.' Why? 'Anthrax.' *What?* It turns out Azactam and Ciproxin are two of the only drugs that can fight anthrax, so supplies were being rationed. I didn't know whether to laugh or complain. They changed my IV again and the substitute was not as effective, but my health remained steady.

That June when the women's mini-marathon runners went by the hospital, we watched from the front door as two of the boys who were inpatients at the time joined in, wearing dresses supplied by me and Martha: hers a 1940s blue polka-dot type and mine an awful garish white-and-pink flowered halterneck my cousin had gifted me. The lads put them on and went out to shake their buckets for CF. They ended up making a good bit of money. Watching the runners, I felt a sense of us and them – us, the people with CF, and them, the ones who can exercise freely and run 10k. I had not let myself feel that for a long time. Was there really an Us and a Them? In Lourdes, all those years ago, I had first felt it – that two distinct groups existed. My dad had taught me to be invincible – I would be a writer, I would go to college, I could do anything. This place was making me unsure.

Martha and I talked about exercise and its benefits and she told me that she sometimes did yoga. On nights alone in the CF rooms, she sometimes worked out on the lone exercise bike that was in there. I asked her why she bothered. 'Sometimes it gets your sats up.' I wasn't sure if that was true, but I went along with it. I always forgot why things did what they did and had no interest in exercise.

Martha was discharged first, followed by me a week later. When I went home after that admission I was so exhausted, I slept for days. In Vincent's, I often didn't know whether it was morning or night, there was a strangely flexible quality to time when I was in there. So when, after just a week at home, I jumped on the trampoline, felt a swell in my chest and projectile coughed 25 mls of blood into one of my mother's Denby cups, I knew I'd have to return to hospital. I made a deal with myself that I would create a structure for myself in there. It was the only way I was going to keep my sanity intact.

My article was published in *Teen Times* on 15 June 2005. I can remember the date because it was the same day I attended a CFAI meeting in Buswells Hotel on Kildare Street, opposite Government Buildings. The room was packed – everyone was there, including a girl with CF who was being trailed by a camera crew. My article was quoted in one of the speeches – the bit where I described people with CF as 'lifers' because it was a life sentence and we would always do hospital time. There was a chuckle in the room when it was repeated. I talked to a friend with CF that day on the phone, and she told me that one of the staff in Vincent's had dismissed the article as me 'flexing my muscles', saying that I would soon get used to the way things were. I was astounded. The thing was, I didn't want to get used to things as they were. In hindsight, I was probably having some sort of traumatic detachment experience from Temple Street, which had been so different, but I had no tools to explain or articulate that then. I just wanted things to be better for people with CF. I did not want to die. And right now, I was still sick. That's what was so infuriating: I didn't seem to be getting better. Of course, the stress and anger I was carrying around at the time probably weren't helping matters.

The day after the Buswells meeting I rang the CF team to let them know about the blood in the Denby cup incident. The SHO answered and she let me know exactly what she thought of me and my article. She told me that a lot of people worked very hard in Vincent's and she was very insulted by what I had written. I was shocked by her reaction, but while it upset me, it was also helpful in that it made me gather myself and prepare for what might greet me when I was readmitted. She said she didn't think there was space today. I rang the CF nurse straight away and she slotted me in immediately. Mom drove me up to Vincent's.

We assembled in the small treatment room – me, Mom, the CF nurse and the SHO – and the tension was palpable, but no one mentioned the article. There was a bed available immediately on St Paul's Ward and I was signed in. As I had promised myself, I set about putting a structure in place straight away. At 8.00am I would get up, get dressed and buy a hot chocolate and a raisin croissant in the shop. I would eat and sip, watching the bodies file in for work.

Sometimes the room was cleaned out very early and I would watch the boys in the corridor, speeding up their IVs to see who could finish first and fastest. Then I would buy *The Irish Times* and read it cover to cover, before returning to the ward for antibiotics, morning tablets and phsyio. The day was speckled with doctors and dieticians and talking to anyone I could find to talk to, for as long as possible. Talking was always a good way to avoid the situation.

Some days later I got a text from Martha: *In A and E, so hungry. Can you bring food? They keep 'forgetting'*. I had just ordered Chinese takeaway, so I put together marmalade on toast and some Chinese food and texted to say I was coming, armed with provisions. She replied: *I'm where the cardiac people usually are. The sick ones*.

When I got to her, she was sitting hunched over; she normally sat up straight, with perfect posture. I couldn't take my eyes off her. She was slouched over with oxygen prongs in her nose and the tank turned up to 7 litres. That was a huge amount. She told me that she had been out when she suddenly felt unwell and that she knew her sats were low – How can you even know that? I wondered – and that she had to come in. When she was moved to my room two days later I heard her say to the consultant, 'It's bad, isn't it? It's bad?' She had all this knowledge I thought I had. But I didn't know anything.

The fallout from my article was gathering momentum. A researcher from RTÉ Radio 1 contacted me to invite me onto Marian Finucane's morning radio show and I was also asked to appear on the *Six o'clock News* on RTÉ television. The Finucane show said they wanted me on, then they weren't sure, then they were sure and it was definitely going to happen. A steely determination kicked in. I was looking at Martha and thinking, I will never have fear again because CF is so unpredictable. Martha asked me to wake her for the show but I didn't because the night before she was coughing and I could hear one of the nurses, a woman who normally tries to make us laugh, sounding serious and grim and saying, 'Breathe, good girl, breathe'.

The next morning a taxi brought me over to the RTÉ studios in Montrose and I sat in the studio, waiting to do the show. I was nervous and felt over-prepared. The researcher had briefed me on what would be asked and coached me in how to answer the questions. She teased answers out of me first, to see what I would say, and then based how I would answer on that. It was the first and only interview I allowed myself to be treated like that. I didn't know the rules then; I just wanted to make sure I got the message out. I was so positive about life that I was uncomfortable talking about the bad stuff, like how difficult school was or how there was also accountability in my situation. I had no idea at the time what a big deal it was to be on the Finucane show.

Later that day, after the show, the CEO of the CFAI came to visit me with a woman who worked in the association. He was the new CEO and was visiting as many CF patients as he could in person, and I was on the list. While they were there, they witnessed some of the reactions to my article. Some of the nurses were less than pleased and their manner towards me didn't hide it. Some were fine, but most were not. The ward sister approached the CEO and his female colleague and told them the staff were waiting for an apology from me. I realised that I hadn't acknowledged that the staff were great, but the article wasn't about them. The CFAI woman ended up having to defend me, but she wasn't there later when I was making toast and a nurse told me that I should read about the Lea's Cross nursing home, then I would know what pain was.

It was upsetting to see the staff reacting this way, but I was still glad I had written it and I wasn't ashamed. I recognised that I might not have been as compassionate as I could have been about the elderly patients and hadn't mentioned how hard the staff worked, but then, this was all very new to me. The tension it created made me angry, which made me more determined. My parents told me to stick to my guns and I was encouraged by a call from my ex-dietician in Temple Street, who congratulated me. Over the next few days letters and emails arrived, including one from the CEO of Temple Street thanking me for saying such kind things, and one from the wonderful Professor Fitzgerald, the man who had operated on me through all my portacath surgeries. They all said I was right to say what I said, that it was an underacknowledged problem and that they hoped the people in charge did something about it as a result.

Martha was there to keep me company. But she was so different from the person I had met just a few weeks earlier. Each day I visited her bed and brought trashy magazines to make her laugh. I told her I hated my roots. She said I looked like Debbie Harry, rock chick. We gossiped about celebrities, but she looked so exhausted and there was this wateriness in her eyes that I had seen for the first time that night in A&E. Sometimes she was too tired to walk.

When Anna and Jenn visited me some days later, Martha has been moved to a single room. My friends were uncomfortable with the other patients in my room and after ten minutes asked to go to the coffee shop. We made plans to go on the annual trip to Lourdes with the CFAI for a bit of craic and a free holiday. I can go for free, as can my 'carer', so the girls and I decided to pay a third each for one ticket, then all three of us could go. The visit was a stark reminder for me of how bizarre my world could be.

After they left, I visited Martha in her single room to tell her about the Lourdes plan and the other amazing news: UCD had called and offered me a place on their Back To Education programme. She said it wasn't exactly fair on those people who finished the Leaving Cert, the fact that I was being given the same chance. She was right, but I didn't feel bad about it. I knew I needed to go there.

The day before I was due to fly to Lourdes, they let me go home. Dad drove over to pick me up and while he was dividing my various bags, laptops and drugs into a wheelchair and onto his back, I went to say goodbye to Martha. 'We don't have much time,' he warned me. I sat at the end of her bed and we hugged. I had started wearing different-coloured ribbons on my wrist to remind myself there was colour out there, to pull myself out of the trappings of my own over-thinking head while I was in hospital. Whenever I looked at them I would think, there is theatre, there is colour, there is creativity and it is waiting on the outside for me. Martha asked if she could have one, so that we would both be wearing one. I told her she could have any one she wanted. She said I must decide. I insisted, she insisted. 'Okay,' I said, 'how about the blue one? It's not just a ribbon, it's a kind of bandana too, so you can tie your hair up.' She thanked me and we hugged again.

Martha told me once she always wore a miraculous medal on her bra, but she had lost it recently. She was superstitious about these things. We made a deal that I would bring her back some cool Kate Moss-style miraculous medal. Dad stuck his head around the door and asked me to hurry up. 'Sorry, traffic!' We were about to leave when Martha realised she was having a hypo. I walked out to call a nurse. There was a student nurse outside her door and I said, 'Martha's having a hypo, she needs some juice and carbohydrates.' The student nodded, then continued reading her chart. We got ready to leave and there was still no food in front of Martha. Her hands were shaking. I got angry again, it rose up in me like bile. I ran out to the shop and got her an apple juice. I stood in the kitchen toasting bread, trying to resist the urge to shout at someone. Anyone. I was so frustrated with the place. I walked back with the toast and juice and put it on her tray. A final wave, and we left. On the way home in the car, I was busy making mental notes of what to pack. My mother wanted me to look for some skateboarding accessory for my brother while I was there, but top of my list was Martha's miraculous medal. If I got nothing else, I would get that.

24.

Anna, Jenn and I made it to Lourdes. When we arrived, another person with CF made mock-funny remarks about me being 'faaamous' because of my article. It made me uncomfortable, but the girls and I had fun anyway. One day, when we were walking back from the grotto and everyone but me was drunk, Anna turns to me and said, 'Don't ever leave me. I do love you. You're one of my best friends.' In her equally drunken state Jenn declared, 'You're so brilliant, you're just all such brilliant people,' and they both said they learned more about CF on that trip than anything I'd ever told them. I took notes constantly because I wanted to do another *Teen Times* article about Lourdes and religion and the feeling of energy that made people believe something was there, when it was really human presence.

We had picnics on the grass outside the apartment, ate Italian food, went for dinner with the group, avoided the Stations of the Cross like the plague and felt some bizarre sense of warmth in the grotto at 1.00am, when the air suddenly turned from chilly to lukewarm, encapsulating us in the circle we were standing in. None of us was religious, but we still couldn't fully explain that moment to ourselves.

At every religious paraphernalia stall I saw, I search compulsively for an alternative miraculous medal, a cool but non-cool one. We finally found a shop that sold a variety of non-religious things and I ended up buying myself a little statue of a gold Siamese cat with a red collar and a bell on his tail. On the final morning I found the perfect miraculous medal and the girls breathed a sigh of relief: the obsessive search was over. There were no skateboard shops in Lourdes, surprisingly.

We flew home and I slept for two days straight before Mom suggested I call the CF nurse to check what sputum I had been growing last time I was tested. My mother was used to knowing all of these things and if she didn't, she got nervous. Sometimes I forgot to tell, but she never believed me when I said that. Sometimes I didn't tell her because I needed to keep it for myself, I needed her not to know. That, justifiably, used to drive her equally crazy. But I was eighteen and CF was now my responsibility. I needed to take ownership of it and rightly or wrongly that seemed to me the way to do it. We had argued about a lot, so this time I just called the CF nurse, to put my mom's mind at ease – she didn't think I was better.

When the CF nurse called back later, she told me quite certainly that I had a resistant Pseudomonas. Back then, all I knew about it was that no drugs worked against it; I didn't know about the new drug combinations or different ways to fight it. When I put down the phone I felt like digging a hole and crawling into it. This was my own fault. I had been hanging out with a person with CF in hospital when I knew we should have stayed apart. I was such an idiot. The problem was that I kept thinking I was immune to it all, that I was invincible. I wasn't. I sat on the couch, irrationally angry with my dad for making me believe that I was not like other CF patients, that I was stronger. I went for a walk in the crisp air of Hawkfield and breathed in the freshly spread silage. I was so happy to smell it, to see the luscious grass and to feel that this was my home. This was reality. Martha texted me two days later to say she'd be in touch soon.

A week later I was sitting on the couch at home, contemplating going for a cycle, when I noticed two missed calls on my mobile from the friend who probably gave me the resistant Pseudomonas. I didn't want to talk to him. My thoughts wandered to other things. The director of the Youth Theatre had offered me a job in the Arts Centre, answering phones and organising events. If the UCD course didn't work out, that was what I should do: write in the mornings, work in the evenings and rehearse plays at night-time. That would be the perfect life. My phone flashed again. Still him.

I could always get a flat with rent allowance and the food allowance benefits Martha was telling me about. That would be great. I wouldn't live with my parents, we'd all argue less. My phone flashed again. I sighed, pressed the green button and took the call.

I sat up straight as he talked. Listening. Digesting. It happened during the night. How did I think he felt? He had been in the cubicle across the hall. Martha wasn't in the cubicle? No, she was in the bed by the window, the one you were in before you left. And then? But why? He was sorry, so sorry for telling me.

When I put down the phone, I opened my mouth, but nothing came out. Then noises came and my mother ran down the stairs and my brother Jack ran in from the room where he was doing his homework. She was dead. My friend was dead. How was this possible? And she had died in the madness of that room, that bloody ward. And the goddamn miraculous medal, I kept saying to my mom, the goddamn miraculous medal was upstairs in a pink paper bag.

The next day I had a choice: stay at home and cry or do what I had planned to do and meet my friend Sophie to go to the movies. There's no help in tears, so I headed to Dublin and we saw *The Fantastic Four* and shopped in

Urban Outfitters, where one of the sales assistants complimented me on the way I had put together my outfit. He said my style was so quirky and fabulous and right as he was speaking, it just hit me like a ton of bricks – the blonde hair, the make-up and fashionable clothes, they were so unimportant. What had I even been competing against? Why had I been wasting my energy with this rubbish?

While I was in the bathroom after the movie, Martha's sister called me and I told her I already knew. She was at the funeral home and she had just realised that she hadn't called me. She told me the funeral was the following day, in Dublin. She hoped I can be there, it would mean so much.

I did go to the funeral, but all the while I was thinking, What am I doing here? I didn't really know Martha, so what was I doing here? I told myself this shouldn't upset me, that five weeks of knowing someone shouldn't upset me. I decided I would give the miraculous medal to her sister. I queued up with the others offering condolences and when I looked into her sister's eyes, I felt like I'd been punched. She said she was afraid I wasn't going to come because I hadn't been at the removal. She said that I made her sister's last few weeks brilliant. She said that Martha had told her that she had finally found someone who was just like her and that our friendship meant so much to her. We hugged.

When I got home afterwards, my friend Róisín called to say they were running with my Lourdes article and could I edit it down immediately. I explained that I was just in from a funeral, but the deadline can't wait – they need it now. I sat down at the computer and I edited my own words ruthlessly and it made me feel better, more clearheaded and certain of my future.

When I was admitted to hospital a few days later, I was in a bed on the ward that Martha was in few weeks earlier, after her grandmother's funeral. I was back in the very same bed where I had visited her and drank apple juice and talked about how they could build an art room on that roof where people could write and paint and read and have some peace from the madness. Now I was staring out at the damn rooftop alone, with its overgrown moss and the Elm Park golf club visible behind it. Wealthy people paid to play golf there and all of a sudden those damn golfers with their massive greens made me so angry.

I was trying to contend with the two ladies in my room who had cancer. They were there because there was no room for them on the cancer ward. They reminded me of my aunt Breda; Mom's other sister got upset when she came to visit me. The lady beside me was grey in the face and her eyes were wide and dilated. She wrote in a journal every day and I knew she was dying. The lady beside her had cancer, too, and also a foot problem, so every morning I helped her put on her sock. I wrote in my diary to deal with it all. The woman across from me was the worst. She routinely managed to pour hot tea into her hot-water bottle and scald herself with it. The noises she made at night were unlike anything I had ever heard and I wondered if all of this madness could rub off on me with enough lack of sleep. And then was the hunching. It was something I had noticed about myself, that I was hunched over so much of the time. I was used to moving fast, but when everyone else around me was moving slowly, it made me move slowly too and I had to keep speeding myself up, reminding my body that I was young, that I would be out of there soon.

The things I needed to focus on in order to get out were cross-infection and distance – distance from this damn place and distance from CF. I vowed that there would be no more mixing with other CF patients, no matter how crazy things got. After a week the healthier woman with cancer was moved out and the curtains were taken down. I asked why, what did she have? No one would tell me. So I asked her and she told me she had tested positive for MRSA. We had been sleeping in the same room and using the same sink for a week. Anger and nausea overpowered me. I hate this place I hate this place I hate this place. She was so lovely and said she was so sorry. The poor woman, it wasn't her fault.

I told my mother I needed a holiday. I needed distance. Three weeks later, at the end of July, I was out of hospital and boarding a plane to Paris, with my mother. When I woke up in my hotel room at 7.00am to the smell of fresh baking from the patisserie outside, I was satisfied that we were far enough away for now. I told my mother this could be the only time in my life when I was in Paris. She told me not to be ridiculous. We fought again.

'You don't know that, Mom, you can't know that. Look at what happened to Martha. Look what CF does. You can't know.'

She left to go for a walk and when we planned our days, I said I wanted to go to EuroDisney. All the way there on the RER she said she felt guilty because Jack wasn't there, that he would be so upset. I told her they could go again some other time. When we got there, it was magical and beautiful and a complete sensory overload. That night, as we watched the parade, I wondered how all the children weren't scared of the flaming eyes of Jafar, the baddie from *Aladdin*. I can't say why the giant man in the costume gave me the heebie-jeebies, but he did. Good versus Evil. Life would be so simple if it were all Disney fairytale happy endings, but that's bullshit. Imagination is null and void. CF is real, death is real, scientific things are real. In the moment, that's how I felt.

25.

At the end of August I woke up in hospital – admitted for a chest infection – and I was in a room with a girl who had something similar to CF, and who couldn't stop talking about how sad and unfortunate we all were and how she wanted to help us. I tried hard to be pleasant and calm with her. She talked far too much for this place. It was like something happened to my brain in hospital, like the cognitive ability to string proper sentences together deserted me. I was exhausted from lack of sleep. The woman in the middle bed across from me was from Germany and she was a hoot. She told me a fabulous story about dodging bombs to return home to her husband after having gone out shopping during the war. When she got home, he called her name, but it sounded different. 'When I walk inside, he is naked and there is woman in my bed!' We laughed for a good ten minutes before she went on to say that he took her to court, alleged that she stole from him, then took all her money. The room became somber again. The lady in the corner frequently told me to 'Shut up, Bitch! You fucking bitch!' She murmured prayers when going asleep and sometimes throughout her sleep. When I opened the window: 'Bitch!'

The woman beside me was gentle and reminded me of a robin for some reason. She was in her eighties and forgetful, but wore headphones all day to remind her of her choir songs on the outside. One day, when my wardmates had pushed me to the max, I started singing choir songs with her to see if we had any in common. The German lady complained that she didn't recognise any of them and I suggested 'Edelweiss'. For the next four hours we had our very own choir and the nurses walking laughed and asked if I'd gone completely cuckoo. It was actually great fun, but it started to fall apart when choir lady refused to sing anymore because the harmony was out of whack.

A few days later I was sitting in the day nurses' office on St Mark's ward when I got a sudden pain in my side. It started like period pain and then moved around my back. I felt like I was going to vomit, it was so bad, so I decided to get back to my bed. I had to walk hunched over, with my hand clutching my side, feeling slightly crazy. By the time I got to the ward I was twisting into a cat pose on the bed, but nothing eased the pain. The nurses paged the intern on call and I walked around feeling like those horses I used to see that had colic, being walked up and down the stables. The intern gave me a shot of painkiller and I fell asleep. The next morning an x-ray revealed a kidney stone, a calcium build-up in the kidney, and I lay there, flummoxed.

When a member of my team came to see me, he said I would probably pass it on my own. He would have to wait until the radiographer consulted with the kidney people, though, to be sure. He told me that most people say having a kidney stone is more painful than childbirth, so at least there would no surprises in the future if I ever decided to have a child. That afternoon the radiographer gave his verdict: the stone was too big, I would not be able pass it so they would have to blast it out. I knew there no other option, so I agreed. This was my fourth time in hospital since switching to Vincent's. When I looked at the windows, all I could see were grey walls. It was suffocating. When the weather was bad, the cylindrical building seemed to sag and droop, taking us all down with it.

After I woke up from the general anaesthetic after my kidney stone 'blasting' – where I imagined they sent a hoover-like tube up to bomb the stone into smithereens – I remained on oxygen for a day. The kidney doctor came around and said, 'This patient should be mobile by now, why is this patient still in bed?' Well, mister, clearly I'm not lying here on oxygen for the fun of it. 'Hi!' I said. No response. 'HI!' I said loudly. 'Hi, I have cystic fibrosis, so I think the anaesthetic may just be slowing up my recovery a bit.' He looked unamused and walked out. I wanted to rip my drip from the wall and throw it at him. I am a person, not a thing in the bed that you operate on.

Finally, about two weeks later I got out, back to reality once more. I was going to college in October, a whole new experience was waiting for me and I was determined to make the most of it.

26.

The Belfield campus of UCD is near my aunt Eilis' apartment in Booterstown, so I stayed with her from Tuesday until Thursday to attend lectures, then went back to my parents' house in Newbridge from Friday to Monday, so I could study for the Christmas exams. I was doing first year English and Greek and Roman Studies and I needed to do well, to cement my place in college and prove that I could do it. I passed the exams and spent Christmas with my family, feeling stronger.

For our second term I chose the Politics module, and an illuminating lecturer taught us about Liberalism, Conservatism and all the other ism's involved in Irish politics. This was made more fun by one of our classmates, a John Lennon look-alike who hated Politics and The Man. We usually sat around talking conspiracy theories and singing Johnny Cash songs in the Arts Café before classes. As this was a Back to Education college program, it was mainly populated by people over thirty who were returning to third-level education after a long gap, mostly spent working or travelling. I was the youngest person on the course and I was worried that this would leave me on the periphery, but in fact I became good friends with a group of the guys. Al had been a bicycle courier, cycled everywhere, owned a house but lived with his mother. Uisce was the Lennon doppelganger who challenged all authority. Danny was a pale, black-haired, broody type who didn't always show up. One evening I met Danny for coffee in the Arts Café and he showed me his poetry. It was dark and heavy and when I told him what I thought it meant, his eyes lit up. We missed him in the last few classes and he never turned up for the exams.

We were all on the course due to life experience and a good autobiographical essay. And, on my part, good luck. The guys talked about how they knew they weren't ready for college before, how they had other things to do first. Some said they had 'pissed away' their Leaving Cert. I felt like I had too. I wanted college, I wanted the degree, I wanted to make my parents proud. If I could study and write at the same time, that would be great. College would feed my writing, teach me new things, recharge my batteries. I was really getting into it in second term, feeling reinvigorated and up for the challenge of studying and writing.

Just as I started feeling good and things were coming together, I had to go back into hospital, this time with a nasty resistant infection. Second term would go on without me. After three nights on a trolley in A&E, I was finally given a bed in St Paul's Ward, in a room with three other patients with CF, two of whom were on the transplant list. One of them was sarcastic bordering on mean as she struggled to cope with her situation, the other talked really fast, was super-intelligent but immature. There was something extremely unnerving about being in the room with them. I knew we had the same illness, but I could never imagine being as sick as they were. They both needed transplants, but they dealt with it very differently, and they were different degrees of sick. I felt like a complete phony, like I shouldn't even be in the hospital. We all had CF, but next to them, I felt so healthy.

One evening the girl in the corner bed was listening to our conversation about models. The hyperactive girl was saying that she thought Victoria Beckham was gorgeous. The sarcastic girl nodded in agreement. I said I thought that she was dangerously thin and it was unattractive and a bad influence on young girls, that I felt her tiny body could trigger eating disorders. What we needed, I argued, were proper, Marilyn Monroe-shaped role models. The girl in the corner bed joined in then and told us that she had an eating disorder and CF. She had been suffering from the eating disorder for years.

'When did it start?'

'In college, when I started living on my own. '

'Did they put you in a program or anything? '

'Nah, I didn't want to, but I did talk to the psychologist and stuff. There's no hope in recovering now, sure I've had it forever. '

My heart sank at that idea. There's always a way out. I was proof. 'A similar thing happened to me,' I told her. 'I had a problem too when I was younger, but I went to therapy everyday and I got over it eventually. '

'Really? That's not for me though.' We moved on to more celebrity chat.

The next morning I walked out of the bathroom to find the psychologist standing in front of me, arms crossed. She told me not to talk about anorexia as it was none of my business. I asked her to what exactly she was referring. 'You upset some people, so keep yourself to yourself,' she replied and walked off.

It was like a hit and run. In physio that day, I cycled harder than I ever had. This situation was nonsensical. Okay, if I upset someone I was sorry, but no one was forced to take part in that conversation. I didn't realise that by sharing my experience, in confidence, I would hinder more than help. It didn't make sense to me. Not then, anyway.

A few days after this, it was the day for the dreaded once-a-week full room clean. Everyone grumbles because it takes place early – usually at 8.00am – and you have to move all of your personal contents out of the room and into the corridor, just at the time when you need to be doing nebulisers and other medication. So at 8am on this day I was sitting in the day room with a few other CF patients, all of us groggy with tiredness. An inane television programme was showing us how to cook something colourful in a pan. Bodies came into the room behind us, talking loudly. It was three men and two women, who told us they were all there for the sleep apnea clinic. One of the men, sporting a purple bandana, sat down on the couch and asked us if we had CF. One of the girls replied that we did. The man's friend then piped up and asked the girls if they were waiting for a transplant. He pointed to one of them and said, 'I'm a healer and I know you'll get one'. He looked at the other girl and said nothing. We sat there in silence, stunned by his blatant stupidity. They kept asking questions and I answered short and fast. I wanted to be a writer because you can do it anywhere – on the top of a mountain, in a hospital bed, probably not under the sea. But right now we were all really tired and just wanted to rest. Exhaustion hangovers. I was just trying to get them to shut up, but they kept asking questions.

When our room had been cleaned and the beds wheeled back in, I lay down for a nap. When I woke up, the three men were standing at my bedside, looking down at me. They hoped I didn't mind, but they just wanted to talk to me because the skinny guy, with the sunken eyes and the cheesecloth top, was a healer. The biker with the bandana, it turned out, was a lounge singer. They liked my attitude and the healer wanted to help me. I let him continue, only because it was easier than listening to the nun in the corner preach yet again about how Jesus would save me. He told me he had helped a woman with cancer to wake up and see her husband before she died. Murky territory; he could commune with the dead. My bed pooled with light from the window illuminating the madness. That is when I should have asked them to leave. The healer sat on the left of my bed and the biker sat on my right. I had a friend who had died, right? She meant a lot to me and I was hurting because I didn't get to say goodbye? An easy guess, but my stomach heaved with an ill feeling. He told me if I let him place his hands on me, the pain would go away.

'You can cure CF then?'

'I can lift the pain away.'

'There is no pain, there's just mucus.'

The healer's eyes were watering as he told me that I needed to open my 'third eye' to heal, to see what I had previously seen and was locking away. This would free me from CF. I told him, 'CF is scientific. You can't help me.' He said he would do a free healing session with me, if I consented. I told him thanks for everything, please leave. After they left I coughed non-stop for what felt like an age and then hid under my covers until the physio came to get me for my session. As I exercised, I tried to imagine their negative energy rushing off me. I felt violated.

Looking back, I don't know what their motives were. Did he really believe he had the power to cure CF? Whatever he believed, he made me feel uncomfortable, but I didn't know how to ask them to leave in a polite way. I couldn't shout at them because they weren't being overtly threatening, just unnerving. I only wish I'd thought to ask him why he hadn't healed himself of sleep apnea. I needed to figure out how to say, 'No more, get out. Now.'

This wasn't a new situation to me. There always seemed to be someone – whether someone I was in contact with or a random person who just heard I had CF – who wanted to help me. It annoyed me, but then I think I probably gave out the vibe that I was open to it because I was so friendly and obviously wanted to learn more and experience more. In truth, I was in a bad place at that time. I had given up on the authority figures in my life and just needed a break from everything. I felt like my world was changing and I had no control over it. Leaving a place and people you've known for eighteen years was very difficult, and then trying to make new connections was equally hard. I wasn't an instantly charming child anymore; I was an adult.

So what did that mean? I wanted to get away from Newbridge and my family home, like anyone at that age. I ended up kissing Henry, a boy much older than me because it was thrilling and different. Despite the fact that he had CF. Despite the fact that, in retrospect, this was physical and emotional madness. I told the CF nurse and she checked our sputum to find out if there was a risk of cross-infection. I had Pseudomonas; he didn't. This meant that he was at risk of infection from me, so it was his choice to continue or finish the relationship. He could decide to be with me and risk his health, or not. Now, it is unfathomable to me that I let that be an option, but then I felt like Henry was one of the very few people who understood me. I felt like a freak who didn't know how to make real, meaningful connections with other people. With him, I felt like I had found a space for me in the world, not that I was, in truth, hiding.

Our relationship was intense and fraught with some difficulty. I was extremely naïve, but after spending the entire summer with him and as far away from my parents as possible, I realised I hadn't been taking care of myself properly. There were a good few people with CF dating other people with CF. I think I was trying to be a rebel in the hopes that someone would show me a better idea of who I was. I didn't realise I could find that out all on my own.

27.

That May, summer 2006, after I handed in my final assignment for the Back to Education diploma, I started looking for a summer job. The Hoky Poky, the coffee shop where I had worked the year before, was not hiring. I felt a bit unsure as to how to go about getting a job. I was having so many hospital admissions that I couldn't guarantee I would always be there, but my CF wasn't going to stop me from applying. By all accounts my CF had changed, in the sense that it was slightly trickier to manage because I was getting more infections, so I needed more IVs now, both at home and in Vincent's. Should I be straight-up honest with employers about my possible absences? I wanted to do the job properly and well, but there wasn't much I could do if I had an infection and had to be admitted to hospital.

I applied for a job in Mothercare and got it, but it wasn't due to start until the same week as my theatre group was travelling to Italy. In July, we were going to visit an Italian theatre group in Florence, where we would work on a joint drama project exploring the issues of xenophobia and racism. It was a choice: take the job and start immediately, or go to Italy for two weeks. My parents wanted me to take the job because I might not get another one. I wanted the theatre and Italy. I imagined myself shackled to the bibs and rattles in Mothercare; it wasn't the summer I had planned. I hopped on a plane to Italy.

My mom sorted out my travel insurance and I packed my travel nebuliser, which was a machine a little bigger than a video camera that was carried in a blue satchel, so it looked like a camera bag. I shoved Ventolin into the secret pouches and placed the rest of my drugs in my backpack. They had to be on me at all times, which meant travelling was frustrating. When my hand luggage went through the security screen at Dublin airport, the machine started beeping. The security guard snatched it up, sternly eyeing the girl in the long skirt with curly blonde hair. I waved my medical letter at him, but he still felt the need to unpack my entire backpack, complete with underwear and socks I had thrown in last minute, until he found my drug stash at the bottom.

'I have Cystic Fibrosis, if you'd like to read the letter.' He glanced at the letter, then left me to repack my bag.

Aidan and Niall, my friends, stood there gawking. 'I'm going to tell him to repack it for you!'

'No, it's ok,' I sighed.

The Italian theatre group had visited Ireland in February that year, and we had completed the first half of the project together. We had put them up in the same guesthouse where I used to work out with Isobel. They each had single en-suite rooms and enjoyed the use of a pool and the gym. About twenty of us travelled to Italy and our digs in Florence, by comparison, certainly had an Italian feel to them. We stayed in an old Carmelite monastery that had been renovated into a hostel. Upon arrival, the owner, an Italian man with long floppy hair and a muscular body, led us from the monastery courtyard up two flights of stone stairs to the living quarters. The walls were adorned with frescoes and the large living area was open plan, with a fridge and a massively high ceiling. The sleeping quarters presented a problem, though. We were four people per room, sleeping on bunk beds. The rooms were tiny and with all the bodies crammed in, it was like sleeping in a coffin. The owner brought us into a small room that was probably the old chapel, and informed us of the house rules. No smoking inside was, thankfully, one of them.

Our schedule was hardcore: we worked together, Italian and Irish actors, from 10am to 6pm in the Teatro della Limonia. It was a 20-minute walk from our Carmelite home through the streets of Firenze to the bus stop, where we boarded the local bus that took us to the theatre. The air was humid and our route seemed to get longer each day as the heat rose to 40 degrees. On our bus journey we passed high-rise flats and a barren playground. I saw a machine on the street where drug addicts could deposit their syringes and needles, something I'd never seen before.

The theatre was a large period house that looked like something straight out of an Evelyn Waugh novel. Inside, it was a hive of creativity and bohemian style. During our first few days we spent hours sitting in the garden, listening to men of different nationalities describe their experiences of xenophobia in Italy. Throughout the day we drank water and cans of soft drinks from the machine in the theatre building. The machine didn't stock Diet Coke, which was my mainstay. On the first day I made Aidan walk with me outside the gates and ten minutes up the road to a nearby shop. It didn't stock Diet Coke either. Or any diet drink at all, for that matter. We bought ice-pops and walked back. I would drink the full sugar drinks in the theatre and it would be okay because I was using so much energy anyway.

By the second week in Italy I knew I was in trouble. There was a random weighing scales on the street – another thing I'd never seen before – and when I stood on it to check my weight, it was clear that I had lost a lot. I started doing less at the theatre, but even so, by day nine I knew I needed a break. I headed to the beach with some of my friends and the salt air helped and made me feel better, but when we

returned to the city, the humidity immediately had me tired
again. On the tenth day there was a taxi strike, so Aidan
and Niall walked the streets of Florence, trying to find me
an air-conditioned hotel room. Finally, Aidan found a place
and booked it for me.

The boys carried my bags for the thirty-minute walk to
the hotel and by the time we got there, we were all sweating
and breathless. I walked up the stairs to the room, but one
look told me it wasn't a runner. I apologised to the
crestfallen Aidan, but I just couldn't do it. It was a box-
room and if I had to stay there longer than a day, it wouldn't
work. We roamed the piazza for another half an hour, like
the holy family looking for room at the inn, as one of the
lads remarked. On our third attempt a woman with a lot of
young women hanging around her ushered us out a door
and along an alleyway of cobblestones to two large brown
doors. Inside, the marble floor was breathtaking. We took
the lift – thank goodness, no stairs – up to the room, where
we stood open-mouthed, like fish. It was a carpeted living
room with a bathroom attached and up some steps were a
bedroom and a balcony that looked out over the city. The
boys left me with a bottle of water and they raced off to the
theatre. I was content.

After an hour I realised I needed food as my blood sugar
was low. I left the apartment, clutching my Laser card, and
made my way slowly to a nearby pizzeria. My lower lobes
were definitely not taking in enough air. I felt like a dufus
for being so under prepared! I should have chilled out
earlier, but I didn't want to look weak and 'sick'; years later,
I read a statistic showing that people with CF go on longer
than they should, to prove themselves to their peers. A
familiar trait. When I arrived at the pizzeria the man behind
the counter would not accept my Laser card – cash only. I
did not have enough money on me and now I also didn't
have the energy to walk in search of an ATM. I hobbled
back to the hotel and as I walked in through the big brown
doors, I started to shake. There had to be sugar upstairs. I

was focusing so hard on putting one foot in front of the other, I bumped straight into a cleaner in a grey dress. It all got a bit Hollywood movie then.

'Juice? Can I get a drink? Room service?'

She stared blankly at me. I sat on the steps, waiting for the lift, and showed her my shaking hands. My last chance now was the sugar sachets I knew were upstairs. I made my way painfully slowly, but finally I got into the room. A buzzer sounded. In the back of my mind, I prayed this was not a brothel – it was so hidden and the woman had so much make-up on and there were all those young girls and the two boys did bring me in and leave me. My mind was all over the place as I opened the door. It was the cleaning lady – with orange juice and *biscotti*. I wanted to throw my arms around her, but I reckoned that a woman screaming in fear and a drunk-looking tourist might fetch the wrong kind of attention. I say a heartfelt *grazie* and when she left, I wolfed it all down and felt better.

At 6.00 that evening the boys and one of the girls returned to me, bearing pizza, and I sent them out on a mission to find some hypertonice saline. It's a miracle nebuliser airosol that always loosens up my chest. They had seen a chemist open on the way, so they headed off in search of it while the girl and I stayed munching pizza. If they found this stuff and it didn't make me feel better, I would go to hospital.

The found it but unfortunately it only provided small relief. The next night found us sitting in A&E. After twenty minutes of waiting I was moved to a room with two other people. The Italian woman in charge looked friendly, like the woman from the Ragú ads. She wanted to access a vein, but I explained that I did not have any, that I had a portacath instead. I showed her the port and she went away and came back with two other nurses. They stroked my head and brow as she advanced towards me with a needle. It didn't look like the proper needle for a port. I said 'no', but her helpers held me down by the wrists and shoulders and I couldn't move. I screamed as she pushed the foreign body into the wrong place. If she breaks my port, I will fly back to Italy and hunt her down. 'No! Get away from me!' I roared. Micheala, the Italian theatre director, ran into the room, panicked by my yells. He rubbed my brow before chasing the nurses out the door, flinging furious Italian in their wake.

Micheale, the most amazing Italian man in the world, called my mother. Her advice was to ask for an anaesthetist to look after the IV and needle insertion. They called for an anaesthetist. When he arrived, I was eating chocolate wafer biscuit. He took my hand and said, 'I have not done this since I was a student, but I will do my best.' My heart melted. He did it perfectly right, first time, and my drugs started to go in. For once I was thinking that Vincent's had its benefits – so many nurses there could put needles into ports properly. Things could clearly be a lot worse.

I spent that night in the HDU, where I shared a room with two men and a woman. The next morning I was seen by a consultant, who apologised for the wait in A&E. He told me that things were bad in Italy, that Ireland must be very different. I assured him that a twenty-minute wait and sharing a room with two other people overnight was actually great. He wrinkled his nose, as though the language barrier was in the way. Later that morning I was moved to a single, en-suite room, where I could order whatever food I liked. I was feeling utterly exhausted and sleep felt so good. I kept taking notes about the whole experience because I knew it would make a good column; I texted Roisin to tell her.

The Kildare theatre gang moved on to Rome without me, but the Florentine actresses came to visit me and told me about the performance. The result of all the workshops and talks, it was a physical theatre piece, with no words, depicting the experiences and struggles of immigrants. I was gutted to miss out, but the girls told me it went really well, and I was grateful for their visit.

That afternoon my poor mother arrived on a flight into Rome, frantic with worry, and came straight to Florence and the hospital to be with me. When she walked into the room I was relieved. Up until then I had been listening to Tori Amos on a loop, awakening only to take drugs and keep an eye on my surroundings. She teased me about being a drama queen and hugged me. Her humour and good grace were exactly what I needed.

Roisin rang about the column I wanted to write, telling me that it would be perfectly timed as a girl with CF had just stood up to the Minister for Health, Mary Harney TD. 'It's like what you did, but with cameras there,' she said. She sent me through a link and it was fantastic – the girl was on the front page of three newspapers, wagging her finger at the minister. She had done far better than I did. When I had approached Mary Harney, it was some time after my friend Martha had died. I knew the Minister was touring the hospital that day, so I sat in the CF sitting room, waiting for her to come along the corridor. A ward sister came in and told me the minister had already gone and to close the door so that I didn't get cold. I did as told, then waited a minute and opened the door again. Mary Harney obviously wasn't gone. When she came out of the conference room, I smiled at her and asked if I could say hello. She asked, 'Do you work here?'

Smiling back, I said, 'No, I'm a patient on one of the wards, the CF ward. Except it isn't really a CF ward, it's respiratory ward masquerading as a CF ward and only two of the beds are allocated to a CF person at any given time. Did you know that?'

She listened and then the guys flanking her tried to move the group on, like a floating island.

'Do you know people are dying because of this? My friend is dead. Have you read the Pollock Report?'

'I hope your situation improves soon,' she said, and moved on. I understood how things worked, how she couldn't give an inch or I might have taken a mile, but her

apparent lack of empathy left me shaking as I made my way
back to my six-bed room. We were so dismissable, so
inconvenient. Now here was this girl, wagging her finger at
Minister Harney and letting the whole world know what we
thought of the politics and priorities of the Department of
Health.

Five days later I was released from hospital and my
mother and I travelled home to Ireland by plane. During the
flight, I started my piece for *The Irish Times* and I kept at it
doggedly, even in the face of the irritating singing from a
bunch of kids in the front seats. When I arrived back in
Dublin, I was immediately admitted to St Vincent's. I
finished my piece, got it printed out in the hospital and the
newspaper sent over a courier to pick it up. I was
completely exhausted by this stage and had suffered a
complication of my now prevalent diabetes. I had been
ignoring it, hoping it would just go away. Instead, it had
caught up with me.

As I lay in the six-bed ward, I knew I would have to
change my life. Ever since I had failed to get the course I
wanted to study, I had been skittering around like a spooked
horse. I felt my life had shifted and here I was, six months
into dating someone with the same illness as me – Henry. It
was pure madness. But somehow, in its madness, it made
sense because nothing else did. Without school and Temple
Street and the people I had been attached to for eighteen
years, I just fell into a heap. Was this really all there was? I
was frustrated all the time and didn't know how to fix it.
Deciding to take care of myself properly was a good first
step, but it would take time to implement it. There was no
magic formula for doing my treatment perfectly and fully
every single day, or for changing from eating whatever I
liked to checking the carbohydrate and sugar values of every
mouthful. Because I had lost control before, I was a bit
afraid of food. I was afraid that if I got too involved in
weighing up every morsel, I would lose myself again. I still

didn't really understand that I had a choice in the matter –
it felt more like a trap that I could fall into.

It was positive, though, this desire for change and to put
a more coherent order on my life. I realised that I would
have to be committed to managing my diabetes full-time
and that I would have to be more organised in order to
achieve this. I realised that because I had CF, I would have
to have a plan. It was funny because my dad had always
advocated that, but at the same time he had always said it
was important to go with the flow. I think that's why I had
a conflicting idea about making plans – they meant
structure, which meant discipline, which meant lack of
creativity, which was to be avoided at all costs. Now,
though, I realised that to preserve my creativity in terms of
writing, acting and living, I had to plan around them to
keep my body healthy and my mind free to focus.

I also realised that I had to end the relationship with
Henry. Things were becoming more difficult between us,
and I knew that I would have to let go of whatever past I
was hanging on to and move on. So I broke up with him and
clung to that determination to go forward. I was heading
into first year in college, as a proper undergraduate, which
was all new and meant the world to me. I was moving away
from everything and starting afresh. Running away made
complete sense.

28.

I was due to start at UCD as an undergrad in September 2006 and as part of my 'be more organised' approach to life, I decided to move into on-campus accommodation. Living in Roebuck Hall would allow me to focus on college properly, and to have fun. During the week it was bursting at the seams with Irish and international students, holding parties and study groups. I was living with a two psychology majors, a physiotherapy student and two international students: Marie France from Quebec and Sophia from Germany. The other three, Clare, Grace and Alex, were Irish and we all got on pretty well – most of the time. One of the girls smoked in her room – campus accommodation windows opened only a crack, some nod in the direction of suicide prevention it was understood – and the fumes that wafted into the apartment made me crazy.

On the first day of college, I walked out of the apartment at the Owenstown entrance to UCD, along the green, and said Hi to the only guy unfortunate enough to have a 9am lecture on Monday morning. His name was Patrick, he was from New York originally but lived in Cavan. He was studying to be an actuary and, it turned out, lived just across the hall from me in Roebuck. He said to pop over some time, so later that day I did. I hung out with him and his friend Fionan and it was pretty chilled out compared to an apartment full of girls.

Children's Literature and Critical Theory were the main English modules for first semester and lectures on Roman History and Greek Philosophy made up the Ancient Greek and Roman syllabus. The 9am lecture I was headed to when I met Patrick was concerned with the Peloponnesian War and consisted largely of a barrage of dates and ancient names. Children's literature was more inviting, with *Huck Finn* and *The Wizard of Oz* compulsory reading. The library was the best place to study and near the back on the second floor, past the History and Greek and Roman books, was my favourite spot. I went there between lectures, intent on learning the prescribed texts, but usually ended up rifling through the shelves and unearthing gems that I just couldn't put down. The smell of the older books and the silence there were calming. One floor down and people were chatting and studying Bebo together, until 'Libocop' came along. This was a particularly persistent female librarian, who lurked in the shadows of the shelves and floated up behind you, silently, to challenge your behaviour with an icy glare. There was a €10 fine for using a mobile phone, but it was more of a threat. In truth, everyone feared the glare more than the fiscal punishment.

I took notes ferociously in lectures. The only way I was able to learn was to write it all down and go back over it because my memory can be really poor at times. I would like to think this was courtesy of all the chemicals I've had to ingest over the years, but I think mainly it is just me. My aunt Bridget had told me, 'The most important thing about college, lovey, is to introduce yourself to the person on the right and left of you in your lectures.' I introduced myself to people, but then ended up taking so many notes that I forgot what they looked like and never spoke to them again. A girl sat beside me one day and introduced herself as

Sarah. She managed to break through my mammoth note-taking and years later, she remains one of my closest friends. She later told me that she had chosen to sit next to me that day because I took so many notes and looked just as nerdy as she did.

Living away from home for the first time was tough. My mother had warned me not to share my cutlery because of cross-contamination, but people used it anyway. My milk got drunk and the smell of air freshener mingled with the cigarette smoke that often hung in the air of the kitchen. It made me gag and cough and we fought a lot about it. Some nights random boys walked up and down the corridor outside our apartment, although the worst was the night someone stumbled drunkenly into my room thinking it was someone else's, about five hours before my 9am Psychology exam.

One night, after a birthday party, a few friends of one of the girls stayed over and we sat in the living room, chatting. One of the boys, who was a model, asked me what it was like to have CF.

'Ah, it's no big deal,' I said. 'You just get on with life.'

'But what does it feel like to know you're going to die? Doesn't that scare you?'

No one knew how to react, or told him to shut up. I said that death was just a part of life, but I probably appreciated life more than others, which was why I didn't drink or smoke. He was drunk, and I knew he smoked.

'I feel like shit, man,' he said. He went on and on about how he was going to stop drinking and smoking and that he would spread the word in the morning about how we should appreciate life. I smiled, told him good luck and goodnight. He came after me and pulled me into a hug, the aroma of sweat from the nightclub, cigarettes and cheap beer making me want to gag. The next morning my flatmate apologised for his behaviour, but his reaction wasn't exactly new to me.

Patrick and Fionan's place across the hall became my

refuge. We'd hang out and play *Dead or Alive*, a computer game where scantily dressed women and steroid-filled beefcakes would battle it out. You'd end up dead or alive, believe it or not. On Tuesdays the boys and Sarah would come over to watch *Lost* or *Desperate Housewives*. A woman Patrick knew used to send him a fruitcake every week, which was nearly always stale by the time it came to TV night. We'd eat it anyway, watch some glossy programmes and hang out. When I was with girls, I was always competitive, sometimes irrationally so, but with these guys it was so much easier to just be myself.

I liked my own apartment less and less. Most of us had never lived away from home before and dirty dishes lay in the sink, butter-smeared knives on the counter-top and the floor was often filthy. Neither Frankie nor I were very happy with it, but Sophia, our German roommate, was at her wits' end. She started to eat dinner in her bedroom most days and although we still chatted, tensions grew. She was used to living on her own in Germany. She was also used to budgeting, unlike us Irish girls who bought groceries twice a week in Tesco or picked up readymade comfort food in Marks and Spencer. She tried to communicate with us by talking about Joyce and Yeats, but she knew more than we did.

I hadn't truly discovered or exploited Dublin yet. To me, the city still meant hospital, Writers' Museum, Walton's music shop and Aras an Uachtarain in the Phoenix Park, where the President lived. It meant MacDonalds, too, on those journeys home from hospital as a child. It took a while for the full potential of Dublin to seep into my mind, the fact that it held so many things that I loved and was interested in. For example, I was discussing the greatest living poets with my tutor one day and he told me that Seamus Heaney lived nearby and had recently given a talk to first years. Embarrassingly, silent tears started streaming down my face. I had never considered the fact that Seamus Heaney lived down the road, that he was accessible. The

writers I loved were holy to me and spoke to me so
personally that the possibility that they were pouring out tea
a couple of miles away just didn't enter my brain space.

It was a brilliant learning curve all round, although I
think I probably took everything too seriously at the time to
realise just how much fun it was. Of course, it wasn't long
before it was interrupted – that autumn I was admitted to
hospital again. I was there for my blood sugars to be
monitored, so they didn't have to put me on IVs. It made it
all the more frustrating to be free from infection and in
hospital – it was such a waste of time. I was sharing a room
with two other girls with CF. One of the girls had extreme
bowel and liver problems, while the other needed an NG
tube, but was so traumatised from her experiences of having
tubes inserted when she was a child, that she couldn't face
it. Apart from the cross-infection, which management had
'no choice about', the worst part was the quite healthy
woman in the room with us who cried to her doctor daily
about how depressing it was 'to be around all of these sick
CF children.' We had to hold back the giggles whenever she
said it because it was hilarious. Of course, having listened to
her repeat it several times, the feeling became mutual.

After a few days of mind-numbing boredom I noticed a
white dot on the right of my chest, where the portacath was.
I showed the nurse and she got the doctor to come up and
check it. He poked around my chest with his fingers and
said it was an infection in my port. He prescribed Fluxopen
to clear it up and told me not to worry. By the end of my
six-day admission my blood sugar levels had cleared up, but
my chest didn't feel great. I went back to my apartment and
straight to classes at UCD. Over the next week the white dot
on my chest didn't clear up. I stood at the mirror and felt
crazy. Had it gotten bigger? I called the hospital and was
advised to come in. I saw the same doctor again who
assured me that it was no big deal and that it was clearing
up. I said I wanted a second opinion; I had already missed
too much of the beginning of college. He walked out,

frustrated with me, and the CF nurse came in. She called another doctor who did an x-ray and got a surgical consultation.

The white mark was not, in fact, an infection clearing up. It was actually the place on my chest where the skin had ripped from overuse: the white was my portacath peeking out into the world. It was an open wound created by a device attached directly to the vena cava in my heart, just waiting to be infected by something from the outside world. The surgeon said to bring me in immediately to take out the port. By now it was November 2006, and keeping up with college was getting tough.

I had never yet had a surgery in Vincent's and the mere thought made me nervous. I said I wanted to see the surgeon before he performed the removal operation. I informed him that I had made a decision not to have another port inserted. I knew I could get picc (peripherally inserted central catheter) lines put in if I was sick and I wanted the option of a year without a port. I just kept thinking, the next port I get I will probably die with, which didn't scare me, it just made me feel a sense of urgency to live. Maybe I would feel better if I didn't have one for a year. In hindsight it was insane thinking, but it made sense at the time.

There were two surgeons who would perform the operation together. We asked to see the one Mom had trained with years ago. He arrived, and I explained that I preferred the gas to put me asleep, rather than the needle. He said the needle was easier, although he knew it hurt. The thing was, I didn't mind the needle, but I knew he'd never find a vein for it. He asked me to pull my top down to show him my port area again and he asked why there were such large scars on it, what had happened with it? So I told him about the previous operations in Temple Street, and he said the scars he would leave would be nothing compared to these. I knew that – I had seen the results of his work on my friends and their scars were small and neat and it made me kind of jealous. But this port had caused me such problems,

I just welcomed the thought that soon it would be gone. He tried to convince me that he could just 'pop' a new one in on the other side after he had tidied up the scar tissue, that it would be no big deal. But I had made my decision.

When I got to surgery, they decided to try and get a line in a vein as well as give me the gas. Gassing was easy. A figure in a blue gown held my hand and from behind a mask was slipped over my face, covering it entirely. 'Take deep breaths and count backwards from three,' a voice said. After my third breath they flipped a switch and the gas filled up my lungs. At the fourth breath the sound got blurred and the team started to look like cartoon aliens, waving at me, then there was a white and warm feeling and then ... nothing.

When I woke up, my chest felt sore and when I tried to sit up it was heavy. My shoulder was hunched up and I had to force myself rotate it, to loosen it up. I felt completely elated that the port wasn't there, and slightly nervous too. It was like throwing your airbag out the window mid-journey.

The next day I prepared to get a picc line put in for IVs that I needed. In my mind it was no big deal, like any needle experience – it had never bothered me, needles were just a part of my life. But because this was new, I kept asking everyone I met to describe it to me, so there would be no surprises. I lay in radiography, waiting. They were reluctant to give me mild sedation and said they would place a sedation cream on the area instead. Being in adult hospital, things were different. I lay on the slip of a table in the room and someone to the left took my arm. There were two doctors, a nurse and a radiographer in the room. The doctor started feeling around my arm before introducing himself, so I said, 'Hi there!' I didn't care how busy he was, I needed to know he was good at his job. He said he was feeling around for the vein and then he moved to the right arm, before deciding the left was better. He injected local anaesthetic into the area and said I wouldn't feel much and to turn my head away. I hated when people said that. I preferred looking. It wasn't painful, just uncomfortable. He was effectively threading a catheter up through the vena cava from a hole in my arm. After the fourth go they got it and I wondered for the first time about my decision not to have a portacath. I would have to get this done every time I was in. But then, it was worth it to be free of that foreign device for a year.

During that stay in Vincent's, I walked into the kitchen one day and bumped into a woman whose daughter had CF. She told me her daughter's condition was not improving. As she ran the tap in the sink she said, 'I hope you fight when your time comes.' She told me how her daughter had been admitted to a single room, but never got to stay in it because she was immediately moved on to a ward where they knew nothing about CF. As she moved away from the sink, she said that whoever had authorised her daughter's removal to a ward was an idiot. They left her there on the bed, with her stuff unpacked, and didn't come back, so her daughter, being the independent girl she was, got off the bed and started to unpack her things. She was so weak that to do this she had to slide down to the floor and sit on the ground. That's where a member of the team found her, breathless. I listened to all this in silence, until the woman asked me to visit her daughter. I told her I couldn't, that there was a risk of cross-infection. She persisted and I gave in, against my better judgment.

I walked into the ward where the woman's daughter was sharing with five others. She was lying on her bed, unmoving, collapsed like a doll. My insides trembled as her mother started to list which organs were working and which were not. I repeated that this was not good for cross-infection, sorry, and kicked myself for my own stupidity as I left the room. I walked to the hall and jumped up in the air. I'm alive, I'm alive, I'm alive and I'm never doing that again. I was glad I had seen that, though. In a strange way, it kicked me in the ass and reminded me to fight harder. Sometimes I was lazy, I skipped things, ignored nebulisers, stayed in a friend's house on a whim with no medication, was disorganised. But after looking at that girl, I vowed I'd never do that again. Up until now, I had made these promises to myself regularly, then broken them because I had that invincibility delusion that I had held to so tightly. I just didn't think I would ever get that sick. But the girl lying in that bed had probably felt that way, too. The truth was staring me in the face: I couldn't afford to think I was different.

29.

In January 2007 I got an email from the author Sarah Webb. She was putting together a charity book, with the theme of motherhood. The royalties from the book would go towards the CF unit in Tallaght Hospital and she wanted me to be part of it. I could write a poem or a short story, whatever I wished. Kate Holmquist, Anne Enright and Cathy Kelly were already signed up to contribute.

I sat there and stared at my overdue Roman History essay. The life stories of the Gracchi and Sulla and Caesar were contained in that little cream book with red borders. In front of me was the email. At nineteen, I knew that angsty poetry probably wouldn't cut it for the book, but could I manage a short story? Would exploring my own experience of CF and my mom open a can of worms? We had a funny relationship. Sometimes it worked and sometimes we both annoyed each other. How much should I say? How would I say it? I knew I was being asked purely because I had CF and I wanted to give something that was relevant, but that didn't give away too much at the same time. I stopped and started, crumpling up many pages, but in the end I just went for honesty. When I read it now, I see

something where my perception wasn't fully developed,
something probably a bit unfair, but also true to my
experience at that time

'... One thing that tweaked incessantly at my brain
was [my mother's] inability to understand me. It
seems like typical teenage stuff, but there's a minor
twist. I have cystic fibrosis, a long-term chronic
illness, and sometimes when life goes too fast it can
get you down. I had a penchant for spending time in
my room when I was younger. Losing myself in
Emily Dickinson or even my own writing was
cathartic for me. I wasn't dwelling, I was dealing.

She called it 'navel gazing'. After countless clashes
and an extensive period of 'navel gazing', which to
me was an attempt at starting a first novel and not a
demonstration in morbid mulling, she took me to a
psychologist 'for a chat'.

In the psychologist's office the tension creeped out
like a detonated grenade. We left the place in silence.
Somewhere between there and my house I ended up
on a mucky road in the middle of nowhere watching
the sun bounce off the car bonnet as she drove off. It
was mostly my fault. There was a lone sheep in the
field across from where I stood and I watched it. I
imagined living in its field, eating grass all day. After
10 minutes, just as the tears were being snorted up
my nose, she came back. In silence the door swung
open, I glanced at the sheep and sat in like a folding-
down box, exact and rigid. I knew I was learning a
lesson, I just wasn't quite sure what it was. We drove
home and didn't speak for the next two days.
(Edited extract from *Mom's the Word* [2007],
published by New Island.)

A month later, in February, I got a call to say a friend of
mine, Olive, was dying in St Vincent's. She was the editor of
a magazine for people with CF and had won the Young

Scientist of the Year award when she was in secondary school. When I went to Lourdes at the age of fourteen and one of the drunken boys kept trying to kiss me, it was Olive who had taken me by the hand and walked me out of his way. The phone call to tell me she was dying came from someone I barely knew. I stood in the kitchen in my apartment, on my own. The space echoed around me and I felt so drained. Luckily, my flatmate Alex was home, studying in her room. We called over to another friend, a guy I had dated at the start of college, and asked him to drive me down to the hospital. Everything was a haze and I just went along with it. I was putting myself in a situation I definitely shouldn't be in, but in that moment, shock, grief and naiveté ruled.

I stood next to Olive's bed in the ICU, wearing a protective mask and gown, saying goodbye. I told her a ridiculous story about how I had made pancakes for Pancake Tuesday, and I think she smiled. She was so much stronger and together than I was. When I went home, I cut my hand while chopping carrots. A while later, someone called to tell me she had died. I walked out of my apartment, took off my socks and stood on the grass. I took in a deep breath of the cold February air and I held on to that feeling. Life, life, life.

In March, we had a reading week and during that week my theatre group reprised *The Importance of Being Earnest* for a young audience. The play was on the school curriculum that year, so the plan was to perform three shows a day for five days, to accommodate all the school kids who wanted to see it. That meant my study week was shot, but I was determined that I would throw full focus onto catching up afterwards. The play was easier for me this time: I could do three shows a day and eat all day to keep my energy up. God, college life was great.

I celebrated my twentieth birthday on March 22nd and resolved that for the next while I was going to forget about CF, theatre, improving hospital services and dying friends and focus solely on my exams. For the next few months things went according to plan and I worked steadily, but then in May, something happened that changed everything. My friend Michael and I sat down to watch the pre-general election leaders' debate between Fianna Fail's Bertie Ahern, then Taoiseach, and Fine Gael's Enda Kenny. Michael was having a relationship drama with some boy, so we decided to order pizza and bitch about politics instead. The pizza had not yet arrived when a question was put to the party leaders about cystic fibrosis. Both men skimmed over it; Bertie Ahern started talking about osteoporosis. OSTEO-FUCKING-POROSIS? The Taoiseach, the leader of our country, couldn't even *say* cystic fibrosis. Did he even know what it was? Did he know we existed? The message wasn't getting through, not on any level. I was livid.

I told Michael he had to leave, that I had to write something, he could take the pizza with him. 'Go, Orla Tinsley, go!' he giggled as he went out the door. I went into my room and sat in front of my laptop. Eventually, I started typing, and every word hurt.

> '... There is a constant fear of infection when we come through A&E. My latest jaunt there was over two days, where I was exposed to infection and left coughing on a plastic chair. At 3pm I got a drug line inserted, whilst awake, into my arm. I watched it all on the big screen in fascination, then returned to my plastic chair in the waiting room.
>
> I waited again before being transferred to the actual A&E bed area, where I waited on a larger plastic chair. I then spent the next 10 minutes waving furiously at a porter I recognised. Half an hour later he emerged with a trolley.
>
> He worked hard to get it. When I returned from the bathroom the pillow he also worked hard to get was gone. With a respiratory disease and gloopy, mucus-filled lungs, lying flat is not acceptable. Without a pillow my trolley was useless as I had to

sit up anyway.

This situation is unfathomable. People with CF are sick of hearing the statistics. We are sick repeating the same line: 'We have the highest instance of CF in the world with Third World facilities.' We are sick of hearing that money is coming, that somebody somewhere just has to sign something. We are sick of waiting and I am sick of watching my friends die while we wait ...' for full article, see Appendix 2]

I emailed the article to Róisín Ingle and she called me after fifteen minutes. She said 'Hi' and then was silent. 'What's wrong?' I asked her, thinking to myself, Oh God, was it awful? If it was awful, this would be really embarrassing.

She sniffed. 'It's amazing,' she said. Oh. She started laughing. 'Oh you thought I was quiet because . . . no, it's because it's so powerful.'

We sat in silence for a minute and then she mentioned one or two things that I should maybe look at again. In the meantime she'd call the sub-editor and see if he had space for it in the morning edition. I edited it and when she called back to say the sub-editor wanted it, I fired it in. It was going to be published on 22 May, the day before polling day.

The night before publication, my flatmate Alex and I sat up eating popcorn and I was anxious about the article, whether it was saying all it needed to say, but it felt right. When I woke up the next day there were numerous missed calls and text messages waiting for me. One of my good friends with CF called me and told me that her dad, who was a political journalist, said he had never experienced anything like the reaction to my piece. People were angry and the politicians were talking about it. People wanted the situation to change. I went into town because I had to meet the old fundraising team from Temple Street to discuss speaking at an event they were holding. I arrived at the

Shelbourne hotel in the taxi they had ordered for me and as I walked into the lobby, my mobile rang. It was Róisín, telling me that the *Daily Mail* wanted to republish my article in full the next day and would pay me whatever I wanted. *What?* I wasn't sure about working with a tabloid paper, but then, it would reach a broader demographic, right? Right. I knew it was the bigger picture that mattered and I gave my permission.

The meeting in the Shelbourne was interrupted by my phone's constant ringing. The Temple Street team hadn't seen the article, so I explained to them what was happening. We chatted about the forthcoming talk, the progress with the unit and what things were like in Vincent's. When we were finished and I was waiting for the taxi to take me home, my phone rang yet again. It was the CEO of the CF organisation and he was concerned. He advised that I should have spoken to him first and kept him in the loop. He said he was getting threatening emails from someone purporting to be affiliated with Fianna Fáil, who wanted the article retracted on the basis that Fianna Fáil had done more for CF patients than any other government to date. The CEO asked me to retract the article, for everybody's sake. I told him that would not happen. When I got home, I talked to the sub-editor as well and they agreed to print a letter from the CEO on the next day's letters page.

By the end of the day my ear was burning from taking phone calls and I sat in the hall of my apartment listening as a man from a film production company told me he wanted to do a documentary with me. He wanted to film me in my day-to-day life and promote the CF cause. I called Róisín for her advice and she offered to check if anyone knew of the man's company. After he left, I finally got to reply to the six missed calls from my mom. When I did, she told me that a man from an Irish publishing house had called and they wanted me to write a book. I walked into the kitchen and told this piece of news to my flatmates, who looked shell-shocked. '*What?* Dude, your life is insane. More things happened to you today than happen to people in an entire lifetime. A documentary, a book deal?'

This *is* all insane, I said to myself. I was finally happy in college and now here were all these other things I felt I should be doing. The publisher wanted me to write a book about my life with CF, but my life is so much more than CF. It was the old fear again: I didn't want to be known only for having CF and fighting the government. I walked back to the hallway – the only place where there was decent mobile reception. My head was spinning and I called Róisín yet again. She asked me to give her a few minutes so she could make some calls and when the phone rang again, it was her, telling me that her literary agent wanted to meet with me, could help me develop the idea first and then secure the best book deal. When I walked back into the kitchen we all have to just sit down and order Chinese food. I need to do something utterly normal because the world was so crazy, and takeout was a quick solution. I felt like the world was spinning around me and I didn't know which way to go with it. I could ignore the opportunities and stick with college, or I could take a chance and probably leave college to pursue this. Ideally, I'd like to do them all, but that sort of planning had never worked out well for me.

In the past month I'd been pulled three ways: exam commitments, CF commitments and theatre commitments. From 7th to 20th May the theater group had headlined at the International Gay Theatre Festival in Dublin with our performance of *The Importance of Being Earnest*, playing in Andrew's Lane Theatre. Going in and out to the theatre in the centre of the city daily was exhilarating, but tough physically. In the dressing rooms we marvelled at ourselves for playing the same characters for three years and the different ways they had changed and developed from when we first stepped into their shoes. Gwendolyn was now calmer and shrewder, but still maintained her fantastically overbearing campness when it was needed. Most of the other cast members were doing theatre and college, too, and it made me envious. I knew that, health-wise, it would be impossible for me to do this for long and that I was constantly playing catch-up in college. A friend with CF told me I shouldn't worry about college deadlines and just ask for extensions. The problem was that extensions made me lazy. Deadlines scared me and made me work. My father had taught me that there was nothing I couldn't talk my way out of and that people were essentially fair and understanding. I tried not to think of this when it came to college.

After the play, the exam study, the article and the reactions, I ended up in hospital again. This time I went in through A&E to the old faithful window bed in the six-bed room on St Paul's ward. The elderly patients still made unearthly noises at night, but I kept my iPod earphones in and focused on getting better. I didn't want to be numbed to this place, but really, nothing shocked me anymore. For CF patients, weekends meant some time outside the hospital, once you had not suffered hemoptysis during the week. Since Vincent's is a few miles out of town, a trip to the city centre was troublesome, so most weekends either Mom or Dad came up and took me to Dun Laoghaire for a walk on the pier. The air was crisp and pure when it fired up my nose and nestled down into my lungs. It was like diving into a swimming pool on a foreign holiday when you've had too much sun, my sun holiday destination being the slow-moving grogginess of Vincent's.

When I was living on campus, I didn't really go home at weekends. I didn't want to take breaks and miss something and my mother hated that I wasn't home more often. 'You are disorganised,' my parents frequently told me and I knew it was true, but that was just me and as long as I was getting my work done, it didn't matter. Sometimes it was hard because I really wanted to take a proper break, a holiday, but when I had free time I always wanted to write something or be somewhere or see someone. I spent so much time stuck in the damn hospital that I didn't want to waste time when I was released. So instead of going home for weekends when I was well, I stayed and tried to catch up on college work because I did not want to fail my exams.

Now that I was back in hospital, my parents had to travel to see me at weekends, but it had benefits for me and my mom. Our trips around Dun Laoghaire became a bonding experience, a chance for me to hear things about my mother's life before me that I'd never known. We would be driving along and my mother would randomly tell me a memory from her past. She had lived in Dun Laoghaire in her youth, as it happened, and I was shocked to hear of the mad, hippy motorbiking world she had once belonged to. This wasn't my mother – who was this woman? I loved it. She would point to a particular corner and suddenly say, 'That's where I fell off my hog', or another time she pointed out St Michael's and told me that was where she had edited the nursing newspaper. It was such a revelation. I always thought I got all my creativity from my dad. I loved learning more about my mom. Our favourite restaurant on those jaunts was GTI, where you could buy a bagel with cream cheese and smoked salmon or a veggie dish or a devilish Death by Chocolate. Their food was what I looked forward to most on weekend release.

After the article in the *Times* and all the interest it had generated, I was starting to get recognised by people on the street from time to time. Once, soon after I had been on the TV news, the owner of GTI gave us our food for free and then threw in some free T-shirts as well. Being recognised was a strange experience. People were generally very kind, but some people could be both extremely affectionate and intense. They felt they already knew me, which affected how they behaved with me. At times it was strange because I felt I had to be on best behaviour all the time, that I was 'on view' and had to always be doing the right thing as a result. And some people who actually knew me acted differently around me too, making a fuss over me because they didn't know how to react. They wouldn't have been my close friends, though, who still treated me as the messy, procrastinating layabout I am. At that time it felt episodical, that it would simply blow over after a while and I'd get back to normal anonymity, so I didn't think about it too much.

Of course, the book and the documentary might change all that. That's if they ever got finished and into the public domain. My literary agent had been calling to ask when the book would be done and I didn't want to talk about it. The truth was, I was stuck in limbo with it. At that point I had written just one chapter. I was surprised by my sense of fear in chronicling my life and closely examining my own behaviour and experiences. I didn't want extra attention; I just wanted better services. If I wrote the book, the focus would be on me – what would that mean for better services? It was the documentary I was most worried about though, because the suggestion was that a camera crew would follow me around college and in hospital, recording my everyday experiences over an extended period of time. They were hoping to turn it into a reality TV show over a year or even more. I knew my responsibility didn't lie in that, but I was still worried about missing an important opportunity, so I agreed to meet with the production team to discuss it.

In the end, the documentary turned out not to be what I was looking for. I didn't think I would have a problem doing nebulisers or physio on camera, but for some reason I did. And I wanted to keep the focus firmly on better services, not on me as a subject. The focus had to be the services that were needed, not me and my life. I wasn't the subject.

I turned down the documentary-makers and tried once more to focus on writing the book. I moved into Glenomena residences in UCD for the summer, determined to try to get some work done, but was crippled with uncertainty. I was uncertain whether I could write a book and at the same time catch up with college work and then start afresh next year. I was feeling like I was always behind and it was driving me mad. I felt I was missing out on some things and willingly didn't go to every college event because I felt I had a responsibility to get everything done. All of these responsibilities were starting to weigh me down.

30.

That summer in Glenomena I was kept sane by my flatmates: a girl called Zoe and a Brazilian man called Marco whom we loved because he was gentle and kind and saved us from spiders by gently putting them out the window. I am not scared of many things, but spiders have gotten me since I was three and sitting in my childminder's with the older kids watching *Arachnaphobia*. Zoe and I spent our time writing in our rooms and going to the movies and chatting about family and boys. She had her eye on a French boy in the on-campus, which meant we made routine trips for 'necessary provisions'. None of this was getting the book done, of course, but it was a welcome bit of fun.

On my last stay in Vincent's there had been a boy in one of the cubicles who I used to chat to online or sometimes outside his cubicle as I was zipping by. He had CF too, so there was a risk of cross-infection. We made silly jokes about how, after his lung transplant, he would be rifling through a bookstore in Paris and would hear my voice reading an extract from my latest best-selling novel. Sometimes when I walked by his door I would do the move from the Bangles' song, 'Walk Like An Egyptian', just to make him laugh. When I was checking out, I waved a goodbye to him – he wasn't going to be leaving anytime soon. He was on my mind in the weeks that followed, and I remembered him saying that his favourite books were the *Ross O'Carroll-Kelly* series. Ross is the creation of Paul Howard, who is a good friend of Róisín's, so I decided to ask her if she thought there'd be any chance of Paul agreeing to visit my friend in the hospital – I knew he would be bowled over by it. Róisín asked Paul and he said he would go, but only if I went with him.

We met at the door of the hospital and introduced ourselves. Paul told me he hasn't been there since his mom died, and I thanked him so much for coming. I told him I had known all his books off by heart when I was in sixth year, but then I couldn't actually remember any quotes, only random words, and stood there feeling like a faux fan. I walked him up to my friend's ward, where he was still waiting for his transplant. It was to be a surprise – I hadn't told him his favourite author was coming to see him. When we opened the door and walked in, he recognised Paul immediately and was gobsmacked. I told them I'd wait outside and as I sat on the corridor, I could hear animated chatting and laughter coming from the room. They were both rugby lovers, so they hit it off well.

The physios arrived then, so Paul came out and joined me outside the room. He asked if my friend would be back playing sports soon and I told him that my friends has CF and needs a lung transplant or he will die and that donor availability was difficult as people with CF are so small. Lungs are different sizes, so my friend was really waiting for a kid to die to get the right lungs. It's down to blood type, size, luck and mentality. You have to be well enough to survive the operation, but sick enough to need it. Paul looked like he'd been punched in the face and was quiet. I apologised to him for being so blunt. When the physios were finished, Paul went back into the room and chatted to my friend some more. Afterwards he drove me home and we had a great talk about the writing process and the madness of writing highs – those incredible moments when you finish something creative that you are proud of. It was nice to hear someone talk about it the same way I did. He said he would like to visit my friend again and later in the week he texted me to say he had just put the finished manuscript of his new book into the car and was going to give it to my friend as a gift. That would make him the first person in Ireland to know what happened next to his fictional hero. Paul asked me to arrange a mid-week visit. I really appreciated him doing that because I knew how much it meant to my friend.

The next morning I woke up and there was a text on my phone to say my friend was not well and to pray for him. Shit shit shit. I texted his sister back, but she didn't reply. The next day I called the hospital and tried to get some information. I was told that he had passed away; I texted Paul to let him know. I was sick to my core and I decided I would no longer do this, I would no longer get personally involved with people with CF. I had no idea if I could stick to the plan, but I had to try for my own self-preservation.

A week later my parents were on holidays in Portugal, but they said they would come home to attend the funeral with me. I told them not to worry, that I wasn't planning to go to it. Then Paul rang to tell me that he planned to go. He was new to people with CF dying and I realised how jaded I was. I agreed to go with him. He drove us to Tipperary for the funeral. The turn-out was huge and we couldn't get further than the back of the church, where we stood. It felt strange to be there because I didn't feel I knew my friend well enough to be at his funeral, but I suppose really I was just afraid of facing up to another funeral, another death.

I returned from Tipperary and back to Glenomena with a new sense of purpose. After that whole experience I knew I had to put aside my ego and write the book. I knew I had to stop caring about what other people would or might say and just write. But it was still extremely difficult. All I wanted to do was to write fiction, so this opportunity was strange to me. I knew that if I could just get past my own feelings about it, the book could do a lot of good, but I didn't know how honest I could be, as in whether I had the maturity for it. I had to do it properly, so making a lengthy inventory of myself would be the only way and it could be awfully depressing. But I was the only one standing in my way. Paul and Róisín had both suggested that I write in segments – recording scenes, memories, episodes any time I thought of them. Then later I could sit down and piece them all together to form a coherent whole. So that's what I started to do – I started to remember and I started to write.

31.

In July I went back into hospital again, with a chest infection, and I was placed in a six-bed ward. My mother was visiting me when a woman in the ward started vomiting and we immediately left for the pier in Dun Laoghaire. When we returned later that evening, some of the other women in the room were throwing up. So the 'reflux' they told me the first woman had was actually the vomiting bug, as I'd suspected. I started to pack my things, telling the staff that I wouldn't stay there, in that room. The evening staff said they could do nothing for me, so Mom and I sat in the coffee shop until she had to go, and then I waited for the night staff. When they arrived I explained to one of the nurses, who knew a lot about CF, about the vomiting and she said she would mention it to the night matron.

As we were standing there talking about it, the night matron herself came by and she told me there was nothing she could do about it, that I would have to stay in the room with the vomiting women. She could not move me because the only places to move me to were A&E or to a bed in the coronary care unit. I told her I would sleep in the corridor. She said she could not allow me to do that. I told her I had slept in the corridor in this hospital many times; she looked shocked. Did she really not know that so many CF patients ended up sleeping in chairs because of the gut-wrenching madness unfolding in their rooms? She said the only other option was to wheel my bed into the day room. I said, 'That's perfect, let's do that.' She looked at me, alarmed, and said the nurse would have to consent to it; she did. An hour later I had packed my stuff and my bed was being wheeled into the TV room. I lay awake, watching the lift doors open and close through the glass doors. This was probably not very physically safe, but the nurse would be checking on me from time to time and at least I had a bed instead of a chair.

When I woke up the next morning a CF nurse walked by and stuck her head in. 'You're a lunatic! Are you ok?' A minute later, the ward sister arrived. She said she understood, but she was angry. She told me that the vomiting problem was throughout the hospital. I said it wasn't in my room until yesterday. She said it hadn't been 'confirmed' yet, but that always annoys me because it's quite obvious what it is. She tried her best to get me back into the ward, but I refused. She said, 'Please, Orla, because the other CF patients will think you are getting special treatment.' I told her that they had a choice, too, they didn't have to sit in there. She said the only place she could put me was in the CF sitting room until the team came around because they needed the TV room and did I realise she would now have to get it cleaned and then the CF sitting room cleaned after me?

Yes, I realised.

She said I couldn't move into another room in case I had contracted the vomiting bug when I was in the last one, in which case I might spread it; it can be inactive in your body for up to forty-eight hours. When the doctor came to see me in the sitting room, he laughed at me jovially and called me a troublemaker with a capital T.

That evening they moved me into a quieter, three-bed

room on the ward, in accordance with infection control, and the only other woman in my six-bed room who hadn't been vomiting was moved in too. She was the noisiest of the lot and now there was less space between us. I had won and lost, but it felt like a success.

I passed my first-year exams and got out of the hospital and enjoyed the rest of the summer. Then autumn came round again and with it the beginning of second year in UCD. I started out well, but then things began to get tricky. It became more and more difficult to get up in the morning: my eyes were sticky and I usually had a headache. I didn't want to call Vincent's and end up missing out on the beginning of college, so I let it go for a while.

One morning at 9am, about a week after college had started, Sarah knocked on my apartment window and kept knocking until I got up. I had missed a week of lectures and when she came into my room, she asked what was wrong. I told her I had no idea why I was so tired all the time, that my cough wasn't any worse. She urged me to call the hospital, so I did and went in for an appointment. It turned out to be the diabetes progressing, and they took me in to sort me out.

I now needed long-acting insulin to regulate my sugar levels, which meant I had to monitor them more closely and take insulin every time I ate and at nighttime. I also had my fifth infection of the year, and my picc lines were getting tougher to insert. I knew I had to get a portacath refitted, but I really didn't want to. I talked it through with the surgeon, the same kind man who had taken out the other port, and he understood my concerns about scarring and the possibility of a faulty port being fitted, necessitating further surgery. In order to calm my fears, he did a full work-up and took a deep x-ray of my veins. My request that I get the port in my arm was not an option. I liked that the left side of my chest was still smooth, untouched, unscarred skin – but I knew I had to give it up. I agreed to the surgery.

When I woke up afterwards, I was anxious to see the

scar. I didn't really mind so much about it – my absolute primary concern was that the port worked properly and stayed put and I could go back to doing home IVs. Mom was there, waiting for me to come round, and I was so glad to see her. She said Fionan and Sarah were there, too, but they had just gone out for a sandwich. 'All Fionan had this morning for breakfast was left-over lasagne!' she laughed. From then on every time she talked about the boys she said, 'Fionan eats leftover lasagne for breakfast! They're such cool cats!' and the thing is that they are, and I love them and she's happy because I'm happy.

After this port surgery I had a physiotherapist who I'd never had before post-surgery. She was big into exercise and pushing me to do my daily quota, and I was really tense about the port and needed a way to manage that stress, so I decided to give it a shot. I had tried some workouts with my first-year room-mate, Frankie, but I never knew if I was exercising the right way for me. I knew that if I didn't do it properly I was at risk of desaturating (dropping oxygen levels), so I couldn't afford to do it wrong or to overdo it. Working with the physio and her enthusiasm for exercise was the first time I realised that I could start thinking about my body in a positive way, without becoming obsessive or focusing on body image. I had grown up and now it was time to test myself and my self-control, but it still made me nervous. I could feel the pull of the past and the strange way of thinking I had fallen into before and it made me uneasy. What if I became addicted to exercise? What if my body became an unhealthy focus rather than a healthy activity? I was scared, but I had to trust myself and try it.

Initially, the treadmill made me breathless and I immediately tensed up. 'Am I okay? Are my sats okay?' The physio assured me that everything was fine. After cardio there were core exercises. Now I was forgetting about my worries, forgetting about everything outside this room. Where had this stuff been all my life? It felt positive and challenging and it was good for me – exercise could help maintain FEV1 lung function[2]. Each day I learned something new and trusted myself more. Finally, the day arrived for the stitches to be removed and when I saw the scar, I laughed – it was tiny.

Why hadn't I listened to my physios and my dad years ago and stuck with exercise? Maybe it was just the teenage rebellion thing and the fact that I thought I knew everything. It was the eating problem thing, too, of course. I'd been afraid I wouldn't be able to control it if I started caring about exercising. But now I wasn't looking at celebrity magazines and torturing myself with ideas of the 'body perfect', I was learning instead that exercise is about building muscle and maintaining health. I was armed with the knowledge that I had a type of addictive personality, which I think was either a natural part of my make-up or else my way of coping with things. As the whole body image, food and portacath trinity had stunted my life before, I was afraid it would happen again. I didn't fully believe in my own power to stop it and control it, which seems mad now, but that was just how I felt then. I countered this by being as aware as possible going into it, but as the physio and the exercise started to work their magic, I began to let go of the old fears and just enjoy the new feeling of strength and vitality it was giving me.

I got a bike for Christmas and started cycling the fifteen-minute journey to my lectures each day. Exercise was doing something to me, it was straightening me out and making me confident, and so was college. It was so much easier to just be me. I finally felt like I had returned from the Land of Oz. Exercise had woken me up.

32.

It was Christmas 2007 and I was sitting in Fire restaurant, next to the Mansion House, talking nineteen to the dozen with my fellow bookclub members. I had joined the club in the summer. It had about ten members, on and off, all working in media and including my good friends Paul Howard and Róisín Ingle. Our Christmas get-together was a combination of food and talking, as we trawled over the various news stories of the day. In particular, we talked about the recent death of Katy French, a twenty-four-year-old Irish model who had died from a suspected cocaine overdose.

I had never heard of Katy French until a few weeks previously, when I had seen her image splashed across the front of the tabloids in my local shop. There was some debate over how she had died and the group was discussing her life and death. I said I felt sorry for her and her family, but that I was angry at the media: over thirty people had died from CF in Ireland in 2007 and they were giving acres of column inches and air-time to someone who possibly took drugs and died as a result. 'We take drugs to live,' I said and I knew I was losing my cool, but I couldn't stop talking. I knew I had to write about it. In January 2008 *The Irish Times* published an article I wrote about CF in Ireland that referenced the coverage of Katy French's death:

> '... At the end of November another girl I knew called Tracie died aged 24 from the disease. Her death got one column 'Tracie feared if care would kill her' in a newspaper.
>
> That was the weekend after the death of socialite Katy French. In any situation it is devastating to lose someone so young but I found myself not talking about Katy like everyone else, because secretly I felt guilty at the anger raging inside me. Of course it is tragic that she died at 24, but to watch it reported and debated so exhaustively wore me down, so much that I felt like arguing about the girl who has been called 'intelligent and caring'. I never knew her but I was envious of her, or rather the coverage she got after her death.
>
> It made me feel for Tracie, who played music with Phil Coulter in New York, and her family, when she died from an illness she couldn't control. I also thought about my dear friend, sports enthusiast and all round charmer Damien who passed away last year and for my magazine editor, scientist and encyclopedia of knowledge-friend Jean, who passed away last March. I only got to two funerals, and that's just 2007 and just the people I knew of.
>
> Progress has been made on the issue, meetings are being held, talks are ongoing, but we don't need to hear about meetings and conversations. We need a public commitment, a promise that we will have our dedicated unit, and we need it now. As the public mourned Katy French and the lens on cocaine in Ireland started to get focused, I thought wildly that maybe if I got engaged and broke up with a slightly well-known person, did some lingerie modelling and

then died, if I fought off my illness long enough, maybe something would be done. Maybe the Taoiseach's aide-de-camp would come to a Cystic Fibrosis funeral and see something he would remember, something that he might report back. He might see friends and family congregate, he might hear Leonard Cohen's 'Hallelujah' or Tina Turner's 'Proud Mary', funeral songs chosen sometimes years before the funeral took place.

He might see some lucky transplant recipients hovering outside the church waving and mouthing words from a distance to their still suffering friends, that they can't mix with anymore for medical reasons.

And we don't like that word suffering in the cystic fibrosis world, but we are suffering. Watching three of my friends die last year and going on to their tribute pages on Bebo hurts, out of sadness for the event and a personal fear of the unpredictability of life. Each of these people had just as much life as Katy French, and they were making their way through science, through selecting hurling teams, through study. Privately and steadily they mapped their future in a country that seemed to deem them insignificant. It makes me feel like I need to give up college and get out there and smile for every photo, tirelessly self-promote because physically I cannot do both college and public relations, but maybe if I did then people would notice the tragic ignorance of our Celtic Tiger. A television programme did a segment that linked Katy French to other celebrities who died young like Marilyn Monroe and James Dean. It made my younger cousin tell me all about the model she never knew until she died and how her classmates are now infatuated.

Maybe it is better for her to be infatuated with the glamorised death of a model than with the gritty realism that people like her cousin are dying, because that is what we are teaching our young people today – get famous and you will be remembered, if you are famous your death will matter ...'

Once the article was out there, my phone started ringing, but people were unsure how to react. Some said I was right, others thought I was too harsh. I said to myself – if they had seen what I have seen in relation to CF, they would have done the same. Sometimes it is necessary to push harder.

I was walking back from buying milk in a shop on Roebuck Road when my phone rang yet again. This time, it was a researcher from a popular radio show. She asked me if I was Orla Tinsley, then told me she was doing a piece on the show on the response to my article about Katy French and particularly my reference to lingerie modelling. 'Her parents are justifiably upset enough about the recent death of their daughter without you rubbing it in.' I told her that it hadn't been my intention to offend anyone, that my sole concern was CF. Then I realised that it might be best to say nothing, so I said I would call her back and rang off. I headed to Vincent's for my appointment, all the while hoping that I hadn't gone too far and damaged anything to do with what people were now referring to as 'the CF cause'.

When I arrived into the nurses' office, they were listening to a man with CF talking on Liveline (RTÉ Radio 1) about his sister, who had died from CF and to whom I had referred in the same article, in the context of her being failed by the services. He was so driven and articulate and it made for compelling radio. While I was waiting to get my bloods taken, my phone recorded four missed calls from Liveline. I knew they would like me to talk about this, but as we were listening, the direction of the programme changed. Instead of my article and the fallout from it, they began examining the real issues of CF and the human experience behind all the words. It was a relief for me to hear the shift away from the article to the reality I was getting at all along.

For the rest of the week Liveline dedicated time every day to talking about CF. People from all over the country called in to tell their stories. So many voices and experiences were coming together – it was very emotional, both upsetting and uplifting. I deliberately stayed off Liveline throughout this time so that listeners were hearing new voices, fresh angles on CF. I was glad not to be 'the voice of CF' and to let everyone have their turn to describe their own experiences and build up a comprehensive picture of the illness that no one should ignore.

Four days later, I agreed to participate in a radio discussion with Dr Ronnie Pollock on NewsTalk FM. Dr Pollock was the author of the Pollock Report and I wanted to hear what he had to say. I had also been waiting for a bed for a week and was feeling a bit desperate and out of control, and I knew this was exactly the sort of problem that had to be highlighted again and again until our calls were heeded by the government. Straight after the NewsTalk programme aired, I got a call from Liveline and I agreed to go on at 1.45pm. An hour after Liveline, the CF fundraiser asked me to appear on the Nine O'Clock News on RTÉ that evening. I was exhausted, but agreed to do it if there was no one else available. A half an hour after that, I got a call from RTÉ to ask me to appear on *Prime Time* that night – live. I explained that I was in my parents' house in Kildare, waiting for a bed in Vincent's, so I could only do it if the team came to me. I had to contact the fundraiser again because I couldn't do the news and Prime Time, and he fretted about who could take my place, so I found someone for him. Then I gently broke it to my mom that the *Prime Time* team was coming to film me. 'With cameras? When? *Now*? LIVE?' She ran for the mop and bucket. Our house was really clean, but she is Mom.

We decided that the big sitting room was the best location for the interview and she started cleaning it. I couldn't focus on helping her because I was trying to formulate the points I wanted to make. When the camera crew arrived, they quickly discovered that the lighting in the big sitting room wasn't going to work for them, so they moved the whole show into the kitchen. Mortified, my mother hid the ironing board and we all pitched in to tidy up. The piece was a live link-up to the studio in Dublin, where Miriam O'Callaghan and a HSE spokesperson were waiting to discuss CF services. I couldn't see them, but I could hear them through my earpiece. It was the single most nerve-wracking experience of my life.

Three hours after speaking on *Prime Time*, I was sitting on my bed in St Michael's ward. I was alive with false energy from the adrenalin pumping through my system. It seemed surreal to be in that place, to be assaulted by the faded pong of faeces and disinfectant after such a defining moment in the campaign. Campaign, now there was a buzzword. It made me nervous if I thought about it, so I just didn't. Another buzzword was 'activist', which was how Pat Kenny described me on the *Late Late Show* a week later when he interviewed my mother and other people affected by CF. Except I wasn't an activist or a 'national heroine' or a 'brave girl'. I was just me, being me. I was just doing it and at the same time trying to detach myself from all the things that spun around it – the names, the praise, the letters and phone calls and emails.

Over the following week, the things I heard said about me astounded and entertained me. Some, like the letter from a six-year-old girl with CF, were heart-warming. Her writing was big and wobbly and you could see the effort it had taken her to keep within the lines. She probably used her thumb to count the spaces between the words on her orange paper with purple butterflies. She told me, 'Thanks for your hard work'. These types of letters kept me positive. The others, like the one from the boy who told me that we were around the same age, that he admired me and that I was good-looking, kept me laughing. Others, like the poetry about deadly lungs being ripped from chests of poison, made me feel ill. Each letter wanted to help; everyone wanted to reach out. Finally, after three years of talking and talking, people were talking back. Not just a handful, but hundreds, thousands. I felt like the weight was shared out now, but I also felt overwhelmed by the attention.

By my third day in hospital I was getting up to fifteen calls a day to my mobile and people were regularly calling the CF wards, asking if they could visit me. One woman succeeded in finding my room and arrived in, unannounced, behind my drawn curtain. I was half-asleep and when I opened my eyes, I mistook her for Patsey Murphy, the magazine editor from *The Irish Times*. In my exhausted confusion I started chatting with her. When I realised it was a case of mistaken identity, I asked her who she was. She explained that she had shared a room with me once, years ago. I remembered her; we didn't know each other at all. Now she was standing there asking me if the girl who used to visit me – Sarah – was still my friend? Did I have a boyfriend yet? How were my parents? My skin crawled. Who was this woman? I didn't know her and she didn't know me. After a while more, I asked her to leave, saying I was exhausted. I should have said it in the beginning, but I felt like I owed something to people. I owed them time and words. If they supported me, then I had to give back. And I liked talking to people and finding out about them. But it was like a landslide had been triggered and an avalanche of helpers and supporters had fallen down on top of me.

Some aspects of it were amazing. The sense of hope that came from all of these people collectively wanting change in the Irish system was incredible. I didn't see how such support and honest passion for change could be ignored by the HSE and by the government. But other aspects were less so, like the poem that was posted to the hospital in which a woman fantasised about how I would die a terrible death and how she would dedicate her life to saving me. I also found it hard to know how to react to the dripping sympathy from strangers, the empathy and pain in their faces when they looked at me. Then there was the article in the UCD newspaper suggesting that the government needed to act fast lest the disease kill me before they did. My classmates were reading it, my lecturers and tutors, and I felt uncomfortable in the glare of the attention. My head felt so cluttered with the sheer weight of it all that I was beginning to disconnect.

I knew I could handle all of this, but it was hard to wind down. I needed space and privacy to get better, so that I could keep going. My CF nurse sat with me one morning after reading the piece in the *University Observer*. 'You don't believe what they're saying, do you?'

I paused a moment. 'Of course not.'

'They're just writing what they think they know.'

I knew that too, but it still made me uncomfortable that someone my age, in my university, would type the words: 'act now before we lose another great woman'. I knew they were trying to understand something they couldn't really fathom, but it made me feel sick, seeing those words in black and white. I wasn't going to lose and I wasn't going to be a victim. I hated that someone would think that about me or put me in that position in such a public way. Which is mad, of course, when you think about it, given the topic and the circumstances I'd been writing about all this time, but it was a strange feeling. I guess that's when it started to dawn on me that I couldn't control the perception of me that was out there. I could put stuff out in the hopes that it did good, but then it was gone and at the mercy of the masses. I hadn't really realised that until then. I had thought I had some control over it. I didn't.

Then there was the HSE and its promise to deliver the CF unit by the end of 2010. Could we believe it? And then there were the calls from mothers of children with CF, who had somehow got hold of my number. Some left messages of thanks on the voicemail, others left medical questions and there was one message that timed out the voicemail as a woman talked about the fears she had for her daughter. I think these women wanted comfort from me and knowledge, which I didn't have, on how to navigate their children through childhood and adolescence with CF. Many other people left fundraising ideas. I wanted to respond to them all, but I couldn't. It was physically beyond me to deal with the huge torrent of information, goodwill and generosity sent my way.

I sent out a mass text: 'I'm in hospital, please don't call in unless I reply to your text. Otherwise, I will get back to you when I'm well enough.' I put the message on my Facebook page and my Bebo page and told my mom to tell the now frequent callers to her house the same thing. She was being inundated with well-intended unannounced visitors – an old teacher, the neighbour up the road who never called, friends she hadn't seen in some time – all offering support. Mom was trying to support me and deal with a stream of visitors, while also warding off media calls from random journalists.

Then there were the people within the CFAI who were trying to overthrow the then CEO. They were calling me with their ideas; he was calling me to look for my support. An emergency meeting of the CFAI regional groups was convened and people yelled, argued and walked out. People had lost faith in the Association, and so had I. Then I got a call from an old acquaintance who told me that I should vouch for the CEO, that he was doing all the work behind the scenes. He said it was the CEO who was doing all of this campaigning, not me, and that I was going to ruin the good work the CEO was doing behind the scenes.

'Remember when you thought you were going to save us all with that newspaper article back in the day? It doesn't work like that. It's politics.'

He was ignorant of the fact that I knew that only too well. It was hard to listen to, but I let him talk on. He was the perfect example of how not to play the situation. There was no black and white, no one was good or bad – there was just the reality: what do we need to keep us alive and how do we get it? That was it. It was like running through a shootout in a bullet-proof body suit – I had to just imagine the negativity bouncing off me.

Five days into IV treatment at the hospital and it all got too much for me. I wanted to jump off a cliff. 'Can't you switch off in here?' my consultant asked. In truth, the room wasn't so bad and the nurses were consistently great on St Michael's Ward. I rarely had any trouble or bother with them. One nurse, in particular, had a brilliant habit of going through all the expiry dates on my drugs and sodium chloride bags before they dripped into me, showing me visibly that they were in date. She also wore gloves administering the drugs. Three years in Vincent's and it seemed so absurd and obsessive to have someone do that – though it should have been the norm. It was exactly what my childhood nurses would do back when it was protocol in Temple Street. It was what my mom did when she gave me IVs at home. It is what nurses do in other countries. I really respected it.

But by now I was exhausted, both mentally and physically. I would sit in the day room for some peace, staring at pictures of gorillas in *National Geographic* back editions and day-dreaming about being back in Italy with my theatre group. I missed the freedom of the stage. Here in the hospital, I was stuck in a loop. The elderly women in my room still kept me up all night with their noises – not their fault at all, but I simply couldn't get the sleep I needed there. I complained, and the noisiest woman was moved out. But this really got to me – I knew that because of my writing and profile, they were catering to me, but it was a band-aid solution that didn't really help me – or her. As if caring about my situation once was going to help anybody. Helping out of fear was not conducive to long-term results.

The only real break in my day was the half hour in the evening that I spent in the physio room. Since I had started my exercise regime the October before, I had been attending the gym about three times a week, all through the first semester of college. Regular exercise was making me feel positive and responsible and once I hid the Jaffa cakes and got up off the couch, I enjoyed it. The treadmill in the hospital seemed like an antidote to the chaos surrounding me. I had built up a good base since October and was now lifting 1kg weights. At first I'd been afraid of developing *Popeye* muscles, but the physio had assured me this wouldn't be the case. I'd taken note of the posters on the dressing-room walls of the UCD gym that supported this contention: weights were good for women because they helped prevent osteoporosis, helped burn fat and built muscle and helped prevent diseases, such as diabetes. I had osteophenia, I had diabetes, and I wanted muscle, but not at the expense of much-needed, infection-fighting fat.

Fat. That was a word that still had the power to make me uncomfortable. In my head I didn't want to lose weight or fat, I just wanted to tone up. I didn't want to bulk up, but I wanted to be able to carry my groceries from Tesco to the bus stop without having to hurry or stop for a break. I was a twenty-year-old college girl and I was only now discovering that I could help myself. I could support my body, but I still feared my past behaviour would get the better of me. So from October to January I'd taken it slowly, but now I walked faster and faster. I had too much energy and my physio told me to use this time to reflect, to focus on something other than the CF campaign. But as my speed increased, so too did my sense of serenity. My calves ached every day and I alternated upper body weight-lifting one day with squats and lunges the next. Gradually, my body started to respond.

The gym became the focal-point of the day and helped me to relax – and to move the sputum more effectively from my chest. One day I asked if I could try running, just to give it a shot. I had watched the joggers in UCD as they ran along the green outside Roebuck Hall between 5.00 and 8.00 in the evening. I admired their dedication and it made me wonder if running could help me out. My physio was a runner herself and talked about it a lot. Maybe if I moved faster, I would feel even better. During one session on the treadmill it was agreed that I could try running for one minute and see how I went. If my sats weren't okay, I would have to stop. The machine was connected to me by a little probe on my finger that measured my oxygen levels; 97 was normal for me, and pretty good in general. My first minute running was so exciting and full of pain that I almost forgot to breathe. My body felt like concrete and I panted hard. My oxygen levels were fine: I was just panting because my body wasn't used to it. I ran for one-minute intervals for several days.

Running wasn't that simple, though, it turned out there was a lot involved. Posture was a big problem for me – it could have been the osteophenia, or the propensity for people with CF to slouch when they cough to protect their chest, or it could just have been a hangover from my teenage habit of slouching around. Whatever it was, I didn't stand correctly and it affected my running posture. The physio made me stand with feet apart and 'rock' into a neutral pose, where I was standing without slouching or arching my back. It was hard to stay in that position for very long, so I had to practice. Neutral was natural, but natural for me, like so many others, was ass out, stomach in, shoulders back, peacock model style. It was wrong and was damaging my back. For me, it was even cosier to stay in that wrong position because my body was used to maintaining a certain shape from a combination of poor core strength from excessive coughing and osteophenia. Now I made myself stay in neutral when I lifted weights, when I ran, when I walked and gradually I began to feel taller and healthier and the demands and stresses swirling around me seemed smaller and more manageable.

33.

When I finally left hospital that February 2008, after a two-week stay, I went back to college for a week and then took a holiday. It was a bit mischievous, but Róisín was taking a break to celebrate wrapping up her newspaper column, so two of her friends and I went along with her. They flew to Inchydoney Island, in County Cork, while I took the train. I had misplaced my passport that had been on my dresser two days before and I didn't find out until later than you don't, in fact, need a passport to travel by plane within the country. I stepped off the train in Cork City and hailed a taxi. Despite the jovial jabber from the taxi man, a native Corkonian, I managed to take in some of the scenery as he delivered an animated explanation as to why Clonakilty black pudding was something I had to try while I was there.

As we left the city behind, the concrete and greyness faded, replaced by the luscious greenery of the West Cork countryside. It enveloped me in its beauty. Apart from a house here or a barn there, it was untouched landscape and the drive through the mountains to the spa was magical. I was no longer in the Ireland I knew. I was somewhere new.

Despite the fact that my friends had flown down, I was

the first to arrive. Sitting around waiting in the lounge
wasn't really my style, so I went for a mini-adventure
around the grounds. Directly outside the hotel door were
steps leading down to a private beach. The air was cold, but
already my blocked sinuses were starting to clear. I climbed
over bumpy stones to reach the sand and threw off my socks
and shoes to feel the sand between my toes. I stood there,
took a deep breath and listened. '*I hear lake water lapping,*
with low sounds by the shore.' Yeats was playing in my
mind. I held my arms out and let the breeze whoosh over
me. The sea and the salty smell cleared my airways and I felt
at peace. I listened and heard nothing but the mild breeze
and the lapping water. After some minutes the sound of
gravel scraping interrupted my thoughts and I climbed back
up the rocks to greet the girls.

At Inchydoney I felt like I was letting fresh air into my
lungs for the very first time. Gradually, things began to
move and cogs and wheels that had long hidden themselves
started working again. I had been weighed down, mentally
and emotionally, due to the chaotic busyness of my life, but
now it felt like that burden was lifting. In Inchydoney, I felt
free. The sea air cleared my mind as well as my chest.

One evening when we were walking back to our rooms
after a lengthy chat I turned to Róisín and said I needed to
tell her something. 'I think I might be gay.' She laughed.
'Why are you laughing?!' She replied 'I just knew you were
going to say that!'. The next day at dinner we left the spa
for a restaurant in town. We were sitting at dinner talking
about our respective days. We were talking about our
masseuses for the day. I said mine was good lookin'. One
of the girls looked at me and then Róisín just said, 'She
thinks she's gay.' My jaw dropped in horror. 'So is my sister,'
said one of the girls. And then that was it, we chatted about
gayness and coming out stories for the rest of the night.
Finally I was having proper dialogue on a subject that for so
long had been kept internal. Now there were words and

descriptions and other's experiences. I didn't want the weekend to end.

On the third day the hotel organised horse-riding for me – something I hadn't done in over ten years. The girls wished me luck and off I went to the stables with Cork's purveyor of Clonakilty pudding as my chauffeur. When we got there I explained to the owner that I hadn't been on a horse in ten years, but that I used to be quite good, had actually won a few competitions and was a bone fide member of The Pony Club. He put me on a 'safe but challenging fellow' for our cross-country trek, but brought me into the arena first to check my style. The feel of the reins in my hands felt familiar, my feet in the stirrups felt natural, but style was something I didn't have anymore. I flipped up the saddle flap and tightened the girth before adjusting my stirrups. The smell of leather, the dust of the arena and me – wonderful. Heels down, sit tight, shoulders back … I was ready. I walked around and felt the horse's shoulders slump underneath me. Slump, slump, slump from side to side. Boring. So we tried a trot. I was good at trotting, but better at cantering, I knew that. Off I went, up and down, but soon I could barely breathe. Breathing? When did breathing come into this? I focussed on breathing correctly, but the up and down was still tough. What had happened to my core muscles and my leg muscles and my body? What sort of shell had I been living in? I was so breathless, I wasn't sure I could actually do this.

'CANTER!' the instructor yelled.

I squeezed my heels and sat tight and the horse started to canter, but fell into a trot within seconds.

'SQUEEZE *HARDER*!'

I was squeezing as hard as I could. Finally, I got him and off we went around the arena twice. And then I just wanted to do it again. You'll be grand, just relax, I told myself.

A half an hour into our hour-long trek, after navigating hills and calming the horses when the passing trucks rattled the country roads, we found ourselves at the beach right outside my hotel. Were we ready for a gallop? It was me, the instructor and two teenage girls from England. I really couldn't fall in front of these kids. Plus I had been diagnosed with osteoporosis by this stage, which meant falling was definitely not an option. What the hell was I doing on this horse?

We hit the beach and they were off; my 'challenging fellow' and I were just along for the ride. After the first minute, when I felt like these might be my last few seconds on Earth, I suddenly got the rhythm. The sand flew up behind us, the waves crashed against the hooves as we rode along the edge of the sea. My horse and I started to move together, and it was glorious. At the end of the bay the horses turned and moved faster towards home. My arms jerked in rhythm, nearly threatening to pop out of their sockets. This was what it meant to be alive.

When I arrived back to the girls in the Presidential Turret, they were lounging and chatting. I stank of sweat and horse.

'Well?'

'It was beautiful.'

'Did you go along the beach by any chance?'

'Yes! That was us!'

'We saw you! Jaysus, you were moving fast.'

'We were, and it was amazing, exhilarating, life-affirming!'

We headed for lunch and a few hours later I went in search of the pool. There was only one other person in it, so I tried a length and stopped halfway. I was panting. I started again. I reached the end and started to cough. I left the pool and sank into the Jacuzzi. I began to realise just how much my body had changed over the last ten years. It was funny because I had just assumed that I would be able to pick up swimming again whenever I wanted. I had assumed that I would still be able to do the things I had done as a kid, without any consequences arising from being inactive or having CF. It made me realise that I had been living in my mind, in my assumptions and ideals for so long that I had neglected the reality of what was happening with my body. My thinking was a somewhat unrealistic 'constant positive mental attitude'. I had forgotten to back it up with actual work and an investment in my physical self.

Just take the drugs and keep moving forward, I had always told myself. Just keep swimming. Just keep going. That was what Ted Hughes had said to Sylvia Plath when she started to doubt herself. Just keep going. Or what Dory, the blue fish in *Finding Nemo*, sang to the broken-hearted Marlin: '*Just keep swimming, just keep swimming, swim, swim, swimming …*' But the reality was that in keeping going, I hadn't made the space to find peace with myself. I hadn't allowed myself to just feel the thing that I was running from the most. I really liked girls. A lot of the time I liked them more than boys. And I was starting to like my body. Starting to say things like 'I am beautiful.' Without rolling my own eyes or bursting out laughing. It was the first time that I had dared to think it and really, really mean it. I realised of course this could be my reality and of course I was so close to it, I just needed to keep it. I don't know how long I sat in the Jacuzzi, but when we left Inchydoney I felt renewed.

34.

On 21 March, the day before my twenty-first birthday, about-three quarters of an hour before my dad was due to pick me up to bring me home to Newbridge to celebrate, I went for a run through UCD. I had a good exercise regime going by now: running five days a week, swimming on Wednesday and resting on Saturday. My life was more organised, my body felt strong and I felt like I was beating CF in a way that I never had before. As I made my way around the final lap of the field, I felt a gurgle in my chest and stopped. I bent at the waist and let my body hang down, taking in deep breaths. I coughed and noticed red blots hitting the grass. This was the first time in a few years this had happened to me and my first reaction was annoyance. I was doing so well. I had done my clearance before I ran. Why had this happened? It was 6pm and if I called the hospital, I would end up having to go to A&E because it was the weekend and you're not meant to get sick at weekends, there are no beds for sick people at weekends.

As I was standing on the pitch, I saw Dad's car pull up. He got out and slowly walked over to me. I told him about the blood and he suggested we ring Mom, to see what we should do next. I already knew what to do next, I just didn't want to do it. We waited fifteen minutes and the red mucus turned back to light green as I spit it out into a tissue. We got in the car and went home. I spent my birthday at a local hotel, with my family and extended family, having a few drinks and catching up with everyone. Dad dropped me home to UCD on Sunday and I was feeling better, so I didn't bother going to the twice-weekly drop-in clinic at Vincent's. I was afraid they would panic and bring me in; hemoptysis is taken very seriously for CF patients. At that stage I was sick of Vincent's and the hyper-awareness of who had what infection, what risks threatened me and the inevitable sleepless nights, so I decided to stay away from it.

That week in college was a reading week, and by Friday I had had enough of Catullus and his '*I want to rape you front and back, you queer you nymphomaniac*' poems, so I took a break and went for a run, out to the main road and down to Patrick's house. There was something beautiful about the spring air and the way the dewy grass glinted in the fading sun. The peak-hour traffic was bumper to bumper and the runners passed each other throughout the sprawling campus. I was almost at Patrick's when that feeling came over me again. Bam. I leant over and coughed. Blood. Shit shit shit. I couldn't go back when I was just outside his door, and I couldn't say, 'Hey dude, I can't actually rehearse for the open mic night in the student bar with you because I just coughed up a crap load of blood.' Well, I could have, but I really didn't want to.

The coughing fit subsided and I called into the house. Patrick was strumming a guitar in his room and we just chilled out before trying out some Pixies and other rocking songs. I hadn't sung in so long and my breath was all over the place, but it was fun and didn't sound as bad as I had expected. Afterwards I told him that I had signed up to do the women's mini-marathon in June, which was just ten weeks away. He told me I was crazy, but I had nothing to lose.

That May I was back in hospital again. The hemoptysis had happened for a third time, so I had to let Vincent's know and go along with their course of treatment. The consultant stood at my bedside, trying to talk over the noise of the ward, and suggested that the reason I was having so many chest infections was because I was developing diabetes. I told him I had had it for the past two years, annoyed at such a mistake. I understood that there were so many patients, but it was very easy to feel invisible at moments like that. When I left the hospital I remained on home IVs for a week, but I kept up with the mini-marathon training during my stay in hospital, so my stamina was still good. I knew I probably wouldn't be able to run the whole distance, but I reckoned I could do a straight 5k.

I did take one day off training, the day after I left hospital, to go to the UCD ball. My gang of friends went together and we had the best fun boogying at the silent disco. Then we ambled over to the stage, where the Wolfe Tones were about to play. I didn't know their music, but it turned out to be a raucous set that had people moshing and jumping about. Five minutes into it, I felt my feet lifting off the ground. No, the Wolfe Tones weren't making me float with happiness, it was the two guys either side of me, squashed against me. The swaying crowd was shoving them, and I was caught in the middle. I saw Patrick's face for a second, then got swallowed into a black hole of sweaty bodies.

As I lay on the floor with my hand over my portacath, I cursed myself. Damn, Orla! I rarely went to nightclubs or went right up to the front at gigs for this very reason. So how had I ended up on the floor at a Wolfe Tones' gig? Suddenly, a pair of sturdy arms reached around me and scooped me up off the floor and out of the crowd. It was Patrick's friend, Jim, who was built like a tank, and beside him stood Patrick and Sarah, looking panicked. All I could do was laugh – my standard reaction to shock. They pointed out my scratched knees while I slowly grasped the fact that my foot had started to throb uncomfortably. I had twisted it. They carted me off to the first-aid tent, insisting I needed attention while I insisted I would be fine. There were three of them, so they won.

At the first-aid tent I recovered enough to convince everyone I was fine and we continued on dancing and then walked home through UCD. The next morning my mom gave me strict instructions to RICE my sore foot: Rest, Ice, Compression, Elevation. The morning after that I decided it was better and that I would go for a run around the track. On my way there I met Patrick and he gently suggested that I was mad. Couldn't I just rest my foot some more? No way. The power of the mind controls and I controlled the pain and got on with the run.

A week later I hobbled out of the Markievicz swimming pool to the bus-stop for Vincent's hospital. At clinic a week earlier, they had told me I had a stress fracture and that as the mini-marathon was now just four weeks away, it was highly unlikely I would be able to take part at all. But the physiotherapist said I could still swim and cycle after a few weeks. If I kept up that tolerance, then maybe I could walk the 10k instead. I really didn't want to walk it, but I cut myself some slack and considered it. Now, though, as I hobbled out of the swimming pool, I knew I was in trouble. I got to Vincent's and went straight to the physio room door and knocked. They gave me a crutch and that was it for the summer.

In one way it was good, though, because it made me really think about running. Every day, as I elevated my foot in the bed or at the dinner table, or hobbled slowly to class, I thought about how amazing my feet were. Sure, my toes were freakishly long and ugly as sin, but my God, weren't feet amazing? A spindly network of fragile little bones and yet they carried us so far. I came to the conclusion that I wasn't invincible after all and that if I wanted to enjoy running regularly, I would have to be more responsible with my body and avoid injury, no matter what.

The day of the mini-marathon, my crutch and I stood on the sidelines and cheered on the runners and walkers as they went past UCD. My friend Laura was doing it, so my flatmates and I were there to support her. It was a really hot day and we devoured ice creams as we watched the thousands of entrants go by. Suddenly a familiar face emerged from the crowd and I recognised my CF nurse. She stopped to hug me and it was a nice marker for the event, even if I was slightly jealous. I didn't know then that two years later I would be running the race myself – and coincidentally would end up running beside that very same nurse.

35.

Although I had missed out on the mini-marathon, the summer did have a highlight: in July I went to New York for the first time. My friend Sarah and her sister Becky were working over there for the summer and staying with their aunt and uncle in Queens. They invited me to stay there too, and Sarah's relatives turned out to be two of the nicest people I have ever met. Their house was warmly inviting and beautifully decorated with interesting antiques.

The heat in New York that summer was so intense that on my first day wandering around Times Square while the girls were at work, my feet bled from heatburn. I bought some new shoes in the Skechers store and headed back to Queens. I spent most of my first week hanging out in the East Village and that weekend we went to Montauk, near the Hamptons, and met up with some girls we knew who were working there for the summer. We made a barbecue on the beach near our motel and an American girl asked me if I was the same Orla Tinsley who wrote about CF for the *Irish Times*. It turned out she had studied some of my work in her college journalism class for some kind of social issues module. That bowled me over. While we ate, fireworks from a party across the bay lit up the sky and the water. It was 20 July, which was also the anniversary of the death of my friend Martha. Sarah knew that and asked me if I was okay. In truth, I had forgotten what date it was, but I only felt mildly guilty – I felt I didn't need to hang on anymore, that it was okay to forget, to let go. She started singing 'Hallelujah' – the song they sang at Martha's funeral, the song in which I had searched and searched for meaning for months afterwards. The song that came on the radio in a café in Dun Laoghaire when my mom and I were having a stressful conversation about the campaign. It would be ok, I knew, when I heard it. For so long afterwards I felt like she was with me, helping me out, guiding me. Whether it was grief or truth, it was there, sustaining me. But it had left me now. She sang to me and I kind of wished she'd stop. She was always being amazing like that, trying to do whatever she could to make me feel better. I was mostly grumpy and cynical, perhaps determined to be the opposite of manically positive. In the strangest way we grew together as polar opposites, learning to balance ourselves out individually through the other. Sarah's probably the best friend I ever had and that summer was the fulfillment of a life's dream, just being in New York.

Some days later I stayed in the Chelsea Hotel, where I had booked a suite for one night. Having been obsessed with both Leonard Cohen (still) and Andy Warhol (abated) at different stages in my life, I really wanted to stay there. There was a famous Irish singer staying there at the same time and I met him in a funny way. I was walking down the staircase when I became aware of someone behind me and immediately thinking of 'stranger danger', I turned around to glare an accusation at whoever it was, only to find myself glaring at Glen Hansard of the Frames. We ended up chatting and he told me that the longer you stayed at the Chelsea, the more they dropped the price, once you were an artist.

Next I went to Brooklyn and stayed with a well-known

New York family who were kind enough to take me in for a day or two. Staying with them gave me a real sense of Manhattan working energy: all of the family members were focused and dedicated in their approach to their careers. Their daughter, who was my age, was interning at a major news network and was working even when she was at home that evening. She took me to a barbecue in her friend's house and it was amazing to meet a variety of American kids my own age. A conversation about making Smashleys, a type of alcoholic drink, turned into a heated debate on climate change, which I tried to join in on. I wasn't too bad, but they were so much better than me – more informed and more articulate. Their wealth of information was mind-boggling and their hunger for knowledge and change was fascinating. I didn't know anyone at home or in college who talked like this. It was an experience I'll remember forever.

After I left Brooklyn I spent the remainder of the holiday back in Queens, trying to arrange interviews with the Boomer Esiason Foundation. It had been set up by a National Football League player of the same name after his son was diagnosed with CF. The foundation did amazing work in the USA and I was eager to talk to them about it. I went to Vincent's Hospital, near Chelsea, and got near the CF ward and into an office, but unfortunately I never got to speak to the team I wanted to see. I then spoke on the phone with Jerry Cahill, a member of the foundation, who had CF and was forty-five. He was shocked when I told him about the situation for people with CF in Ireland and said it sounded like a legislative issue. He said that every state in the US had to have a proper CF center – it was mandatory in law. Ireland was so far behind.

I went to meet my friend Al in an Italian restaurant called Frank in the East Village. The food was exquisite and afterwards Al took me on a tour from the Bowery upwards through Manhattan. Looking across at NYU and the hustle and bustle of the city, I wanted New York so badly. I felt like my heart was there, like it was where I was meant to be. It would be so hard to say goodbye and go home. The hardest part was when my friend's uncle pulled me aside and said that I could stay there, if I wanted. I could stay there with them, in their beautiful spare room, to get proper CF care and not have to worry about a system ruining my life. The honesty and love in his eyes as he said this made the situation unbearable. I knew I couldn't stay. I felt responsible for Ireland and the Irish situation – like I had started something and had to go back to see it through. I still occasionally wonder to this day if I made the right decision.

The day after I came back from New York I lay in my bed, my mind foggy and my body limp with exhaustion. I wanted to zoom through the college campus to tell everyone about my experiences, but instead I lay there amidst the mess of clothes from the half-emptied suitcase I had borrowed from my Nana. Presents spilled across the already invisible floor, buried in the carnage of tops, jeans and stacks of paper. The desire to blitz the place made me roll my body up from the duvet for a split second. One look at it made me thud back down, just in time to hear my phone vibrate beneath my pillow. It was a private number. I answered sleepily.

The caller was Paula, one of my CF nurses. I was actually planning to ring her anyway about coming in to see her at some stage, but I still hadn't processed the reality that I was back in Ireland. She asked if my mom had called me. I said no. Why? She asked me to hang up and call my mother first. I did. At first, my mom was silent on the phone, then she took a massive deep breath. She didn't know much, Paula had called her just before calling me, and she didn't want to upset me during exams but ... it was Henry. Something had happened to him. He had been found dead in his apartment.

My mouth gurgled spit in disbelief and my stomach throbbed with an urge to vomit. Tears came out as I took three sharp deep breaths and then I pulled them back in. I told Mom it was okay and then called Paula. Did she know anything else? What? How? When? Why? She didn't know much more. I wasn't sure whether it was the right thing to do or not, but I rang Henry's mother. He was meant to call to her that evening, but he hadn't turned up. Normally each morning there would be an exchange of texts between them, she told me in a calm and clear voice.

As she spoke about him, my mind swelled with the memories of mornings lying next to him. Henry would usually be awake by now, phone in hand or fiddling with his guitar or doing a nebuliser on the other side of the room. Sometimes he wasn't there at all when I woke up and I would climb down the steep and narrow wooden stairs from his attic room into the airy corridor of the house. The smell of sizzling bacon and blaring music, like the Levellers, would greet me in the kitchen. Or maybe the Rolling Stones, because he knew I loved them. We would joke and fall around the kitchen laughing. Stretching over him to put bread in the toaster, he would stop me suddenly and kiss me. It was moments like those that made his snoring forgivable, that dissolved the worries of cross-infection, that fizzled away any concerns I had about our love. The memories played like an endless reel of film across my mind as his mother spoke about him. Each time the scene faded, my insides jolted in fear, so I played it again, grasping wildly at the memories.

'Please can you let me know what the arrangements are?' I was whispering. It felt as though there was no air left in my lungs. I hung up and paused for a second. I walked out into the corridor. Hannah was in her room and Zoe was in the kitchen. I sank to the floor outside my door, the intersection of the six bedrooms in our apartment. Hannah sat on the carpet with me as I tried to explain. I wanted to cry, but I couldn't. I felt defeated.

I decided to go home to Newbridge, to my mother. On the train I sat listening to 'Tiny Dancer' by Elton John on my iPod. Henry had liked to play it for me on his guitar. It was like hearing an eerie version of my life play out. It was

The Truman Show, it was *Groundhog Day* – an unreality that had me in its grasp and I no longer knew what was true and what was not. Here was another friend dead.

The scenery of Clondalkin, Celbridge and the Sallins and Naas stops sailed by outside the window like a never-ending sea of green smears. The fields melted together and blurred shapes entered my vision. I would glimpse a stream surrounded by grey stones, or a horse standing in a field, then the shape whirled into the stream of countryside. Nothing outside was concrete. There was a woman in the seat behind me, talking loudly on her phone. She was 'dying from a cold'. In my mind I got up from my seat, walked to her seat and told her just what I thought about that expression. But my feet were rooted to the ground and I sat rigid and tense, almost pious. My insides churned.

My mother picked me up from the train station and said she was so, so sorry. I said it was okay, it would all be okay. When we got home I drank 500mls of diluted orange and laced up my running shoes as tightly as they would go. I strapped the heart-rate monitor around my chest and walked out into the bog air. The songs of birds could be heard darting around the garden and I remember the sharpness of the wind. Flopsy, our playful black Labrador, hung her tongue out at me as she clawed at my running tights. We set off down the bog road together, slowly at first, both wobbling on the unsteady path. The dry muck tracks and grassy knoll that ran along the middle of the lane from my house to the bog bear testimony to the summer days of tractors and turf and heavy loads. Right now, they were testimony to my pain. These jutting rocks were my challenge, the hard slap of the ground through my thighs was my punishment for the way I had treated him.

I hadn't spoken to Henry since that last time, in February of that year. I had been standing outside the physio room, waiting for my morning treatment as an inpatient. A physio came out and told me to stay around the corner until I was called. Even for cross-infection guidelines, this seemed a bit excessive. I sat where the corridor dipped between the physio room and St Paul's Ward, on the steps of the lecture theatre. After about a minute, I couldn't resist sidling to the corner. I saw his back as he walked away from the room. Then they called me.

'Why did you tell me to wait around there?' I asked.

'We didn't want you to cry!'

'It wouldn't be me crying!' I said.

Later I lay in my bed on the ward, wondering if I should text him. And then my phone beeped. 'You're schtuck here too? For long?' it read.

We agreed to meet in the coffee shop of the new building in half an hour. We met and went outside to the fresh air. It was like talking to someone from a past life. I had dived into a relationship with him because I needed something different, and we had made a mistake that could have seriously damaged both of us. Now, as I listened to him, I realised that there was so much I hadn't known about him in those ten months we were together. In fact, I hadn't really known him at all, only what he had let me see. I had been caught in the trap of dreaming, instead of doing, and so I had slotted into some kind of 1950s housewife role and simply accepted when he didn't tell me things. At first I had tried to open him up, to change him, but then I got complacent. Now he talked freely, and I was shocked to realise how little I had known.

He was still playing with his band – what band? He was still acting – what acting? I was the actor in the relationship, or so I had thought. I had talked about it all the time. Yet here he was, doing all of these things, a man I didn't recognise. I told him I was writing a book.

'What sort of book?" he asked.

'A memoir?'

'What are you saying about me?'

'Em, you're not in it.'

'Jeez, thanks. Am I not interesting enough?'

'No, it's just…I haven't figured it all out yet. I don't know if hanging my dirty laundry in public is part of it – not that you're dirty laundry. And will people get it, considering I campaign about cross-infection and there I was dating guy with CF ...' I really wanted to hear what he thought about that, but I had set him off.

'Oh, so that's what I am? Dirty laundry? Thanks!'

'No. It's just about my life.'

'And I wasn't part of that?'

'You were, yeah, we'll see what happens!'

We talked some more and walked back in together. I put my hand out to shake his. He pulled me into a hug and then we parted. That was the last time I saw him.

The last place I wanted to be just then was St Vincent's, but I needed IVs and there was no choice in the matter. I admitted myself and got a bed on a semi-private ward with four other women. Eventually, and for the first time, I was moved down to a single cubicle. It was the one in which I had said goodbye to Martha before the trip to Lourdes in 2005. It didn't bother me though, because I knew I had healed the wounds of the past. But being in that space was still strange. I kept thinking of that line from *The Wizard of Oz*: 'My, people come and go so quickly around here!' I ended up listening to *Judy at The Palace* and *Judy Duets* for most of the time I was there. Judy and physio and fitful sleep – that was my days and my nights.

After all of that, I ended up seeing a therapist for a while. I needed to figure things out and get myself back together. One of the biggest things I learned from those sessions was the lesson of living from one moment to the next, taking it one step at a time. The therapist started treating me for an addictive personality and it was funny in the sense that what she said made sense – she told me that I had a choice, that I could actually stop campaigning and that someone else would do it if I stopped. It was a strange thing to hear. I had never really felt like it was a choice. I felt I had made my choice at the start and then had to see it through; giving up wasn't an option as far as I was concerned. But she didn't mean that, she just meant handing over responsibility to someone else and getting on with my life. I thought about it for a while and tried to pull back from the responsibility of speaking at events or speaking about anything to do with CF. I had been running around, trying to do so much and then beating myself up when I didn't get everything done. In truth, I had been running away from responsibilities *to* myself, maybe by unconsciously creating too many other responsibilities *for* myself. So I paused, and allowed myself to see the therapist for a while in order to reflect on why I was doing anything. It wasn't easy, but I started to feel things I had never felt before.

36.

It was now spring 2009, but no work had started on the long-promised CF units. When I had appeared on *Prime Time,* the HSE representative had guaranteed completion by the end of 2010, but that didn't look possible now. The campaign hit a lull as we all stopped ramming our heads against the brick wall for a while. I took the opportunity to highlight another angle in the HSE's and the government's failure of people with CF: the transplant system. I wrote an article for *The Irish Times* outlining exactly what was wrong with the current system (for article, see Appendix 3).

One morning in March, a few days after my birthday, I woke up to a text message from my friend Sarah: 'Can you call me asap? Are you coming in to college today?' It was alarming for her, so I woke up quickly and called her. The 'asap' emergency was down to her new green flats, which she'd worn into college that day. She hadn't even felt the blood trickling down her heels from the shoes cutting into her, and now there was blood all over her tights. In fairness, it was hilarious and we chuckled, but she was mortified and so I got out of bed, did my nebs, dressed and cycled up to UCD. On the way I stopped off at a shop to buy some tights. It was a beautiful day and I could definitely make it up the steep hill from Merrion to RTÉ and then cycle the stretch to UCD.

The air was calm but cool and I was glad Sarah's mishap had forced me out of bed. Another friend of mine, Bernadette, had died a few weeks earlier from CF – this had shaken me and left me feeling unable to tackle anything. This was my first real day back in reality since then. I was really trying to be lighter and more optimistic. The prospect that the documentary might do some good was positive. We had chatted about it in the Arts Café the day before. Sarah and Lorelei wanted to enter something into the Human Rights Film awards and we sat in the café as they discussed which human rights issue they could write a script about.

'CF care in Ireland!', I said.

They weren't sure if that was a human rights issue. I explained to them that people dying prematurely in a country that had so much wealth was most definitely a human rights issue. We talked it out and finally agreed on the topic. Two other girls and I would research it and get in touch with people with CF for their input; Sarah and Lorelei would be Director and Assistant Director. It had to be a short – less than fifteen minutes – and we had only two weeks to pull it together, but I was confident that some of the people with CF I knew would be willing to take part. I thought it could be a really strong piece and show the difficulty of the life-threatening situation facing people with CF in Ireland. We agreed to work on it together and it was exciting.

I walked the tunnel from the Arts block to the library and swiped my illegal library card in the machine. Technically, I wasn't supposed to be able to use it as I was on a leave of absence, but I wrote better in the library and it didn't hurt anyone. Besides, I still had some overdue assignments to complete. I found Sarah on the fourth floor and delivered her fresh tights. It was now 11.15am and we decided to meet for lunch in Elements at 12.30.

I took a seat in a corner of the library, opened my laptop and read what I had written a few days ago. I was learning more about myself as I wrote this book, and the more I wrote, the more time I had to take to reflect and come back to it. I was opening up parts of my life that I had forgotten or taken for granted, and really understanding what it all meant. For the first time in my life I was taking responsibility for it all and just saying, Here It Is. People called me a role model and an inspiration and I had never felt comfortable about it, although I also knew that they were just labels that people put on things and that, in reality, they didn't even know a quarter of me. The more I wrote, though, the more I realised that I had some sort of complex shame about who I was and how I had got to where I was. I blamed myself for my eating disorder in my teens, and that was my biggest fear in writing it down: would people judge me for my imperfections? I sat at the computer, staring at the blinking cursor, and let things like Bernadette's death float into my mind. She had died less than one week ago. I turned it all over and the conclusion I reached was: it doesn't matter what the hell anyone else thinks; we are who we are; you only have one life, one shot. It made me pause and at the same time filled me with conviction. I'm not here forever, why sugar-coat it? I had just started retyping a passage when my phone beeped with a text message.

'Heather Dolan passed away'.

Heather. Dolan. Dolan was Heather's second name. Was that her second name? My friend? My brain refused to recognise her name, clutching at the notion that it couldn't actually be my Heather that the text was about. I read it again.

It was my Heather.

I took a deep breath, made some guttural whisper. The library seemed to swell and I ran across and crashed through the door to the bathroom. A girl's reflection flashed me a look in the mirror. I bundled myself into the toilet and shook with tears. I started to cry heavy and loud, as though I was coughing, and I couldn't stop. I just couldn't.

I sent a text to Sarah: 'please come to bathroom'. She came in and I showed her the message as I leant against the wall. Heather had CF, she had been a massive part of the campaign in 2008 and she was such a lovely girl. Sarah hugged me and I said, 'I'm fine', and hugged her back. It hurt so much. She took my hand and we walked outside to the UCD lake. Once past the smokers hovering at the door, I took in massive deep breaths. Stupid, stupid smokers, ruining their lungs.

'I have to call my mom, I have to call my mom,' was all I could say. I called her and told her about Heather. I wasn't crying anymore. I realised this was the first time I ever called my mother about anything truly emotional. It made me cry again. Sarah and I sat on a bench and watched the ducks and the swans. It made me feel better, watching them float along slowly.

'I don't know what to say Orls,' she said quietly.

'Neither do I.' I sighed, watching one ugly grey duck waddle on the bank. 'It just can't keep happening like this, it can't. Ireland is such a fucking joke.'

We sat with our arms around each other for a while. 'Let's go and see Lorelei,' she said. So we walked to Glenomena residences and sat in the hallway until Lorelei came back and then we sat in her living room, eating biscuits that belonged to someone else. We told her what had happened and she said she was sorry. I said sorry for putting it on them. I felt awkward in the situation. I could usually deal with these things alone, or else call one of my friends with CF. I now had one friend with CF left. I had resolved to stop making friends with people with CF a long time ago, and yet it had kept happening. Or rather, in the line of work I was in, they found me. I knew now that I couldn't prevent myself from getting close to them. It happened so easily. You're both in hospital, bored, so you text/email each other over and back, you wave in the corridor, you pass in the shop. Then one person is still stuck in there and you support each other still until one person gets too caught up with life on the outside. That's what had happened with Heather – I had got too caught up with life and I wasn't there for her. I knew that wasn't my responsibility, but it still made me so sad.

Lorelei left the room and came back with my birthday present – a book about a cat called Fred, whose alien-like eyes stuck out on the front cover, and a green picture frame holding a picture of the gang from Sarah's 21st party that February. My chest welled again and she hugged me, and I cried again. 'What's wrong? Don't cry.' They were both so helpless, there was nothing they could do. That's why I hated crying in front of my friends. But this was it, this was real life in motion, it just happened. I was going with the flow, just being.

I didn't want to go home yet, but they had classes to go to, so I hung out in the Arts Café with some friends before leaving at 4.30pm. I walked to the gym, got on the treadmill and ran. I did push-ups, sit-ups and I felt alive. I was alive, I was breathing, I could run, I could work my core, I was alive and moving and breathing. When I got home to my apartment I pressed 'reminder' on the TV to record the new episode of *Skins* at 10pm and threw some chicken in the oven, then sat down in front of my laptop and tried to write in my diary about what had just happened.

I had written that exposé piece on the transplant system in January and no one had registered it. Now two people on the transplant list were dead. My mom had told me that a friend of hers who worked in the Mater had mentioned to her that the head consultant there had been frustrated by my article on the transplant system, which was a good sign. I was getting to them, but there was still no real explanation. If there was a higher percent transplant success rate in other countries, then why not in Ireland? And now Bernadette and Heather were dead. I decided I would keep all this for the documentary because I felt that was the most effective medium to get this point across in a way that would impact on people, but at the same time, someone had to know about this. How? What was the best angle? I didn't want sympathy. I wanted action and realisation. We all deserved answers.

I was one paragraph into my thoughts when my phone rang. It was the subeditor of *The Irish Times*. 'Where are you?' his voice sounded breathless, 'I have to tell you something.' He sounded grave. As he spoke, I collapsed back into my chair. The HSE had indefinitely postponed funding for the CF unit. There had been a written answer embedded in a massive Oireachtas report on the matter and those few words decided our fate. It was part of cutbacks, part of the new agenda in recession Ireland. The CF unit had been promised for the past fourteen years, all through the ostentatious wealth of the Celtic Tiger years and I had wanted so much to believe the HSE when it said it would happen this time, but it was a false hope, a false promise. The subeditor passed me over to the Health Correspondent and she filled me in on the details and asked if I was okay. Anger was simmering in my gut and I was so tired. I replied in monosyllabic answers: Yes, Yes, Okay, Fine. I could barely breathe.

'Would you be able to write something about it for tomorrow, to be in by eight o'clock this evening? Do you want to do that? Do you think you can do that?'

'Yes, absolutely. Two of my friends have died in the past ten days. I had just started writing something anyway.'

I put the phone down, ran to the bathroom and projectile vomited into the toilet. How could this happen now? Did I really have it in me to campaign again right now? I was out of hospital a month and my bowels were just starting to get on track. I cleaned myself up, went outside and sucked in the fresh air. I thought about Bernadette. I thought about Heather. I thought about Martha. I thought about all those with CF who hadn't been given a fighting chance. I went back inside, sat down at my desk and started typing.

... THE 30-bed dedicated cystic fibrosis unit that Brendan Drumm promised in January 2008 would be available by 2010 is not happening. The news that the funding will not be available until 2011 is heartbreaking. As CF patients we should have seen it coming.

Eight single en suite rooms were made available at St Vincent's hospital in August 2008, and that gave us hope. On Wednesday I sat beside the lake in UCD holding on to my friend. I had just gotten a text message to say that a close friend with cystic fibrosis had died. All we could do was leave the library and go outside and breathe in the cold, fresh air.

That was the second person I knew with cystic fibrosis who died in the past three weeks, and there are at least two others that weren't friends of mine.

Yes there is a recession and we are all struggling, but trading people's lives for survival is sick and heartless. It is heartbreaking to think that we will not have our unit by 2010. The declaration that the facilities for cystic fibrosis patients in Ireland were in a state of emergency was made my healthcare expert Dr Ronnie Pollock in 2005 so it's hard to see why, with the highest instance of cystic fibrosis in the world, Irish patients are treated like insignificant people.

(© 2009 *The Irish Times*)

On the morning of 27 March deliveries of the newspaper were late into the shop at the top of my road and when I arrived to get my copy, they had none. I stood outside the Toyota Centre waiting for the express bus to UCD. The sky was a pale blue and at 8.30am I was the only person at the bus stop. Ballsbridge was strangely quiet. A green leaf with streaks of white whipped in the wind across my path and landed in front of me. It was so innocent and pure, that little leaf, susceptible to anything nature chose to do to it. That's all we really are – flimsy leaves at the mercy of nature. We try to control things because we know, ultimately, there is no control. That was something else I had started to accept but still struggled with sometimes: I had no control over my life, my birth, my death. My heart felt warm when I thought of it and there was less fear than before – but there was still fear. I picked up the shamrock-shaped leaf and held it before releasing it again. I would read my piece, I would gather my thoughts, I would pray that the media picked up on it again. If they didn't, I would call Liveline and see what I could do that way.

I went into the library, sat at a desk on the third floor, stuck my *Irish Times* piece up on Facebook and opened my book manuscript on a USB key. I couldn't concentrate properly, but I typed blindly and my hands started to shake. I had forgotten breakfast and was about to have a hypo – clever. I went down to the shop to buy a banana and some rice cakes. I checked my phone in the shop and realised I had missed a call. I went outside the library and listened to the voice message. It was the One o'clock News on RTÉ Radio 1 – they wanted to cover the story and they wanted me to come into studio. I knew that I couldn't do Liveline and the One O'Clock News on the same day. The news programme was important, but I knew Liveline had a very large listenership and the added dimension of participation by phone, which would keep the topic rolling for longer.

The CEO of CFAI called me next, and this time he was congratulating me on my article and telling me that he was sending over his new PR people to help me out, if that was okay. I didn't really want that, but it would be handy to have them drive me around and not have to waste ridiculous amounts of money on taxi fares. The third time my phone vibrated I was back at my desk in the library, so I answered furtively, mid-banana bite. It was the PR people. I was too exhausted to leave my seat, so I whispered directions to the woman on the phone, telling them I was in the library and would call them in a few minutes. Behind me, someone cleared their throat. I cancelled the call and bit into my banana. 'Excuse me,' the voice said. It was a librarian. 'That is three violations.'

'I'm so sorry. I never, ever do this, this is an exceptional circumstance.'

'There are *no* exceptional circumstances. Downstairs.'

This was not the day I needed this. Okay, I always ate in the library, but so did many others. I was allowed to because I had diabetes. 'I have diabetes,' I said, 'and this *is* an exceptional circumstance. I'm very, very sorry.'

I followed her down the stairs, the biggest inconvenience in the universe. All I could hear was, '*permanent record ...marks ... banned*' and suddenly tears sprang to my eyes out of nowhere. What the hell was wrong with this woman?

'Look, read the *Irish Times*, I'm on the front of it. The HSE pulled funding for the cystic fibrosis unit and I'm meeting people to do something about it. I needed to use the computer and I needed to eat because of my diabetes.'

She looked at me. 'Eat your banana,' she said and took my library card and walked behind her desk. This was a waste of time I did not need. Yeah, I had broken the rules, but for a higher purpose. Trust me to get caught the one day where time was of the essence. She came back looking shocked and handed me my card. 'Good Luck,' she said and I ran back upstairs, packed my stuff and hopped on the escalator to meet the PR people. The librarian waved, smiling at me on the way out.

I sat at the only table free in the Arts Café and it happened to be the same one I had been sitting at with Sarah and Lorelei the week before when they pulled out a cup cake with a candle on it for my twenty-second birthday. Sarah looked at me, smiling, as she pulled out my birthday present. 'I think you'll like it!' she beamed. I ripped open the present – proper present-opening style – and found a pair of brown and green Roxy surfer knicks and a stringy top. They were probably a bit small, but they were funky for sleeping in. 'You brought me underwear, eh?' I laughed.

'No, it's for running,' she said, deadpan.

Lorelei looked at me and we exploded into laughter. Maybe Pamela Anderson would wear it running. It was the best moment and I remembered it before letting the hum of the café wash over me.

I watched people dash for lunch and kept an eye on the door for the PR people. I took some deep breaths and concentrated on being in the moment, focused on what I felt and revved up for what was to come next. The two members of the PR company, a man and a woman, came into the café, introduced themselves and sat down. 'So this is the famous Orla Tinsley?' they opened with. They asked did I want tea and talked about my article, which they hadn't yet read. The man said they would drive me to RTÉ and help me out in any way they could. We drank coffee and they showed me their portfolio, explaining why they had been selected to be the PR agency for the CFAI. I had never had help like that before, but I had dealt with PR before and I was itching with the urgency of the situation. They sat in front of me, showing me slides of the presentation they had given to win their job. They told me their ideas and asked me if I had met all the cool people with CF they had met. I liked their idea of shaking up the CF logo, of getting a set of advocates and creating a media group.

I told them what usually happened on a day like this: I was going to call Liveline at 12.30 to see if they'd run the topic. They suggested things for me to say if I got on air and I kept an open mind. I told them I was waiting for Liveline to call and if they didn't, I would be doing the One O'Clock News, so either way I had to go to Montrose, to RTÉ. They offered to drive me there and I accepted. When we walked outside they slipped on their shades and we walked along the concrete jungle of UCD from the Arts Block towards the gym.

Liveline decided to run with the topic and I managed to persuade the researcher to let me sit in studio to make my contribution rather than speaking on the phone, as was normal for most guests. She had called back and said I could sit in, but I knew that meant it would be difficult and there was no way of knowing what would happen, but I reckoned if I was there in person, I could drive the point home continuously, so it would be worth it. Nonetheless, I was nervous.

Inside the studio, I sat there feeling very vulnerable. I started talking to the presenter, Joe Duffy, and after a few minutes he mentioned that Heather and Bernadette had passed away recently. He played parts of interviews he had conducted with them in January 2008. My heart stopped. I hadn't expected this. I hadn't expected to hear their voices. I had to mentally kick my brain so I could respond to his questions directly after each sound byte. I don't remember what I said next, but I remember getting angry and just saying what I felt. It was the hardest media experience I ever had. That was the most bizarre thing about campaigning and all of the political nonsense that went on around it – there were so many hoops to jump through, when in fact our message was pure and simple: we wanted to live, and every year people were dying because of CF. They would most likely die of CF anyway, but they were dying in unacceptable conditions when I believed some of them could have lived longer in single en-suite rooms. I knew isolation couldn't prevent CF, but I also knew the way infection works and I knew the psychological and physical toll of sleepless nights in multi-bed rooms. It was spirit crushing.

After one hour and forty minutes of responding to calls from listeners and talking about CF, I got up from the seat and thanked both Joe Duffy and the program producer. They said they hoped it helped the cause and that they'd do anything they could to support us. When I walked out the door of the studio, a massive camera on a tripod and the

RTÉ News Health Correspondent were waiting for me. 'A quick piece for the news?' So I did it there, feeling hungover from the previous show.

I walked from the studio to the canteen, where the PR team was waiting. They clapped. They loved it. But I just felt totally drained. One of them said that my 'best line' was, '"Are human lives the new currency?" You must have prepared that on the way in, how did you pick it?'

I was pretty sure he couldn't miss the snarl in my lips. 'I don't pick lines, I just speak from the heart,' I told them. It sounded so corny and self-righteous, but it was true.

In campaigning I was media aware, and I knew which shows to do and how much to do so I wouldn't exhaust myself but would still get the message out as effectively as possible. Now that my appearances were being organised for me, it was different. I started to do more and it was rolling a different way. Early the next morning the PR head office called me with a list of journalists, to see if I knew any of them, could I call them. I needed my sleep was what I needed, and I told them that.

Over the next week I moved between the girls' apartments in UCD for documentary discussions to my own apartment for rest to interviews on every national and independent radio station I could find. I took numerous calls on my phone from parents and people with CF. Mostly it was very supportive, but there was an odd encounter that left me wondering, the solicitor who thought we might have a case, but wanted to see me alone, with absolutely no one else present. I said someone else had to come with me, but he said he strongly advised against it and gave me directions to his office. He had got my number from a friend, he said. I didn't call him back.

In between the madness Sarah and the girls and I were contacting people for the documentary on CF. There was little I could do to help as my energy was zapped daily, so I just tried to be present and hear what they were doing and help if I could. It was strange the way it all happened, the way the documentary was planned just after my birthday, which turned out to be a week before the HSE pulled the funding. On the slides the PR people showed me they had made it a Human Rights issue too. It was like the universe had aligned it, I knew it was right.

37.

The upshot of the campaign was another promise that the unit would be completed, this time by the end of 2011. Near the end of the campaign I had gone into hospital for a routine check-up, exhausted. My consultant told me that I would have to come be admitted as soon as a bed became available. I had a terrible pain in my shoulder that had been bothering me throughout the campaign. Sometimes when I was under pressure or coughed too much, I hunched up my shoulders – as do a lot of people with CF. I think it's a protective instinct, but it can lead to aches and pains.

This shoulder pain was particularly annoying, though. I was sitting in the CF room, sparring with the registrar about it. He was hilarious and we always fought about whether I should have home IVs or in-patient IVs. If I thought I was well enough to do it at home, I made sure they knew my list of reasons. I'm sure this made me a major pain in the ass occasionally. This day, mention of the shoulder pain was an after-thought. I don't really like making too much of a big deal about pain because other people with CF go through so much more than me, and also running means I create self-inflicted pain. But we were chatting away and I mentioned it and the doctor checked and said my chest sounded clear. The CF nurse was more wary and insisted that the decision about home IVs be left until I had been x-rayed. I went for the x-ray and when I came back down. The doctor looked at the x-ray and said I was grand, but still had to be admitted.

Two days later the pain in my shoulder was worse and on Saturday morning a different doctor came in to see me. She said the official report of the x-ray had come back and the reason for the pain was that my lung had collapsed. She apologised that it hadn't been recognised sooner. It made sense – the inability to lie on my side and the searing pain when I moved in certain ways. I had gotten so good at blocking out pain that I had not been listening to my body. They put me on full-flow 02 and propped me up in the bed. I called my mom, who came straight to the hospital.

What did this mean? When had it happened? Once they described the sensation of lung collapse to me, I immediately knew when it had happened. I had been working out in the gym one evening and I was so tired, but I thought exercise would re-energise me. I lifted heavy weights and then stretched out in cat pose – legs tucked underneath, arms pushed out in front. When I made to stand up, the left side of my chest stabbed with pain. The higher up I moved, the more electrifying it got. I stayed down. No one was around. I was in the dark side area of the gym because I was a bit self-conscious; I was literally in the gym alleyway, so I couldn't be seen. Up again? No. I lay there for about twenty minutes, focusing on breathing, before finally feeling able to lift myself up. I walked slowly over to the changing rooms, showered, got on my bike and cycled home.

By the time I got home the pain was abating, so I called a friend who had CF to ask what she thought. She said I should probably get it checked out. I knew she was right. I figured if the pain came back, I'd go straight into the hospital, but it kind of eased. Sometimes I just got random chest pain, too, so maybe it was just that. What a fool I had been. What an utterly stupid thing to have done. I lay in the bed, debilitated, exhausted and sad. It was one of those moments when I was meant to pull my 'positive mental attitude' out of my gut, but I was so doped up I was almost numb. I was a zombie, happy to stare into space. I fluctuated between that and wanting to run, which was probably a not-too-subtle metaphor for wanting to get better and get the hell out of there.

Spending my first five days with a collapsed lung in a six-bed ward with staff who didn't know anything about CF was hell. I had to walk all the way out to the bathroom and hunch over to clean up other people's crap while dealing with my own pain. I tried to quell the anger with compassion, compassion, compassion. The only relief was the fact that I was on so many painkillers, which meant I slept a lot. I eventually got a cubicle, but by that stage I was much better and walking around. When the day came that I was allowed to run on the treadmill again with my physio, I jumped around like a slightly deranged person. It made me so ridiculously happy. My consultant said I'd have to take my time getting back to weights, and in fact I might never be allowed to lift them. It was a grim realisation. I couldn't accept it and started counting the weeks in my head until I would be able to start again. After three weeks, I went home.

The next month was spent trying to focus on my book. I think what crippled me so much when it came to writing this book was I didn't want it to be all about CF, and yet my life had been so much about CF for the previous three years because of the campaign. In ways it has shaped me, it's unavoidable, but when I signed my author contract with Hachette that month, I was determined to write an expansive, multifaceted book about my life. Naturally, I felt like I was an egomaniac for doing so, but then I thought, well, I'm writing it because people know I campaign for CF and people want to hear what that journey was like, so there's no escaping CF in this story. I could talk to myself about 'multifaceted' all I wanted, there was no escaping CF at any stage. It had always been there, sometimes interrupting, sometimes not; sometimes floating alongside normality in perfect harmony, although not often.

During that first month out of hospital I really slacked off in terms of exercise, until finally I decided enough was enough and ventured back to the gym. In fairness, I had no excuse: eating an entire packet of choc chip cookies the night before probably helped kick me out of lazy gear. But that day, 29 June, was special because I was officially out of the danger zone with my lung: if you go six weeks without it collapsing again, the 80% chance that it will collapse again reduces to 50%. So I celebrated receiving the all-clear by going to the gym. Well actually, I cycled there and took it easy on the treadmill. I did some strength training and core exercises before hopping on the bike and heading for home. I was aiming for little and often to try and get back up there.

The following day I made my way out to RTÉ to appear on the Tubridy Show on RTÉ Radio 1 with Philip Watt, the new CEO of the CF association. I had met him just once before but really admired him and was looking forward to meeting him again. He had cut short his holiday in order to come on the show and I really liked that about him. Our chat with Ryan Tubridy was mostly about the aftermath of the campaign. It was strange because I normally did media interviews out of necessity, in the midst of intense campaigning. I hadn't done one before without that massive urgency attached to it. There were still important things to highlight though, particularly with the plan to put the building contract for the CF unit out to tender in July. The next step could well prove to be our biggest challenge yet, depending on the outcome. The end of the campaign meant I was free to focus on other things – most importantly, and most excitingly for me, on the work placement I'd managed to secure in the *Irish Times* newsroom.

I was absolutely thrilled to get the chance to work in such a hectic, demanding journalistic environment and I willed my body to stay healthy long enough to allow me to really enjoy it.

Five days after the Tubridy Show, things started falling apart. I have a running joke with a friend of mine who also has CF: 'Have you been coughing up ketchup for attention again?' It's a funny way to handle those irritating moments, like yesterday morning, when I woke up coughing 'ketchup' from my lungs. Coughing up blood is never a good sign; the doctors say it's usually a sign of infection, which means you should call the hospital. That's the best thing to do. Or you could just grab some breakfast and get on with your day because sometimes, it 'just happens'. That day, I knew I could choose to be sensible or stupid. I could have waited to see if it eased off and cycled to UCD as planned. Let's face it, stupid is always much easier. But this time I opted for sensible, so I called my team and an hour later I was in one of the two examination rooms being told, 'Blood is usually nothing big, just an indicator of infection ...'

'So, technically, I could go on home IVs?'

'... but sometimes it's about a blood vessel that starts bleeding and won't stop.'

'Well, I live down the road, in Ballsbridge, so what if you just give me home IVs and I swing by if it happens again, eh?' I really didn't want to be admitted. I knew I had to be here, but I was so sick of here. I wanted to be outside, living, working, cycling, running ...

'Orla, here's the deal. If you bleed and it doesn't stop, then you bleed and it doesn't stop. It doesn't matter if you're in Ballsbridge or in Tesco across the road. You might not get here in time.'

You see, I knew that. Deep down, I knew that, and I wasn't a lunatic. But it was just so frustrating: I felt fine, I was ready to cycle to college and get on with my day, but this red stuff was coming out of me, telling me to stop. Nonetheless, it was one of those frustrating moments when

I had no choice but to surrender control and do the right thing. To the average person it may seem strange that ignoring the blood, the medical advice would have even crossed my mind. But it did.

I got a bed that evening. I was extremely lucky. It was a case of refusing to go to A&E but the severity of the situation being so beyond me that I knew I was going to have to go to A&E if there was no bed. Luckily, one became available after a few hours waiting in the CF room. After my first dose of IVs I realised how truly awful I actually felt. I was feeling a nauseous grumble of mucus in my chest. I fell asleep reading *The Universal Journalist*, dreaming about working for longer than three consecutive weeks.

I was kept in hospital for two weeks, but finally the day arrived when I was told I could go home and hopefully get on with my life once more. On my first morning at home I was getting ready to meet Mom and Jack. I was just grabbing my bag and my keys, ready to leave, when I started coughing. Blood. I sat down and waited. It continued and then eased off into streaking. We went to Blackrock and stopped in Superquinn on the way home. I found myself coughing into a tissue beside the bin. I sat on the bench and sobbed uncontrollably. It was so embarrassing. There were people everywhere but all I could hear were my sobs. My mom found me and held me. My brother stood for a minute and then went away for a while. He knew me so well, he knew I didn't want him to see me cry.

The next day my chest felt heavy, so I called the hospital. There was a bed available immediately, but a team member asked if I was sure if it was blood I had coughed up. I went in and the routine started all over again. The next day a physiotherapist asked me if I had been eating anything pink before I coughed up the 'blood'. I wanted to rip apart the bedsheets I was lying on. 'You're seriously asking me that? Because there is no medical reason for this, *I* am being questioned.' In fact, someone told me afterwards they knew a person who had fabricated symptoms of blood to avoid going home. As a result, when a symptom had no obvious cause, the staff had to ask. By that stage I was so on edge, I could feel my fingers pulsing. But I understood.

I was left sitting on my own for a long time, which was not a good thing because it gave me too much time to think, which led to a sense of despair. What was wrong with me? They didn't know, I didn't know. There is sort of a hollow space that forms inside when you realise your medical team doesn't have all the answers. It's a scary space. The next day my consultant came to see me. He sat on my bed and told me that although this sort of stuff – lung collapses, coughing up blood frequently – usually only happened to people with more severe CF than mine, it still happened. But why? He said 'We don't know. But it's not your fault. This is not your fault. It's just CF.' . I wanted to hug him. The bleeding happened five times that summer.

I knew that, somehow, I was going to have to find the strength to stay positive, to stay focused on all the things I wanted to do and achieve outside those walls. It was getting harder as I got older, though – I was tired, weary of the same routines and protocols, the same conversations, the same building up and dashing down of my hopes for my health. But I also knew there was no point complaining about it – this was life with CF, so this was part of my life.

That summer while I was in hospital my mother got a call from the former teacher of the school room in Temple Street Children's Hospital. She was not the principal and she was calling on a sad occasion. Mrs Dawson, the woman who had been the principal when I was very young, was dying. She was in St Vincent's Private and she had requested to see me before she passed away. I was flabbergasted. Of course I knew I had to go, and my mom came with me. The private ward was glistening when we walked in, but the corridors felt narrower than the public hospital. It was like entering a different universe walking from one to the other. When we entered the room the woman I hadn't seen in over 12 years knew me immediately. She told me I looked the same as always. Such a great girl, she said. We talked a while and I held her hand. When we left I burst out crying in the car. She had recognised me and she had wanted to see me. It was the most humbling feeling and it validated all of the stuff I couldn't fully yet understand. Children's Hospital had been like a second home to me. But it was the past and this was the present. And I was so lucky to be here alive with my future ahead of me. Anything was still possible, I just had to be sensible about it. I had to be my own guard and set my own pace. It was just growing up.

38.

In mid-September, a month after my last admission, I developed a nasty chest infection and was admitted again, to St Clare's ward. I was reading Eckhart Tolle's book about the power of inner transformation, about how we are ultimately insignificant but that there is something in us, the Self, that transcends death. It was about being at peace with the world and your situation and believing in your inner power. It sounds so corny, but it really resonated with me at the time. It made me feel at peace about being there, that it was where I was meant to be. Everyone was where they were meant to be and this was the cycle of life. There was thought and ego and energy behind that, energy – unperishable energy. I found it and floated in my mind. The ward seemed slightly obscured to my eyes, as if by a mist, and movements became slower. Peace and Love. Love is all you need. No judgment, no labels, no definitive. No past, no present, just this very moment. Yes, this one. Now, this one. Each minute blew my mind and I stayed in bed for three days, apart from attending at the physio room, but that was purely perfunctory because my body didn't want to exercise – I was too exhausted.

After a few days of this, my doctor came around and I told her I was feeling what I thought was inner peace, that it had started about five days ago and was getting stronger each day, so I was starting to worry. Was it the new drug I was on? That morning I had walked to the shop and felt a little dizzy. She examined me and said my balance was fine. She sat in front of me and told me that acceptance was important and that I needed to realise that I didn't have to be strong for everyone the whole time. I told her that wasn't what I was talking about. It was so annoying because she was only about three years older than me and I didn't want to hear this stuff from my doctor, particularly not one I could easily bump into on a night out. She started to tell me how she sympathised with my sinusitis because when she had it for a week, she was bedridden, and she didn't know how I dealt with it everyday. I knew she was trying to help, but I just didn't want to know. She said she had no idea what I was going through, that CF was so complicated. I wanted to clobber her over the head. This wasn't her job and it wasn't appropriate.

'Do you think it could be the Minocycline?' I asked firmly. I had started taking it around the time this high had escalated. 'Do you think it's chemical or physical?'

'I don't know.' She told me that sometimes acceptance brings peace and a high feeling. I asked her to please take me off the drug. She agreed, and after twenty-four hours I was once again a healthy mix of cynicism, judgment, love and consciousness. Love is all you need, man, but you need your wits about you, too.

That same admission they did a CT (contrast) of my sinuses. I sat in the waiting room for an hour, waiting for an anaesthetist who was going to insert the needle into my vein so they could administer the contrast. A member of the team had already tried to insert it three times, but respected the fact that he couldn't do it and had requested an anaesthetist. I sat with an intern, who did his best to distract me as the nurse waited patiently for the anaesthetist. When he finally arrived, I explained the situation and the reluctance of my veins in the matter of needles. He tried the veins in the back of my hand, my thumb, my upper arm and the back of my other hand. He squeezed my wrist and said he was sorry – he couldn't do it. All I could think was, How did I just sit there and let them do this to me when I was five years old? I gave the nurse the name of the anaesthetist I knew and she left to bleep him. The intern looked at me. 'How do you put up with this?'

'I just do. I don't really feel it.'

The nurse reappeared with another doctor and he tried three times. His hand was shaky and he didn't palpate the veins first. I felt like a zoo animal on display as random doctors walked by, staring and wanting to have a go. As the doctor stabbed away I just kept saying to myself, *The CT looked suspicious, you need the contrast dye. You know you need to rule out whatever they think they see.* Finally, I told him to stop.

'One more try?'

'No.'

'But I am sure, here ...' The needle was already uncapped and pointing at my skin.

'*Fine.*'

When he missed it again he stood up quickly and stared at me, frustration written all over his face. 'Maybe on the other ...'

'NO. Sorry, with respect, no. It's not your fault, they're pretty difficult veins. Someone else can try.'

Finally, another anaesthetist arrived and said he would try, but only twice. He took his time, skimmed his finger along my skin looking for the vein and got it on his second go. I let them wheel me back in a wheelchair after the contrast X-ray, like some sort of floppy doll. They concluded from the test that my sinus problem required further attention, so I was given an appointment in the Mater. For some reason, my left sinus was in almost direct contact with my brain, with nothing protecting it. I got a taxi across to the Mater with the ward attendant from Vincent's and on the way we chatted about the Rolling Stones.

When I got into the Mater, they couldn't find my x-ray. Vincent's sent it over, I insisted over and over, but it couldn't be located. After forty minutes of waiting a doctor materialised and brought me into a room. 'We've seen it before, but we're not sure what causes it.' I told them I had had sinus surgery when I was eleven.

'Oh that could have been it, it depends what they did. So here's the deal - don't let anyone examine you up there, don't let them stick anything up there and if you have any sort of increase in your symptoms, any clear fluid dripping down from your nasal passage, any salty taste in your mouth, call us.'

'Right. But you know I have CF, right?'

'Yes.'

'So I have both of those things all the time. I have a post-nasal drip almost every day. I always taste salty.'

'Just if there's any general change.'

'What would that mean?'

'Well, at the moment your brain is sort of slotted into the sinus.'

'So, effectively, my brain would be falling out of my nose?'

'Eh, yes.'

'Okay. Thank you. That's hilarious. It really is.'

We got the same taxi back to Vincent's and I listened to tales of holidays being exchanged between the ward attendant and the taxi driver. When I got to my room I lay down on the bed and digested all I had been told. This sinus/brain problem was nothing to do with CF; they didn't know how it had happened. Maybe it was a birth defect as a result of premature birth? Oh well, nothing I could do about it. My physio arrived and I told her what had happened. She imitated the guy from *One Foot In The Grave* – *I don't believe it!*

Thankfully, I hadn't coughed up blood again, but my sinuses remained consistently bad, with headaches, so I distracted myself with *The Private Lives of Pippa Lee* by Susan Miller and a handbook on journalism. I looked out my window at the drab grey of the oratory wall. By the end of the month, I told myself, I will be scaring the hell out of myself in the *Irish Times* newsroom and it will be absolutely amazing. I repeated it over and over like a mantra, and it made me feel good. I focused on *The Essential Journalist*, on the work I would get to do in the newsroom, on getting out of there. Out beyond those walls, in the newsroom, that is my life, that is what I am meant to be doing. I will get there.

39.

I was discharged at the end of September. This time, I told myself sternly, this time I will stay well, I will get my work placement at last, I will focus on staying healthy. Five days after being discharged I sat down to watch the *One O'Clock News* before heading off to meet a friend for lunch. The headlines started and with one cough, so too did the blood. I've never been so frustrated. Wearily, I presented myself at the CF clinic and when the consultant came in, I burst into tears. What the hell was wrong with me? Where was all this blood coming from? They still couldn't tell me.

I was brought in, but insisted I wouldn't go to a ward. The blood scared me, but I didn't feel sick enough to waste time and lose sleep and be open to infection on a ward with so many other patients. I was sent down for a chest x-ray and I stood waiting outside the room with a woman opposite me and a man to the right of me. We formed a triangle. I slid down to the ground and slumped onto the hard floor. I was exhausted and no longer cared. Hemoptysis is bullshit. One side of the triangle spoke – it turned out the man was in his forties and had CF. He told me he suffered from hemoptysis, too, but whenever it happened, he didn't tell his team. I wished he'd go away. He told me that the doctors didn't know anything, that he was thinking of moving to Spain for better healthcare. I turned around and said, 'I don't want to be rude, but I'm exhausted.' He said he had called me several times – why, I don't know – and that I had never called him back. I'd never seen him before. He'd got my number from a friend, he said.

The nurse called him and thankfully he left. I took a deep breath. Then the woman opposite started talking to me about her daughter with CF, her difficulty with putting on weight, how she was developing an eating problem. I gave her the best advice I could and we talked CF until the nurse called me.

'Orls, what's the story? You're always ruining my Fridays!'

I had been for the past few months, alright, it was pretty funny. Despite the best attempts of the staff, the hospital was run in a way that getting sick on a Friday or at the weekend made it virtually impossible to get a bed.

'What's going on with the hemoptysis?'

'I wish I knew.' I knew I couldn't control it, I couldn't do anything about it and that was just life. It disturbed me that I'd been saying that for years but had only just grown into it.

I got one of the old single rooms again, settled myself in and opened *Interviewing for Journalists*. The team came around and told me they were thinking of cauterising the lung, depending on the information they received from radiology. I told the consultant what the man with CF outside the x-ray room had said. 'I know you can't legally tell me that I might be okay if I don't present the minute I have hemoptysis, but do other patients not tell you and are they okay?'

I told them I felt crazy, because it the blood would occur once, then stop and I was so sick of this damn hospital. The entire team was in the room, plus the changeover team who would shortly take over my care – roughly ten people in all, staring at me – but in spite of the embarrassment, the tears started to fall before I could do anything to stop them. It was just that they keep telling me to slow down when I wasn't going that fast anyway. I wasn't in college, I wasn't doing theatre, I wasn't running as much as I had been, and yet this damn hemoptysis kept appearing. I felt so crazy because I wanted to fix it, but I couldn't make myself stronger or better or clear my chest or blast my bowels. This problem was beyond me. I hated that this was beyond me. The team made soothing noises, but it was the same as before: they couldn't tell me *why* it was happening, so there was no comfort.

Two days later, I was sitting with my new consultant after the changeover. When we were alone he looked me in the eye and said, 'This is not your fault'. The heaviness weighing me down evaporated instantly. I had needed to hear those words. I told him why I was so upset and how much I had given up to try and fix this – that I should have been having an amazing experience in the *Irish Times*, not lying on a bed like an invalid. He told me we would work it out.

After he left, I sat alone in the room, lost in thought. I knew I needed a break from CF, but obviously I couldn't have one. So the best thing to do was to try not to fight with it for a while. That was why I needed the work experience or the theatre so badly - to distract me and to fulfil me. It was why I needed my book to be finished so I knew I was capable of finishing things I'd started, regardless of constant interruptions. The beauty was that I could let it go, that the past didn't matter, that as Tolle had said, all that mattered was this moment. I couldn't control the hemoptysis, so I had to view it as being freed from that responsibility. I knew I could only live each moment as it happened. I had known it before, but I had never really held onto it. I had said it like a cool platitude and hadn't really meant it. This time, I would make it a lesson to live by.

40.

On the morning of 10 October 2009 I slapped on my
nebuliser and waited for the seven minutes to be up. In the
twenty minutes between Ventolin and physio, I put on high-
waisted navy trousers from Topshop, a black string top and
a flowery chiffon blouse over it. Physio took thirty minutes
exactly – I had it down to a fine art. The morning before
that I had practiced the cycle into town, so I knew it would
take fifteen minutes. I would be there within the hour. It was
the day I was starting my work placement in the newsroom
of the *Irish Times*.

As I chewed my muesli, I thought about how unassuming
I had been in 2006 when I had written my first article for
the *Times*, and how nervous I was now. I was nervous about
my inexperience, but at the same time I knew I could pick it
up. The fact that it might only last two days and then the
bleeding would interrupt things again made me even more
unafraid. I didn't want to get it wrong, but at the same time
it was okay if I made mistakes. I was too long in the tooth
now to worry about that stuff.

When I finally got there and walked through the door,
the newsroom sprang up around me in a wall of colour,

movement and noise. It was unlike anything I had experienced before, and it was mildly terrifying. People worked so fast and seemed to revolve around the room like cyclones. I had to get fast and confident quickly, and it wasn't easy. The days were intense and I wanted to be able for them, so I made sure I cycled in and out everyday. I figured if I did this as much as possible, it would help keep my lungs clear. Initially it was really hard to run on weekdays because my body was just so exhausted. It was the first time since school that I had had such a consistent routine and funny things struck me about my CF in this situation. I realised I could go until around four o'clock and then I needed to do some more airway clearance. My sinuses would drip from maybe two o'clock on and sometimes earlier. I obviously couldn't blow a snotball through my nose in the office, so I had to sort that in the bathroom. Then there was my bowels, which was another reason I was cycling. They were trickier to manage these days, but after a few days in work they were cramping badly. I ate breakfast at around 7am, then did my nebs and meds and was in work for 9.30/10.00. I ate a bagel around 11.30 or 12.00 and then had dinner/lunch at 3.00. It was hard to get used to the change of timetable and eating dinner so early. When it was really busy, I'd leave the later meal and just have a snack to keep me going. But the new regime threw my body out of sync and created all sorts of problems that I just had to deal with as quietly and as efficiently as I could.

These were just minor drawbacks, though. The time itself was amazing. The news editor, who was in charge of my placement, gave me some brilliant books on journalism to read. I wanted to be the best work placement person they'd ever had. The atmosphere was buzzing and yet so friendly. I flung myself into every task I was given and thoroughly enjoyed everything I did. I was interrupted yet again by a stay in Vincent's, but by April I was back in the newsroom again and training for the mini marathon. I couldn't believe how exhausted I was every day from focusing so hard for long periods of time, and it took a while to get back in the swing of things.

In May I was back in Vincent's again, back on IVs again and the mini marathon started to look like a bit of a gamble. I talked to one of my physios about it, about whether I was crazy to be even thinking of doing it, but she encouraged me to keep it as a goal, saying that I could probably walk-run it. She pointed out that the miles I had built up wouldn't disappear. I thought about that and realised that I'd tricked myself into thinking about it the wrong way. When I got sick, I imagined all of the hard work and muscle I had built up evaporating. I had forgotten about Positive Mental Attitude. I wasn't sure where it had got lost along the way, but I decided to reinstate it now and think about the mini marathon differently. I wouldn't be foolish, I'd just be more positive.

I was so happy to be back in the newsroom, although it wasn't always an easy ride. On one memorable occasion I had to cover a parade in Irishtown. There was a host of children in colourful outfits for May Day and a great sense of community spirit. I was interviewing these kids about why they were there when a little girl ran over, pushed her way to the front and demanded to be interviewed. She was being very aggressive, so I was being very calm. I asked her name and she looked right at me, then spat in my face. I couldn't believe she had spat at me and that no one else there thought to comment on it. I kept calm, though, told her it was nice to meet her and then kept interviewing the other kids. It was a very interesting re-start to my career in journalism.

One of the better moments also came during that time, when the *Times* produced a supplement examining forty years of feminism in Ireland. It was called *Sisters* and I was, amazingly, included in it. My picture appeared on the front page alongside lots of women I admired, like Mary Robinson and Geraldine Kennedy. I felt so honoured to be included with women who were my idea of 'proper' feminists. Of course, I had never liked labels – people saying, 'you're a CF sufferer' or 'you're a brave fighter or whatever – but now here was a new label: you're a feminist. It was strange to have that public stamp placed on me, but this particular label didn't bother me at all. I was and am a feminist and I was extremely proud to be included among their number.

I worked in the newsroom right up until the mini marathon in June. I had enlisted some brave friends to run it with me, but between hospital and work, we had never gotten out together to train. It was every woman for herself. I kept telling myself, 'don't start too fast, don't start too fast.' I started too fast. Within three minutes I had raced past one of my CF nurses - the same one I had cheered on from the sidelines the year I wrecked my foot. We high-fived and I kept running. This was a good sign. It was only when I hit 3km, the first water station, that I realised just how fast I was running. I had been trying to slow down, but I got stuck behind people, so the best option was to follow the other runners and weave snake-like through the crowd, runner after runner.

On the way past Vincent's something kicked inside me. I thought of the time I had stood there with Martha and watched other people run this when I couldn't. I thought about how bizarre it was that back then I had thought I was right to not exercise, that I had believed I was doing everything possible to help myself, but I was so far off. I didn't feel like I was even the same person as her, the Orla who stood spectating, not thinking of taking part. Once I hit the bottom of Nutley Lane adrenalin and the sheer feeling of being alive made me want to get to the top as fast as possible: I had to get as far away from Vincent's as I could. Now.

When I hit the RTÉ campus at Montrose my calves were hurting. This had possibly been a supremely stupid idea. Yes, I decided, it was a supremely stupid idea. So I walked for a bit and was grateful to start jogging on even ground. I was back on track as I sailed past UCD and the line of portaloos surrounded by throngs of leg-crossing women. I needed to pee so badly, but I was not going to lose precious minutes to it. I held my pelvic floor muscles like hell and ran on.

It was when I knew I was nearing the end that I felt the most tired. I had to stop and stretch my lower back and calves. My core wasn't ready for this yet and my calves felt like they might snap in two. I fished around in my shorts' pocket and popped the last of my jelly babies into my mouth, felt better and ran on again. I finished strong and when I crossed the finish line, I just wanted to do it all over again. There was no time for that, though, because I had to get myself straight over to the Irish Times offices to write up an article on the race. I made my way there, fuelled myself with an energy bar, typed furiously and filed my copy on time.

The next morning I had to get up early as I was going to talk about my experience on Morning Ireland, RTÉ Radio 1's flagship programme. They had had me on the morning of the race, talking about my expectations, and they wanted me back for a post-race chat. Luckily for me, I hadn't estimated a finish time live on air. I did it way slower than I was capable of, but it was my first race after years of trying for it and never getting to do it. I was so darn proud of myself.

After the programme my dad picked me up from the station and drove me to the airport. I'd been in a new relationship for a few months and my boyfriend and I were going on a trip to Barcelona for a whole week. It was the perfect end to two months of hard work and the mini marathon achievement. It rained for most of the holiday, but we still got to see Gaudi's cathedral, the aquarium and the beach. My last day was taken up with writing an op-ed piece on the fact that the contractors had been pulled from the CF unit. The Irish Times had called to tell me about it and asked for an article as quickly as possible. Damn CF, taking over my holiday. It was important to do it, but nonetheless frustrating for that. As I typed the date on my copy, 5 June 2010, I realised that it was now five years, to the month, since I had unwittingly started campaigning. Five whole years. It was hard to believe, and here I was, still writing pleas for the government to attend to our needs.

When I was walking back to the hotel, I noticed my shoulders were a bit sore. My body was stiff all over from the mini marathon, so I swung my arms around a bit to loosen them up and then headed for the Starbucks beside the hotel. I sat there a minute and the pain abated. I went back to the room and snoozed before dinner. We strolled the short distance to a nearby restaurant, where we ate tapas and talked about how much we'd miss Barcelona. When we left there it was raining and my gallant young man offered to run back to the hotel and fetch an umbrella for me. Unusually for me, I really didn't want to walk. We got a taxi instead and the driver took us the scenic route and drove like a maniac. We were almost at the hotel when I announced that I was most definitely going to throw up. We jumped out and ran straight up to the room and once inside I threw my guts up. 'That did not sound pretty,' he said when I surfaced.

My entire body felt weak. I lay down for a bit and then got up and started to pack. He offered, but I insisted that I'd do it myself. Then we slept the four hours until the flight. When I woke up, I was taking shallow breaths. My left shoulder ached like there was a large pin just sticking in it that couldn't be reached. I tried to lift myself up, but I couldn't. I lay back down, devastated. It couldn't be a lung collapse. It wasn't as sore as before. We don't know anyone in Barcelona. What would we do? It was just because of the race, I told myself. I'm fine. It's fine. I'm fine. I tried again, but couldn't get up. I asked my boyfriend for help and he rushed over and lifted me. It wasn't painful when someone else did.

'What's wrong? Can you still fly?'

'Just let me have a shower and I'll be fine.'

I got into the shower and instantly felt better. The pain was easing, so it really was just another one of those weird pain phenomena. At least twice after the last collapse I had freaked out and made a fool of myself by going in to get an unnecessary x-ray. The team was lovely about it, but I felt awfully stupid not being able to tell the difference. There was no reason why this time should be any different: I was panicked, but it wasn't a collapse. I was definitely able to fly, although I wished we didn't have the whole connecting flight from Barcelona to Zurich to Ireland thing.

In Zurich we had some chocolate milk and I got a massage from a beauty therapist. I felt better. On the coach to the train I kept closing my eyes. He eyed me suspiciously, 'What's wrong with you?' I was just so tired. I wanted to curl up on the floor of that coach and just sleep. 'I'll just sleep here, leave me in Zurich,' I feigned a dramatic face and swished my hand. He laughed. I really didn't want to get on the second plane.

When we got home I was in some sort of delusional state. I had convinced myself that I could tolerate this mild pain and it would be okay. I pulled my luggage from the air coach to the apartment and then called Vincent's. They had no appointments until the next day. This suited me fine as my favourite band, Tegan and Sara, were playing that night and my friends had given me tickets for my birthday. I had been waiting for it for months. I could go out and have fun and worry about the pain tomorrow. I went to see my chemist for advice, just to be on the safe side. She recommended a heat pack and asked me if I was sure it was nothing else. At that point I was sure: it wasn't intolerable and I could function, so it was grand. That night, while wedged between a gaggle of girls at the gig, the jumping up and down only started to feel sore near the end. I must be okay.

I went to the hospital the next day and they marvelled at my tan and said I looked great. I mentioned how I probably needed home IVs and, by the way, I had a sore shoulder. The CF nurse said we'd get an x-ray, just to make sure it wasn't serious. The doctor listened to my chest and said it sounded great, definitely didn't sound like there was much there. The CF nurse insisted on an x-ray and in the end he agreed. I was thinking, Maybe I pulled something during the mini marathon. I hoped I hadn't done some sort of stupid injury that would keep me from exercising.

The doctor and CF nurse met me back in the room when I returned from x-ray. The doctor opened the x-ray and we looked and fell silent. There it was, a small but definite pneumothorax. Oh. My. God. I had flown with it and I had convinced myself it was nothing. They put me on high-flow oxygen immediately and gave me Tramadol for the 'mild' pain. I called my boyfriend, but he couldn't come for a while, so Róisín came over to be with me. She was amazing and calm and exactly what you need in that situation. Someone who is just there and makes you feel less like your world is ending. Again.

41.

In spite of everything, the truth was that I wasn't as panicked when my lung collapsed this time. I was kind of at peace with it in the sense that I had spent the year coming to terms with the fact that I didn't really have control over most things. I had talked to other people with CF about it and I knew that you could come back from it. I had come back from it myself. So all in all, I wasn't feeling scared about the prospect or the outcome. At the same time, being on high-flow oxygen – which required a large mask to be worn, with an 'elephant trunk' apparatus coming out of it – and carrying around an oxygen tank is quite debilitating.

On the first day, I was placed on a six-bed ward. I wasn't allowed to walk around and I couldn't get out of bed anyway because I was so tired, but inevitably, of course, I needed to use the bathroom. The nurses offered me a bedpan, but I wouldn't use it because I wanted to preserve some dignity. I knew I had the strength to walk to the toilet. I did manage to do that, without oxygen, which I knew would be okay for a few minutes. It was quite noisy in the ward and a little bit intimidating because I was feeling very vulnerable when I really needed to feel secure. I didn't want to have to worry about anything, like getting the wrong medication or telling staff members to wash their hands, but unfortunately I did have to think about it. It wasn't a CF ward, so while the nurses were absolutely lovely and eager to help, they had limited knowledge of my condition and my needs.

It was very strange to be lying in bed, unable to move. I found myself thinking, I have so much in me and so much I want to do, but it made me so grateful for what I had and so thankful that I had done what I'd done in my life and had gotten this far. It gave me plenty of time to take stock, which wasn't always good. I lay there thinking, This is the second time this has happened to me – what does this mean? I knew it wasn't *it*, I knew I wasn't going to die and that I would recover, but still, here I was again, for the second time in one year. I had read online that lung collapses were indicative of a person at the end stage of CF, but no one was telling me that I was such a person. Then I worried that perhaps they were keeping it from me out of a false sense of kindness. My consultant came to see me, to talk about my lungs and what could be done. He suggested that a pluradesis might become necessary, which would entail sticking the lung back up to lung wall so that it wouldn't collapse again. On the downside, the procedure might have counter-indications for future transplant. He said we wouldn't do it yet, though, that we'd see how things went and if it collapsed again, we'd see what the surgeon said at that point. My reaction was predictably horrified: '*What?* It's going to collapse again?'

In the event, I began to recover and the pluradesis was taken off the table. Recovery was a frustrating time. When I first restarted physio, it was very difficult and sore, but after while I got into swing of it and was back exercising again. When I left the hospital I was eager to get back into my life. I planned to finish writing the book and maybe get back into the newsroom, but first, I was going to take a break. This was about two weeks after leaving hospital and

I felt up to a trip west, to Galway. I went with my boyfriend – our first time away since Barcelona – and we started out in Galway City. I was doing a piece for the *Irish Times*, so we were under orders to fit in as much as we could and have as much fun as possible. No problem! We strolled around the market, browsed in antique shops, hung out by Spanish Arch and rode a tandem all the way out to Silver Strand, where we ate crisp sandwiches and ran into the waves. After that we checked out of our hotel and headed to Roundstone, where we were meeting his family to celebrate his mother's birthday.

When we reached Roundstone, following the curving road round the bay and into the village, I was bowled over by the beauty of the place. I gazed out on the bay, unable to look away, and thought about how refreshing it was to take in a view like that. It was like that was what we were meant to see in the world and what we were meant to feel and that if everything else fell away in the world and left just nature, that would be perfectly okay. It was amazing.

I was tired throughout the trip, but it escalated on the journey home. I put it down to too much training in my bid to recover fully, but it was an odd feeling to be unable to stay awake in the car. I was really grumpy and snappish, but couldn't put my finger on what wrong. When we reached home I did a nebuliser and then decided to lie down for a bit before I did some airway clearance. I didn't even unpack my stuff, just got into bed and crashed out. My body felt wrong. I lay there for a while, but when I tried to get up again, I couldn't move my left side. There was creaking pain and I thought, No, no, this is not happening again. This is not real, I told myself emphatically. Of course it's not. It's just another one of those fake pains that make me think I have a collapsed lung when really, I don't. I turned onto my right side and that felt better, but when I turned back over, the pain was still there. I stood up, walked around, stretched a bit … the pain was still there. I took some

Nurofen, climbed back into bed and prayed it would be gone when I woke up.

I woke up to the same pain. I called the hospital and went to the clinic. The CF nurse met me at the door and looked at me with worried eyes. I laughed and said, 'I'm fine. It's not going to be a collapse. I'm fine.' Strangely, it was like she knew from looking at me, and I didn't know, or maybe I did and just didn't want to believe it. I went down to x-ray and then returned to the room with the CF nurse. The doctor came in and told me that my lung had collapsed again. After he had left, I looked at the CF nurse and dissolved into tears.

I was admitted and this time I got a cubicle immediately, which meant privacy and quietness. While I was lying on my bed, frustrated, my article on Galway appeared in the *Irish Times*. It felt good to read it. Life was still moving. Even though I was stuck in there with a collapsed lung, I felt I had accomplished something in the past while.

It was a stressful stay because the doctors were debating whether or not to perform a a pluradesis – some were saying it was okay to do it; others were saying it would preclude me from transplant when the time came. There were a lot of complications and a lot of arguments and in the end, we had to call in the transplant surgeons to talk it through. One of my friends who has CF said to me, 'I can't believe they're talking about transplant and using that word.' But I told her it wasn't scary to me because I wasn't having a transplant yet. Nonetheless, I decided to investigate it and I found out that there was a list of requirements for eligibility. For example, you must have the right blood type, you must have your diabetes under control, you must not have sinus problems and you must not have had a talc pluradesis. There are two types of pluradesis – talc and blood. The blood one is a fairly easy procedure, with a 50% success rate. The talc pluradesis has a 90% success rate, but performing it makes it more difficult to extract the lungs in a transplant situation. If you have had a talc, there is a possibility that you will bleed out on the table when they try to peel the lungs away from the body, which would be a waste of a lung.

I was really anxious and upset about it now, what with the doctors and consultants arguing as to what was best thing and me not knowing which way to cast my vote. Eventually, I took matters into my own hands and decided to approach it like a journalist. I spoke to the relevant people in the hospital in Newcastle that performs the transplants, listened to the pros and cons being presented by my doctors and ultimately decided not to have the surgery. A week later, my consultant came to talk to me about my decision and the pros of the pluradesis. I got so upset that I actually ordered him to leave my room, telling him I didn't want to see him again. When he was gone, I sat there and cried and cried. I felt utterly helpless. I felt like I was this sort of genderless, human-less thing, like every single piece of energy had been taken out of me. I was emotionless and motionless. I was defeated. I didn't know what to do next, I didn't know how to play it, I didn't know who to call, I didn't know what to think, I didn't know how to get back. The CF nurse came in, took one look at me and said, 'Orla, I've never seen you like this.'

'I've never seen me like this. I don't know what to do. I don't know what to do.'

Sitting alone in that room, I realised there would be a time in the future when I would be completely powerless and that this was a good lesson for me to learn. This emotion that was like the life had been taken from me, that I had no choice, I realised that this was something I would have to confront in the future, when I would no longer have the ability to decide what I was going to do, where I was going to go, what surgery I was going to have, how fast I was going to recover or whether I wanted to go for a run or do more physio. And it was funny because I recognised that only through relinquishing control can true strength come. If you can live your life accepting those things over which you have no power, accepting that nothing is certain, incredible things can happen. There was beauty in that recognition.

But it was strange to think like this, because all through my childhood people said, 'positive, positive, positive', that was always the focus. My father constantly pushed the ideal of Positive Mental Attitude, and I made it my mantra, too. But in the past few years I'd had moments where I'd understood that it was not a simple case of being positive. I had come to understand that it was important to first untangle all the stuff that makes you feel you have to be positive all the time, lay it out there and then say, right, actually it's okay to be afraid of this. Once you had admitted that fear to yourself, let yourself feel it, that was when you could own it and that was when you could rid yourself of it. You cleansed yourself of it and you just said, Look that's going to happen and when it happens, I've now gone through this and I'll know better next time. I'm sure it's not really possible to be prepared when it actually happens, that you can't predict exactly what way it will go or what you will feel, but that isn't the point. The point is that I now know that there is a sort of peace that comes from saying the truth and that peace means I'm not scared and I'm not hiding from it. So I can move forward again with my positive attitude, this time armed with the knowledge that I do not have control.

Also this made me think about my attitude to having a lung transplant. I had ignored the notion of it to a large extent, because I felt that with my sinus problems and my weird veins, among a few other things, I would probably be considered a risky candidate and therefore ineligible. I had coped with that by trying not to think about it. Whenever it surfaced I would say to myself, No, I'll never get one and even if I could, I wouldn't anyway because I don't want someone else's lungs and I don't want some half-arsed life. Now, though, I know it is a medical miracle. I've seen the way people suffered with CF at the end, and it wasn't pleasant. I'd also seen successful transplant patients living and succeeding and going to the European Transplant Games and going back to work, going back to college, having families, living their lives. I often wonder if, when I need one, I'll regret being as aware as I am. But then again, I know I will make the right choice, that it will happen when it's meant to, the way it's meant to.

42.

During all this time, when my health was difficult, there was still the campaign. We still did not have any further progress on the unit. When I came back from Barcelona and was in hospital with my first lung collapse that summer I had written an article for the *Times* marking the fact that it had been five years since my very first article on CF. That article finished with these words: 'If there's such a thing as campaigners' fatigue, I may be experiencing it. I have been writing the same thing for five years. It's a depressing thought that I will be doing it for another five.'

There was a huge response to the article and the CF campaign saw a resurgence in support as a result. It became part of the national conversation again, with callers to Liveline highlighting the case and a Dail debate on the matter of the contractor. The original contractor was now involved in NAMA, which meant a new contractor was being sought so the building work could commence. I found out about the Dail debate from James Reilly, then opposition spokesperson on Health, now Minister for Health in the Fine Gael/Labour government. He was very supportive of the cause and told me that the Dail had debated the matter late into the night and that then Minister for Health Mary Harney was present for it, which he saw as very encouraging as she hadn't attended the previous debate on the matter. His interest seemed very positive to me, so when a new contractor was appointed a few days later, I felt more secure about the plans and for the first time really believed it was going to happen at last.

There was another hugely positive moment for me that summer: in July, I was presented with the Young Medical Journalist of the Year award. I was in hospital at the time as it was just at the end of my second lung collapse, but I was allowed out to the awards ceremony. After some last-minute phonecalls, I secured the company of my good friends Laura, Patrick and Philip at my table. It was an incredible sight – to see so many journalists and friends gathered in one room. I find awards nights very strange because my default setting is 'messer' and everyone else is so professional at these things, but I really enjoyed this one and felt at home among those people whom I so admired. When they announced the Young Medical Journalist of the Year award and called out my name, I was completely gobsmacked. It wasn't that I thought I didn't stand a chance, but I wasn't prepared for my own reaction to it. I had to fight back tears as I rose out of my seat and made my way to the front of the room. I have been lucky enough to win a number of awards, so I thought a win wouldn't feel any different from any other win, but it was totally different, in fact. This award had the word 'Journalist' in it, and I felt overwhelmed to be included in that category. I was incredibly honoured and thrilled to have won. Of course, I was a Cinderella that night – turning back into a hospital patient at the stroke of midnight – but I stretched it out and went to Yamamori with my friends after the event and ate good food, enjoyed good conversation and stared disbelievingly at the award on the table beside me.

When I got out of the hospital in August, I was filled with a renewed sense of purpose, thanks to the award, and was determined to take on the journalism world again and really make my mark. I figured if I could just get a good run at it it would be ok. But I kept getting sick, so that didn't happen for a while. From September to December I was regularly on IVs and in and out of the hospital, which held me up. Instead, I focused on exercising and trying to finish the book. Then a new opportunity cropped up that I hadn't expected. I got a phone call from Ken O'Shea, the series producer of RTÉ 1's current affair programme, *Prime Time*. Ken was hugely supportive of the CF campaign and told me that he wanted to give me a *carte blanche* to produce a programme about CF in Ireland. It could be any story I wanted to tell about CF care in Ireland and it could be an amazing testimony. It was the most incredible offer I think I have ever received. I met up with the producer, Ross Whitaker, in October and we started planning the programme.

That same month, October 2010, I had reason to write another article in the *Times* because a young woman with CF rang Liveline to describe the facilities in which she was being treated. She wanted to highlight how CF patients were being failed by the system and her testimony was very effective: she was being treated in appalling conditions and was under ridiculous amounts of stress and danger as a result. Her call sparked a deluge of callers, and the programme ran with the CF story for several days. One of the key points being repeated was that the newly appointed contractor hadn't yet signed the works contract for the CF units. The truth was that the cause of the delay was being sorted out and signing was going to happen shortly – that's what the CFAI and the journalists knew. However, it's not surprising that people were finding that hard to accept given that they had endured so many broken promises over the years.

I feared that the heated discussion being conducted on the airwaves and the anger it was creating might derail the signing process, so I tried communicating with the young woman who had originated the discussion on Liveline. I said to her, 'Please don't keep going with this. It is going to happen and you're going to do more harm than good.' But as I said, when a government has cried 'wolf' so often, it's very difficult to convince people that they are now telling the truth. The story rumbled on and the outrage was palpable. It was very strange for me to watch the way it was picked up and how it progressed because this time I was a spectator, watching how a story can take on a life of its own. I found it very difficult because some of those involved went to new extremes. Some of the tabloid newspapers ran with images of people with CF, hours before their death, hugging their parents – it was the most private of moments being laid bare on the public stage. It made me feel so sad and frustrated because I really believed the contract would be signed very soon and therefore these private moments were being traded for nothing. I felt for everyone concerned, being able to see it from all sides. It was a reaction to years of waiting, years of untruths, half-truths and hard truths, and now it spilled over into an uncontrollable emotion that threatened to engulf everyone – and the CF cause.

As it was, I knew I couldn't get involved, even the slightest bit, nor was there any point talking further to the main protoganists because no one was listening to me. As always in life, there are those who like you and those who don't and the CF campaign was no different. There were those who felt I shouldn't be a spokesperson for the campaign and anything I said wasn't going to hold any weight with them whatsoever. All the same, it was interesting to see how things divided up: some people supported me and said things like, 'why are they doing this? Can you not stop them?'; other people were saying that I was too much to the forefront in terms of public profile, that I shouldn't be given awards and that I had no right to speak for people with CF. That was funny, really, in the sense that I had never, ever wanted to be a spokesperson. I had gone through a lot of personal difficulty and self-

searching to be able to do it and it was a role that had cost
me an awful lot physically and emotionally. There were
many mornings when I had woken up and thought, I don't
want to do this campaign, but I had to do it. I knew it
would come out well in the end and we would get there and
I didn't want to give up on it. Once I had started it, I knew
I had to finish it; it had blown in and out of my life like a
whirlwind for five years now. That's why it was so strange
to be on the outside, but it was also good for me to let go
and step back. It was really heartbreaking to see it get so
messy, but I hadn't started that campaign.

When it got to breaking point, I decided to write about
it. I did an article for the *Irish Times* about the difficulty of
campaigning and how you will never get the support of
every person because opinions differ. You might think you'll
achieve consensus because everyone has a common goal
that they're fighting towards, but that's not what happens.
You learn so much from being part of a campaign. Now, I
look back at the past five years and think, I could have done
things differently and there are things that, with hindsight, I
would do differently, but when I was starting out I just did
things the way I thought was best. I listened to my gut and
when something felt right, I ran with it. I think that's all
anyone can do. So while it had been a very difficult time, it
had also been a successful five years. That much was clear
when the contractors did sign the contract. I know some
people look at me and think all sorts of negative things
about me, but my only aim in all this was to get the CF unit
built. That was all I wanted and what I fought for. I just
wanted the unit built and us to be using it and for it to be
done so that none of us had to worry about this crap
anymore.

The other reason for my patience with the contractors
and the government during that time was that I didn't have
as much anger as I had at the start of the campaign. After
five years, I just had frustration and this bizarre knowledge
of how long it takes to get something done in this country.

I didn't want to do anything that would adversely affect the process because I also had the knowledge of what happens when it's not done: I had watched my friends not finish their college degrees, not get married, not see the world; I had watched my friends die. CF is a vicious illness and if you have it, you're going to die from it. That's the truth. But CF care must be about keeping a person as well as possible for as long as possible, and that can only be done with proper facilities across all sectors of life for someone with CF. It's the only way. To secure those facilities, you need to keep an open channel to government and keep up the dialogue. It's the only way.

Funnily enough, there was something very helpful that came out of that young woman's call to Liveline and her description of her life with CF. It spurred on young girls of school age to describe their experiences on air, which brought into the light some of the myths about CF. I was really upset when one of the callers said that boys wouldn't go near her if they knew she had CF because they would think she was diseased. That comment showed how much ignorance was still out there and how awful it was for a person with CF to live with that ignorance. If someone doesn't want to touch you because you've got CF, then you shouldn't be with that person. That person doesn't deserve you. That's one aspect. The other aspect that was brought up was the tendency for some people to think a person with CF isn't really sick because she or he looks healthy enough. This really struck a note with me in terms of my own schooldays. One of the girls described how her peers and teachers often didn't believe her when she said she was unwell, which made school very difficult at times. I completely related to that because when I was in secondary school, I hadn't realised that a lot of my tiredness and breathlessness and inability to focus or concentrate was to do with CF, as well as medication. I just thought it was only me being a messer and my parents hadn't exactly begged to differ. In fact, after that girl spoke on Liveline about this, my mother who, along with my dad had always pushed me to stay positive and not to give in to laziness, said, 'We never realised that the IVs did this to you.' Listening to the callers' experiences and matching them with my own, it made me realise that there's still a huge grey area in relation to CF, so much people don't know or understand. That, as much as anything, made me certain about writing this book and about producing the *Prime Time* documentary because it was clear that all these ways of demystifying CF are still badly needed.

All of this thinking fed into my work on the documentary and my focus became to create positive images of people with CF, whether they were waiting for transplant, post-transplant, working, studying, married, having children – all the faces of CF to show the complexity of the illness. I worked hard on it from January to March 2011, albeit interrupted by three hospital stays in that period. But slowly it began to come together into a piece of which I am very proud.

In March I flew to London for a short break. I was worried about flying – it would be my first time in an airplane since the journey home from Barcelona – but I decided to do it. It wasn't a good decision. On my first day in London, I coughed up blood in the middle of Leicester Square. I was devastated. This was a special birthday trip and I was staying in a room once occupied by Judy Garland, one of my heroes. I had been looking forward to it in a state of high anticipation, so to get sick while I was there was so frustrating. The only upside was that I got good use out of Judy's bed because the whole next day I was too sick to go anywhere, so I curled up under the duvet and stayed put.

On day three I was determined to get out and about again, and got as far as Covent Garden. By that stage I really couldn't walk or breathe very well, so I got a taxi to the hospital. I couldn't get into the CF hospital on a Sunday so they sent me to A&E down the road. I was admitted through there, which was interesting in comparison to Irish hospitals. The cubicle curtains were made of disposable paper, not washable fabric like in Ireland, and it was quite clean. I asked for a CF doctor, but was told I didn't need one. I got an ABG test, which showed that my oxygen levels were fine, but I wanted a six-minute walk test because I felt my sats were dropping when I was walking. I ended up being walked around the A&E, very slowly, by a wonderful gay nurse who told me how he loved to go to The George when he was in Ireland. He started talking to me about drag shows he'd seen there and, while it was hilarious, I felt I was going off my head without oxygen. But they insisted I was fine and I was sent home. I called my team in Vincent's and they told me to dump my return air ticket, get the ferry home and come straight in.

When I got back to Dublin I had to wait two days for a bed. The morning before I was admitted, I went to an event in the Burlington Hotel that was attended by the Minister for Health and the head of the HSE. We had a chat and they pulled me into a lot of photographs and told me that everything was on track for the unit and it was all going well. Sixteen days later the *Prime Time* documentary was aired and that evening RTÉ received a press statement from the HSE, the Department of Health and Minister for Health James Reilly: there would be twenty beds in the new unit instead of the promised thirty-four. They had cut fourteen beds without even telling us, through a statement sent to *Prime Time*. It was unbearably frustrating. I turned, once again, to the power of words and wrote an article for the *Irish Times*.

One week later, a contract was drawn up between the CF consultant at St Vincent's, the CEO of CFAI, the building planner CEO for the architect for the HSE, the head of the HSE and the CEO of St Vincent's, which stated that there would always be two beds available for CF patients. This would mean that if the twenty-bed unit were fully occupied and two more people with CF were admitted, then two more beds would be freed up. In other words, there would be a rotation of beds, which would mean there would always be space for CF patients. The day after this contract was signed, I rang the CF consultant to talk to him about it and he said it was what he had always wanted – to have control over the admissions so that he could guarantee beds for CF patients. The unit might have less beds than originally promised, but by the terms of this contract, patients with CF would not be left waiting for in-patient care.

I felt like we actually had done it this time. It was done. It was finished. The new CF unit is due to open in April 2012 and so far work is progressing and the horizon is clear. I am hopeful that it will open on time and make a huge difference in the lives of all of us with CF. I am hopeful.

Epilogue

I have friends who are writers and they're so good, they make it look easy. To find out how hard it is, you have to sit down and try to write a whole book. I started that process four years ago, and it's taken me a long time to find the end. It has been difficult to get to this point because sifting through my experiences, working out my feelings and motives and reactions, has been a strange journey – at times enjoyable, at times draining and at times, if I'm being honest, impossible. The amount of times I've gotten up and literally run away from this manuscript would have written the book twenty times over. As a result, it took a long time to figure out what I wanted to say and then to write it.

A memoir is an odd piece of writing. I was constantly frustrated by the idea that what I was doing was somehow egotistical, that what I was sharing was unnecessary, that I was shouting things no one wanted to hear. After so much thought I just said to myself, Look, if I'm going to write a book it has to be a full circle of me and not a half-circle or a quarter-circle. I don't want to die in a few years having produced a half-circle book to represent me. All I can do is give my truth, which is what this book is. I went through all these things and I struggled and I had a great time and I'm very lucky and this is just one life, just one experience. It doesn't mean everyone with CF has experienced or felt these things, it doesn't mean that everyone is like me. That's the thing, if everybody with CF wrote a book, each one would be very different, and if every young girl wrote a book, each one would be very different, but within that, there are many similarities in both of those groups that I think people will relate to in my story. So that's what I have told: my story.

In writing this, a few key things have emerged for me, some of which I knew before I started, others which crystallised as I wrote. One of those is the notion that what I am known for is CF. That is a loaded statement for me. In the beginning it was a bit strange, but after a while it started to really bother me. When I started campaigning people would say, 'Well done' or 'That was great' and it was funny because I didn't feel we'd gotten anywhere. All my life I didn't want to be the brave sick girl who fought something, that was my worst nightmare. Now here I am, having spent the past five years cementing that idea in people's heads. I find it hard to accept, but it's not possible to avoid it when you devote yourself to campaigning for something. It overtakes you in so many ways. During campaigning, people would approach me on the street, in the supermarket, in restaurants to say, keep going, keep fighting, which is wonderful to hear. But it didn't restrict itself to the campaign, it spilled over into every area of my life. So even when I was just doing my own thing, like being in college, going out with friends or even trying to date people, I found there was an unspoken expectation about how I would be or what I would say because everyone – whether or not they were a stranger to me – already knew I had CF. I've had to work hard to forget this

For a long time I have been putting expectations on myself, always thinking, This person expects me to be like this or expects me to be perfect, and then trying to mould myself to some imagined ideal. This has dogged me since I was young, when my anxieties revolved around the questions: how am I going to be perfect for everyone? How will I meet the needs of this person who expects me to be a certain way? I suppose some people do expect me to be a certain way, but now I think a lot of that pressure is in my own head. When parents of children with CF asked me things, I found it really stressful because I was so caught up in trying to give perfect answers. Often, though, they were asking me about things I hadn't experienced or didn't know, and I'm certainly not qualified to give anyone medical information about this condition. When a distressed person is questioning you like this, your whole instinct is to do everything possible to help. It took me a long time to understand that while I could be helpful, I didn't have to give all of myself, I didn't have to drain myself doing it, I didn't have to answer every letter immediately. I eventually learned that there was a pause button – I had a choice. At the start I raced to help straight away, tried to be the one who sorted everything out, and I had to come to accept that this wasn't my role and it wasn't possible for one person anyway. When you become a public figure – a label I raise an eyebrow to – people forget that you have another life, so you have to learn to preserve something for yourself – that's your duty to yourself.

The problem is, it can be very difficult to carve out your own space and secure your own identity within that situation. As the campaigning went on, and a few months turned into a few years, I found it more and more difficult to reconcile the real me with the public me. The public me was the person people saw and made assumptions about, and sometimes that crossed the line into a violation of my privacy, like the time the college newspaper speculated about the government having another death on its hands – mine. Yes, I was fighting for my own and other people's lives, but it was still hard to see my death become public property, to be invoked and discussed as others pleased.

When that happens, you feel you don't have control over your own story.

I never wanted to be known as someone with CF. I wanted to keep that part private and be known for acting, writing, singing, being a good person, being an achiever. That was what I wanted. But as I campaigned more and more and as college slipped away from me and I chose not to finish my degree, I began to think that all I was was this person who had CF and campaigned, that I didn't have anything else to offer the world. I felt like my intelligence was decreasing, like I had less value as a person. That, of course, meant my self-worth was nil. It was so very strange because while I was feeling all that, some people were looking at me and saying, 'You're amazing, you're doing amazing things', which I couldn't relate to really. Others were saying, 'You think you're so great, you get all the praise', which besieged the fragile part of me. The truth is, I would have much preferred to just be in college, living life below the radar, getting good grades and focusing on *my* life. That would have been so much easier than the constant juggling, because that's what a life lived like this is: juggling health and exercise and campaigning. The campaigning is so brutal, it's like a political campaign – you do every interview you can do, work as hard as you can, on the go constantly, you sacrifice sleep, you sacrifice meeting up with your friends, you sacrifice so much. I don't mean that to sound like a sob story because it's not, it's positive because you get there in the end, but that doesn't change the fact that you give an awful lot to get the bit you want.

I'm sure there are people with CF who don't mind at all being known as such. I think one of the reasons why it was so hard for me to get to grips with it, with the whole 'brave sick girl' tag, was because when I stepped onto the public stage, I hadn't yet figured myself out. I think it was harder for me to realise who I was because I lived in a world where everybody kept telling me who I was. I had doctors and nurses and people who had known me since I was a kid saying, 'Sure you're like this' or 'You love the performing arts' and I did, but there was also this intense feeling of being owned by everyone else, of not being autonomous. When I was fourteen I realised that my entire medical history was documented and that everything I was doing was being written down. It was a strange thought and I became exceptionally paranoid at the time. Looking back though, in a way I accepted the fact that I was like a lab rat and I think it made me feel that my life was not my own, which of course it is. But I think I had put these blocks in front of me of fear and fear of rejection and I couldn't knock them down, so I couldn't live my life and be myself, and yet I desperately wanted to carve out my own future, outside of CF.

I was eighteen when I started campaigning and up to that point my life had been quite sheltered, in that I spent a lot of time in hospital and was close to my parents and tried to be a 'good girl'. I felt I couldn't do or say anything that might make people think otherwise. But then, that's one of the best things about getting older, you stop caring so much what everyone else thinks and start living more for yourself. There's no point knowing that life is short if you can't enjoy it the way you want to, in honesty and freedom. The truth that I was so afraid of was that I was having feelings for other women that were very complicated. I couldn't explain this to myself when I was younger and as a result I was deeply, deeply ashamed of these feelings and afraid to articulate them to anyone.

My mom told me recently that when I was about eleven, that was the first time she thought that I was attracted to girls. She didn't know what to do about it, she just hoped I wouldn't be adversely influenced by anyone, that I would find my own way in my own time. It was only when I got to college that I was able to start exploring that side of me properly and finally come to terms with it. When I started talking openly about it to my parents in 2008, it wasn't so hard for them to accept because they had seen it coming for so long, and yet because I felt I didn't have the dialogue to express it for so long it felt new to me. When I started writing this book and confronting so many things, and the upshot of that was a stint in counselling, where I talked everything through and straightened it all out in my mind. It wasn't that easy, though, because it turned out that the therapist was an Evangelical Christian who did not believe in homosexuality. I had been seeing her for a while before this came out, but I didn't stop going to her because I knew she was helping me solve things. So I went to her for a year and she was really helpful, but at the end of it, when I told her I felt so much happier and that I'd accepted myself and yes, I liked girls, she couldn't accept it. She tried to show me that this was not the case, that I was fooling myself. I went along with that for a while, to see where she was coming from; I didn't want a new struggle. I went out with a guy for eighteen months and I loved him dearly and it was great, but it wasn't what I was looking for.

It took me a long, long time to peel away those layers of myself and accept that and be at one with it. What I also realised was that I don't have to do anything with it, that I don't have to stand up and say, I'm gay, I'm bisexual, I'm whatever, I can just be the way I've always been and feel the way I've always felt. I can date women if I want to and fall madly in love with one or I can date men, and whatever prejudices people throw at me or whatever someone thinks about me, I'll still be me. Once I had accepted that fully, I felt I no longer had to worry about that secret shame I'd been feeling all my life, which was like having a part of my identity that I couldn't claim. When I decided I would claim it and started talking about it and feeling it, I felt more me than I'd ever felt. Maybe I will call it something at some stage, but given my general loathing of all labels, I doubt it.

I remembered one time a friend had come to see me in hospital and I was tired and frustrated and sad, languishing in a six-bed ward. He said to me, 'Remember who you are.' I looked at him. 'Remember what you've done. Remember what you've achieved and what people think of you and how you're revered.' I remember sitting there thinking, That's not who I am, though. That's what I do, but it's not who I am. So who was I? That was what I had to figure out – who was I? Perhaps in ten years I'll look back at this book and think, Oh my God, how embarrassing, why did I say that? Or else I'll think, Jeez, that was pretty impressive for me at that age, look what's happened. That's the brilliant thing about life: it's always evolving and every day is a new adventure, you're figuring out things about yourself and every day you wake up and it's a new day, it's the best feeling and I appreciate that so much. I know that who I am is going to be a journey that I'll be on for the rest of my life.

I don't know what exactly I'll do with all this energy I have now that the campaign seems to be at an end, but I want to give time to journalism, to writing, to politics. There's still so much I want to do. After giving over the formative years of my life, 18–24, to campaigning and CF, now I get to go chase my dreams. Maybe I'll go back and do a different degree, have a completely new experience. I'm enjoying the maybes – it's like a brand new view to look out on. Because in the end, that's what you have to live for – experience. It's living your life and experiencing it fully, that is the most rewarding and inspiring thing about life. If I have lived my life like that, then when my time comes to die, I won't be too worried about it. To be honest, I don't necessarily believe that when you die, you just die. I feel like my spirit could come back and do other good things in the world; maybe elements of me will merge with other people and help them. Anything is possible. The idea of death is too final for me. Experience, creativity, expression, inspiration, these things never die. They are life.

Appendix 1

Fragile lives put at risk
The Irish Times, **Wed, Jun 15, 2005**

Why are people like me dying ten years earlier than other cystic fibrosis patients across the border, asks
Orla Tinsley

In the dim light of the hospital ward, the woman in the bed beside me searches in vain for her long-lost relatives. 'Maire! Sean! Paddy!' she cries, wandering towards where I am lying. As her fingers prod and stroke my back, I can only hope she soon comes back to reality and realises that I don't have her relatives hidden under my hospital blanket.

Such is the plight of cystic fibrosis suffers in this State that this afternoon the Cystic Fibrosis Association of Ireland (CFAI) is meeting a group of TDs and senators to try to impress upon them the urgency of the crisis that has developed in the treatment of people with CF. I am writing this in the hope that somebody, somewhere will take action to address the appalling statistic that, on average, Irish CF patients are dying almost 10 years earlier than their counterparts across Europe because of unacceptable levels of care.

When I was three days old I was diagnosed with cystic fibrosis, a chronic genetic disease that severely affects the lungs and digestive system. Because of this, my life is punctuated by two-week stints in hospital. In the past year my illness has accelerated, leaving me hospitalised every month since October 2004, with roughly a nine-day respite between hospitalisations. My days revolve around nebulisers, inhalers and injections, not to mention my harsh, hacking cough.

That's my reality and I can live with that.

But late on this particular night, as I lie in my bed in St Vincent's Hospital, I realise there are certain things I should not have to live with, not in this booming Ireland of 2005.

Before I turned 18 I took a while choosing which hospital I would go to for care, in much the same way other people my age make those vital CAO form decisions. For most of my life I'd been in and out of Temple Street Hospital and I knew that the leap to adult hospital was always going to be precarious.

Now here I am, officially an adult, being cared for in what is effectively a geriatric ward. As the woman in the bed beside me continues her search for her family members, I am struck by how silly it was of me to turn 18. I will myself to be transported, Star Trek-style, back to the howling babies and hyperactive toddlers in Temple Street. Who cared if my feet hung over the end of the bed? I was safe there. Away from this cacophony of chaos.

The bond I had formed with the children's hospital had been unbreakable. The nurses, doctors, dieticians, phlebotomists, teachers, play staff, physiotherapists, administrators, porters and surgeons were integral parts of my life and they all played a big part in my personal development. It seemed their ethos was that although there is an illness there, there is also a person. A living, breathing, thinking human being. A person with an illness, not an illness with a person attached. I had got used to that ethos.

I've been taught, trained and virtually brainwashed about the way to take proper care of myself by the dedicated team at Temple Street. A structure of beliefs, medical evidence and ideologies were instilled in me so that I could protect myself with regard to my CF.

There are organisms floating around in the air that are dangerous to a person with CF, and one of these is the 'superbug', MRSA. When I was admitted to St Vincent's I spent my first two nights in the casualty jungle, metres away from a man who had the bug. Fear flooded my mind as I thought of the germs floating around, germs that were harmful to a healthy person but that could prove fatal for me. It was a massive culture shock. What was to become of me? Four different beds in three days, that's what. From paediatrics to geriatrics, that's what.

A close friend of mine, who died some years ago, liked to refer to us affectionately as 'Lifers'. Every minute of our life is affected by CF, thus every minute should be properly catered for. We take great care in the 'outside world' to live life conscious of every threat to our very existence. Why is it that the health services, during those times when we are at our most vulnerable, do not do the same? We are not even asking for special treatment, just basic human rights. We need to be cared for in isolation and should not be put at risk of infection. But this does not happen in hospitals across the State.

Another night in the hospital I turn up Andrea Corr on my headphones to maximum volume, to block out a different kind of music. The woman across from me needs to use the bathroom. 'Nurse, Nurse! I need the toilet! Nurse! Are you deaf?' Her glazed eyes turn towards me and her head rolls demonically, her tongue hanging out. 'Maire! Sean! Paddy!' the woman to my left joins in, their cries an unbearable duet of desperation. I flap back upon my bed, my body thudding against the mattress. Then the woman who needs the nurse clambers from her bed screaming 'Help! Help! Help!' and her excreta drop on the floor behind her. All I can do is open my window and wonder how I got here; from safe hospital to what seems a geriatric asylum.

I should point out that my medical needs have not lessened because I have turned 18. If anything, they've increased. Diabetes and osteoporosis tend to set in as people with CF live longer. I am 18. These women are 80. Our needs are completely different. They need bedpans. I need clean bug-free fresh air.

I don't just want to highlight the situation in St Vincent's Hospital. A review of hospital services across the State recently showed that it's the same story elsewhere. According to the latest research, the median age of death for CF patients in the Republic is 21, compared to 30 in Northern Ireland; people born in the US with CF in the 1990s are expected to live until the age of 45.

They have a better system across the Border. They have more funding. The CFAI is currently part-funding the provision of desperately needed specialist staff across the State but it should not have to do the job of government.

The curious thing about all of this is the fact that we are among the richest nations in the world. We have a vast disposable income, we have new cars, high-class restaurants, a higher standard of living. We are no longer the poor relations. Well, except for our elderly, except for our school buses, except for people with CF.

I spent night after night listening to the ramblings of my more senior room-mates and wondering why it is that in Ireland CF patients don't seem to be entitled to life-prolonging hospital care. The blood-stained tray on which I received my antibiotics from during my time in A&E recently proves that.

Disgusting? Yes. Degrading? Absolutely. Normal? Unfortunately. Acceptable? What do you think?

Appendix 2

My life is in politicians' hands
The Irish Times, Tuesday, May 22, 2007

Whoever is the next taoiseach, **Orla Tinsley** *wants the best shot at life she can get, her illness notwithstanding. This is her impassioned appeal to the government we are about to elect*

I watched the Ahern v Kenny TV debate unfold. I was particularly interested because I am still unsure as to where my vote will go. Being a teenager in the throes of exams I am bombarded with calls to 'rock the vote'. It is easy to spurn such rocking, particularly when voting is on a Thursday, in the middle of university exams.

However, I have a very personal interest in this election, a selfish one at that. It concerns my life and the lives of many of my peers, so I've taken time away from study to write this.

I needed treatment in hospital last April for my cystic fibrosis. I have had this illness since I was three days old. Ireland has the highest incidence of CF in the world and yet we have the poorest facilities. In their debate, Bertie Ahern made light of the fact when Enda Kenny said that a 30-year-old machine was in use in a brand new hospital. The Taoiseach quipped under his breath that it was impossible as it was a new hospital.

But he doesn't understand. Machines are exchanged, underfunded and overused. Just like the nurses, doctors and patients who are shovelled through the relentless system.

The last time I went into hospital I left after 10 days. I am usually pretty level-headed about my illness. It doesn't control my life; it's an extension of it. I've learnt to deal with it to a certain degree. However, there are certain things my mind cannot deal with; lack of sleep is one of those. I left hospital a week early. I would like to tell the Taoiseach and Enda Kenny why.

They might not be aware that elderly, senile patients are forced to share rooms with CF patients in a way that poses a threat to us both. In this environment, I have to get used to being cursed at continually.

My crimes include opening windows, running taps and pulling my curtain to change in privacy. I have laughed nervously as psychiatric patients have sat on my bed trying to convince me that the world was going to explode. I have met people who have wandered into the six-bed room where I sleep and attempted to convince me they could heal me if I only let them touch my arm.

I've seen beautifully glamorous elderly ladies urinate on the floor through no fault of their own. I've maintained my composure as other friends with CF are attacked by elderly people or family members for being too loud or for having the gall to have the window open.

Sleep is not possible at night and with breakfast at 7am, cleaners at 8am and a barrage of doctors, blood-tests, physio and medical students to occupy, it's not possible in the day. iPods are a handy way to try and escape unless they go for a walk, like mine did the last time I was there. That theft, along with nine consecutive sleepless nights, instigated my decision to leave.

Checking myself out had fortuitous consequences – a much sicker friend, who had been in a different six-bed room, was moved into a cubicle. A week later I found out that my friend had passed away. I took a small comfort that her last few days were in

the privacy of that room with her family, and not
with five other people and theirs.

I have often observed old and young people dying
in the room I sleep in. The unspoken rule is, if you
can walk out, you leave or if you can't, you put on
your headphones and pretend. You pretend you
cannot see the silhouettes through the curtains,
bending down to give one last kiss. You pretend that
you do not feel guilty for being there, guilty about
your hacking coughs which interrupt their final
moments.

Going home, you pretend you have never seen the
big blue body trolleys rush by. The old lady across
from you, cursing ferociously when you open a
window and praying out loud for hours on end at
night, does not bother you. At least that's what you
pretend.

There is a constant fear of infection when we
come through A&E. My latest jaunt there was over
two days, where I was exposed to infection and left
coughing on a plastic chair. At 3pm I got a drug line
inserted, whilst awake, into my arm. I watched it all
on the big screen in fascination, then returned to my
plastic chair in the waiting room.

I waited again before being transferred to the
actual A&E bed area, where I waited on a larger
plastic chair. I then spent the next 10 minutes waving
furiously at a porter I recognised. Half an hour later
he emerged with a trolley.

He worked hard to get it. When I returned from
the bathroom the pillow he also worked hard to get
was gone. With a respiratory disease and gloopy,
mucus-filled lungs, lying flat is not acceptable.
Without a pillow my trolley was useless as I had to
sit up anyway.

This situation is unfathomable. People with CF
are sick of hearing the statistics. We are sick

repeating the same line: 'We have the highest instance of CF in the world with Third World facilities.' We are sick of hearing that money is coming, that somebody somewhere just has to sign something. We are sick of waiting and I am sick of watching my friends die while we wait.

Recently a newspaper printed an article about another pal who passed away a month before the friend I mentioned earlier. This young woman came up with the slogan 'Sick Waiting' because she felt it encapsulated the mood of people with CF in Ireland. The general consensus is, she was dead right.

My friend wrote a letter, which was published in *The Irish Times*. She was left in A&E in agony for hours without an X-ray, painkillers or a chest drain. Her lung had collapsed and this agony was prolonged. To add insult and torture to an already appalling case my dear friend had her chest drain lifted incorrectly which messed up the gravity and blew her lung out for the second time. She never recovered from that infection.

Outside of hospital, my friend worked selflessly editing a CF magazine and gathering extensive knowledge on treatments and funny anecdotes regarding the disease. She also completed an MA, fell madly in love and won the Young Scientist of the Year exhibition. Her team won the European Scientist of the year too. She fought every inch of the way for her life. Nobody wants to be a victim. This is something I personally loathe.

The idea that someone is poor, fragile, incapable and not in control of their destiny, terrifies me. Yet right here, in this shambles of a health system, the reality is that what we fight so hard not to become has become us, uncontrollably so.

When not in hospital we fight to stay alive. We also fight for our healthcare. Daily we take our drugs, nebulisers and 50 or so tablets. There are also, for some CF patients, enemas, needles, insulin, and bags of diluted feed fed through naso-gastric tubes.

We do it because we are lifers. We have the illness, we deal with it in different ways. Yet most of us work hard at keeping well because we are determined to have the best quality of life possible, because we, like everyone else, deserve it.

Every time we enter a hospital this idea is undermined. Our hard work to stay on this journey called life is destroyed by the broken promises, by the bloody politics of it all. The money was there for staffing but the number of staff was capped. The plans were there and six months later we still 'just need someone to sign off' on them. There is no more time for planning; the time for action is now.

I am in first year in college, have missed 10 weeks of this school year but I intend to do my exams and do well. I will then go on to write, act and live my life the way I want, alongside CF, as I have always expected to. I am not ready to be stopped yet.

Taoiseach, Enda Kenny, our lives are quite literally in your hands. We want an honest shot at it. Even if we have a few limitations the system should not accentuate them. It should work in favour of its long-term patients.

Allow us to recuperate with sufficient sleep and without fear of infection. Enable us to leave hospital without having to take two extra weeks off to sleep, or spend time weaning ourselves off the sleeping tablets.

Bertie, Enda, give us a chance at life and I assure you, as the youth of today who have truly experienced both the ugliness and the miracle of life, we will not let you, or ourselves, down.

Appendix 3

False hope and cruelty of having an inactive lung transplant list
The Irish Times, Tue, Jan 06, 2009

ANALYSIS: Double lung transplants for Irish cystic fibrosis patients is a lottery with a waiting list that doesn't make sense, writes Orla Tinsley

I've wanted to write about the transplant situation in this country regarding cystic fibrosis patients for a long time. It's a difficult and controversial subject, especially when you consider that since the State's first double lung transplant of a person with CF, that of an 18-year-old in Dublin's Mater hospital in 2007, there has been no other CF transplant performed in Ireland.

The Irish transplant list continues to grow while the reality is that those on the list for the Freeman Hospital in Newcastle [England] have a much greater chance of receiving the vital transplant operation than those who are waiting on the Irish list.

Apart from having CF myself, I have friends waiting for transplants and this makes the false hope and confusion surrounding what is effectively an inactive Irish transplant system difficult to contemplate. My friends are among the 25-30 young men and women in Ireland hoping for a chance to start their lives again with a transplant operation.

While many people with CF live fulfilling lives, studying and working in Ireland or abroad, a transplant is necessary at the end stage of the illness when there is no other option available. The 'end stage' means a variety of things, but mainly that your quality of life is severely diminished. It means that your organs are failing, you are zapped of physical energy and you are dependent on a variety of machines to live.

The only chance of survival at this point is a double lung transplant operation. To get this you have to battle to stay healthy or you risk being taken off the Irish or the Newcastle list. Those who are successful also face the risk that they could die during surgery.

When a CF patient needs a transplant they are referred automatically to the Mater hospital. If their needs are assessed as being more complex, they are then referred to the Newcastle list.

I knew two people on the Irish list, a young woman and a young man, both in their 20s. The young woman went on the list in 2006 and the young man in 2007. The man went on the list willingly and had great belief in the Irish transplant system. His understanding was that he was 'the next person in line to get a transplant'.

The young woman originally wanted to go on the Newcastle list, reasoning that the English hospital had more experience in transplant operations. But in the event, she decided on Ireland after extensive discussion with her team. She said it seemed easier to get a transplant as she was closer to home.

I spoke to her mother at the time. She said that they had been promised her daughter would be next on the list.

Both patients who were on the Irish list died awaiting transplants.

Three years ago that young woman and I shared a room in hospital with another female patient who also needed a transplant. That year she received one in Newcastle and now attends college full-time, has a part-time job and has competed in the National Transplant Games. It is impressive stuff seeing someone reclaim their life at 20 but she is one of the lucky few.

In the past couple of years I've written about CF in this newspaper and as a result people have spoken to me privately about how they feel regarding transplants in Ireland.

One young woman with CF contacted me once and said that she felt 'under pressure' from her medical team to go on the Mater list. She had more confidence in the Newcastle list and flew to that city for assessment but was deemed unsuitable for transplant at the time.

Numerous issues can render someone unsuitable whether it is degree of health, infection, weight, psychological state or other factors. And while the Newcastle system refused her, Ireland still felt able to offer her a place on their list. That the Mater hospital would take on a patient for transplant that Newcastle deemed unsuitable makes no sense.

CF patients need double lung transplants because their lungs are riddled with bacteria and severe lung damage because of cystic fibrosis. We need double lung transplants because bacteria grows in both lungs, so a single lung transplant would only deal with half of the problem.

However, Ireland is the only country in Europe that performs more single lung than double lung transplants. There were 84 successful organ donations in Ireland in 2007. Out of these donations, five single lungs and four double lungs were retrieved. One Irish CF patient was transplanted in Ireland that year and six Irish patients were successfully transplanted in Newcastle.

It is estimated by the Cystic Fibrosis Association of Ireland (CFAI) that at current rates it will take 36 years to complete the transplants on the Mater hospital list, which they say is an absurd proposition 'given the life expectancy of the average person with cystic fibrosis'. It's worth comparing the situation internationally. The Belgian system for lung transplants is one of the best on the continent with 94 successful transplants in 2007. In the French region of that country where they have a population of four million people – ie similar to our own – 13 single lungs and 27 double lungs were successfully transplanted.

The Spanish Transplant Authority, which at 34.4 per million people, has the highest organ donor rate in the world, recommends that to have an efficient transplant team, 20 transplants must be performed a year. The Belgian system started transplanting in 1993 and preformed 36 lung transplants in their first three years.

Ireland, on the other hand, has performed only 20 lung transplants since 2005. Out of these lungs, 16 transplants were single while four were double. CF patients waiting for a double lung transplant have to wait in excess of 18 months on the Mater and the Newcastle list. In Belgium the wait is seven months.

According to Godfrey Fletcher, chief executive of the CFAI, when Belgium introduced specially trained transplant co-ordinators into each of their intensive care units to monitor and maintain organs pre and post operation, the number of organs retrieved increased.

With closer monitoring of patients and special patient care in these vital hours, lives were saved. Ireland is currently undergoing an audit of all intensive care units costing €60,000 and funded by the CFAI from 2006. According to Fletcher: 'We do not have transplant co-ordinators in any ICU.'

Fletcher also described the 'strained' relationship between the Mater and his organisation during the first two years of the Irish CF transplant list. The hospital refused to meet the association without other transplant representative groups being present, despite being aware of the difficulty of the situation. While they have since met, many aspects are unclear and there is a lack of communication between those providing the services and the CF patients who need them.

Cystic fibrosis patients need to know whether they will get a lung transplant when they need it. Those on the list know that the longer the wait, the greater the chance that their health will deteriorate. Irish CF patients do not know where to turn and no one is providing any real answers. In the three months after the only CF patient transplant in Ireland, two patients were called for transplant but the lungs were then thought to be unsuitable. It's not surprising that the Irish list is viewed as an abject failure by many in the wider CF community.

So what needs to change? Well, for a start we need someone in authority to provide answers to our questions, and we need a properly resourced, independent transplant body to co-ordinate all aspects of donor identification and transplant co-ordination.

The CFAI also recommends that 'properly resourced transplant teams made up of retrieval teams and transplant teams are made available. These need to be available 24/7 365 days a year and they need to have motivated senior surgeons'. This will ensure that every opportunity is taken so that transplant takes place.

Ireland has one of the highest organ donation rates in Europe with 21 donations per million people compared with 13.2 in the UK. Even if we had a 50 per cent retrieval rate similar to European transplant leaders in Belgium and Austria that would mean 30-

40 lungs, tantalisingly close to what we need in Ireland.

This is not about the law or enough organs being donated, it is about the process of donation, retrieval and transplantation being properly resourced and organised.

As I write, people with CF are still waiting for seven of the 15 single ensuite rooms that were promised last February [2008]. We have eight isolation rooms available for up to 25 CF patients that are in the National Adult Referral Centre at St Vincent's in Dublin at any given time. Usually these eight beds are taken up by those who need them most, those with extreme pathogens, or those on the transplant list.

Acknowledgements

This book has been the single most affecting experience of my life. Since I started, aged 19 (which seems a life time ago now), I have grown so much. It's been with me all this time, and so too have my friends and family. This book wouldn't have been possible without the collective support of a lot of people who listened to me talk, rant, rave, cry, laugh, and be completely bonkers about the darn thing!

Firstly, my mom who has a job unfathomable to most people. She puts up with me and works in the most difficult situations. She deals with health in work and at home. We are so alike and I am proud to have her as a mother. She is a constant source of love and compassion for so many people and I am in awe of her. And to my father who encouraged me to be creative from day one, not that I had much trouble thanks to his genes! For his constant reminders that anything is possible and for his inability to ever give up on me, no matter the situation.

To Jack, who probably had the toughest time of all. For his infectious enthusiasm, his limitless and awe-inspiring creativity, and for understanding from a very young age so much more than he should have had to. He throws me a fruit loop if I look like I'm drowning and puts me in my place when I need it too. The best brother a sister could ask for.

Thanks to my agent Faith O'Grady, who persevered with me and consistently went above and beyond the call of duty to help me out with my campaigning or when I was sick. Her kindness and patience is seriously impressive and I'm lucky to have her represent me. To all at the Lisa Richards Agency for their constant support on what was probably the longest-coming memoir in history!

To Rachel Pierce for being such a clued-in editor and for fully committing to going on this book journey with me. For listening hard when I knew there was something I wanted to say but wasn't ready to say it, and for getting there with me. Her dedication is what made this book possible.

Thanks to Hachette Books Ireland, and particularly my editor Ciara Considine and MD Breda Purdue for believing in me from the beginning and not giving up even when at times I might have been ready to. Thanks for recognising the support I needed to help me work out the kinks and get me through the periods when I was unwell. Thank you for believing in my ability to tell this story.

A very big thank you to my dear friend Róisín – words are just a human concept so we'll skip them! But seriously: you rock, you inspire, you motivate, you are still, and you are always. And you take it on the chin when I beat you at karaoke! NEVER CHANGE X

Thank you to Aunty Q, my hero for life X

To Paul H for his advice and support. I promise not to spill juice in your car ever again!

Thanks to Fat and Pionan, you guys are the best. Homies till the end.

Also to Sarah for her unparalleled support. She rocks, in a Jonas brother/Taylor Swift way. Joanna, for the sarcasm, LOM for the sex cookies. To Zuzu for allowing me to be theatrical at all hours of the day.

Thank you to Rachel Lally, my sister for life, and to Laura McG – she's cool. Aoife, you're always there and it means more than you could possibly know.

Thanks to Mr T for being a friend when I needed one most, for keeping me alive in the early days of Vincent's and always encouraging me to remember who I am, in the darkest of times. Carpe Diem!

To SG, for reminding what life was for when I had forgotten it all. For love, laughter, for encouragement, for reality, for Jeff Buckley, for Jaffa apple juice, sparkles and for fighting and believing in something more.

Thanks to the staff in Vincent's for being supportive when it was sometimes difficult to be. For Charlie Gallagher for always encouraging me, making sure I switch off my phone when I'm sick (!) and reminding me that 'sometimes it's just CF'. Thanks Ed McKone for spicing up the team when he came along and keeping me on my toes!

For Paula, Sue, Jo and Catherine for the constant support, jokes, laughter, mini marathon high fives, deep conversations about life, love and everything in between. Thanks also to the physios for listening to me ramble and encouraging me – sometimes through brute force! For constantly challenging me and showing me the reality when I don't want to see it. For helping me set my goals, readjust them and reminding me to slow down. Thanks Clare for that too: the support, kicking me out when I needed it, listening to me ramble and getting me running. You rock.Thanks to Deirdre Sheenan for practically carrying me through a time I couldn't navigate with Sound of Music songs and belief – look I'm running now!

Thank you to Linda and Valerie the dieticians too.

To my creative writing teacher James Ryan for always challenging me and supporting me. For seeing my journalistic potential and guiding me in the right direction. To my English teachers, Bean Uí Riagain and Caroline Malone, for challenging me in very different ways and showing me the true parallels and depths it takes to be a writer of truth. To Emily Dickinson, Seamus Heaney, Sylvia Plath, Margaret Atwood and most of all, to Nelle Harper Lee.

Love to Anna and Jenn for their unwavering friendship. Thanks to my wonderful Nana and all of my family, particularly my cousins, aunts and uncles and my godfather.

A very heartfelt thank you to all of the staff at The Irish Times for believing in me. Particularly the wonderful and infinitely wise Peter Murtagh for his constant support, belief and love. Thanks to Geraldine Kennedy and Kevin O'Sullivan for giving me such a wonderful opportunity and believing in me. To Joe Humphreys for his patience and encouragement. Thanks to Mary Fitzgerald and Ronan McGreevy for being inspiring, putting up with my numerous questions and for eating my jellies! Thank you to Deirdre Veldon and Anthea Tiernan for their unwavering support. And to Rosemary MacCabe, the best accidental friendship ever! Thanks to all the people who challenge me from all walks of life; your presence helps me grow and learn everyday.

To Joe Duffy for taking on the CF cause with intelligence and love. To Sam Smyth for his support. To Faela Smyth – FLO! Love you gurl.

To the staff of Temple Street Children's Hospital, especially Dr Murphy, Dr Slattery, Susan, Mary, Ailish, Lorraine, all at the Schoolroom, the Playroom and the porters, particularly John and Herman. To Angi and the fundraising office for being such an important, inspirational part of my childhood. To all the CF medical team. And to Professor Fitzgerald, who never gave up on my many portacath operations.

To Philip Watt for inspiring hope and Martin Cahill for his relentless and superb fundraising initiatives.

Thanks too to Jessica Fletcher who always proved she could solve a mystery under any circumstance, and Lois Lane for being gutsy, strong and inspirational.

And finally thank you to the Irish public for their constant support for CF and the important fundraising they do all over the country. It would be so easy to forget about an issue or get bored of it, but you have always been there for CF and I thank you from the bottom of my heart.